Vittorio Gregotti

Manfredo Tafuri

Vittorio Gregotti

Buildings and projects

Translation
Richard Sadleir

First published in the USA in 1982 by
RIZZOLI INTERNATIONAL PUBLICATIONS, INC.
712 Fifth Avenue, New York NY 10019

All rights reserved
No part of this book may be reproduced in any manner
whatsoever without permission from the publisher.

ISBN: 0-8478-0450-X
LC: 82-50502

Contents

- 7 Adventures of the object: the architecture of Vittorio Gregotti
  Manfredo Tafuri
- 31 Ten projects 1964-1981
- 33 13th Triennale (1964): Introductory section to the theme of leisure time
- 41 New Science Departments at Parco d'Orleans (University of Palermo)
- 51 New campus of University of Calabria, Rende di Cosenza
- 63 Research Centre at Naples, Portici
- 71 New A.C.T.V. boat yards on the island of the Giudecca in Venice
- 81 Residential nucleus at Sestiere di Cannaregio in Venice
- 89 Residential building in Berlin
- 93 New centre for G.G. Feltrinelli Foundation in Milan
- 97 Business centre in Milan
- 101 IVI Chemical Research Centre at Quattordio di Alessandria
- 105 Collaborations
- 107 Works and projects

Adventures of the object: the architecture
of Vittorio Gregotti
Manfredo Tafuri

The "generation of uncertainty," as it has been called, was being tugged in two directions at the start of the 1950s. There was the desire to join in an international architectural *koiné* and a canny adherence to the national-popular ideologies bound up with the styles of neorealism. When Gregotti, Canella, Aymonino and Aldo Rossi began work, in the shadow of "masters" like Rogers, Quaroni or Ridolfi, the attitudes that had guided the earliest choices in the period of reconstruction were beginning to become more settled. Disappointments and frustrations that followed on 1948 had already found an outlet towards provisional sublimations: the "school of reality" seemed capable of providing a life-raft for leading Milanese and Roman architectural circles. Then, to people like Gregotti, who had had the opportunity to be in on the BPR studio and take part in the 1952 CIAM on the *Heart of the city*, the opposition of Milan/Rome and MSA/APAO could only appear sterile. And it is quite unquestionable that there was something more than personal bias in this aversion to the artificial split-up into two souls of the new Italian path towards the "modern movement:" the first issue in which *Casabella continuità* began its existence published Ridolfi's towers in Viale Etiopia alongside Gardella's homes in Alessandria and a technological section edited by Jean Prouvé.

Milan was undergoing violent transformation, both the ancient city centre and the outskirts: its cultural circles felt compelled to reflect on the causes of their exclusion on both the urban and the international planes, but possessed tenaciously provincial roots; and here the appeal to "reality" and meditation on history appeared as instruments for the safeguarding of an identity, the preservation of dignity, the identification of a reality. Naturally these were instruments suited to an avant-garde that tried to disguise itself, refusing – in spite of everything – to present itself as a "radical" group, one that made a point of showing that it wasn't afraid of getting its hands dirty: yet an avant-garde all the same, condemned to haunt the margins of institutions and the educational set-up.

Still, one of the functions of an avant-garde is to give its members confidence. With the backing it gave, the youthful Gregotti found a way to reconcile the stimuli derived from his collaboration on the Torre Velasca, an interpretation of populism as a response to a productive level imposed by circumstances, his discussions with Elio Vittorini and Emilio Sereni about the national-popular trend, and the theme of memory. There's no cause for wonder in the fact that the earliest works by the Gregotti, Meneghetti and Stoppino partnership (the Sforza home in Stradella, 1953; standard furnishings for INA-Casa state housing at the Tenth Triennale in Milan, 1954) strike one as stylistically indecisive, not to say mannered. It was the professionals – Nizzoli, Ponti, Mangiarotti, Fiocchi – who possessed an established style, and the younger generation centred on *Casabella* regarded them as the enemy: the complexity of the problems to be dealt with seemed to call for not just an "orthodoxy of the heterodox" – to quote Rogers – but also an openness bordering on the most experimental empiricism. The way towards the abyss of anger and frustration now lay open.

The city cannot be dominated; but the languages inherited from our predecessors express a will to dominate, that now rings false. The themes proposed by the new cultural leaders appeared oversimplified or evasive; the confrontation with the real posed a big question mark over past and recent certainties. A poetic of impatience began to hover over the generations intent on revising elements of a heritage that was meant for different heirs. The responses from the "workshops of frustration" were bound up with this impatience.

In a situation of this sort, the influence of Rogers' architectural teaching and the BPR's architectural output should be carefully appraised. Instead of facile catchwords, Rogers put forward disquieting reflections and open-minded incursions into cultural areas not calculated tranquilly to ratify historicist constructions: in *Domus*, under Rogers' editorship, Starobinski called for reflection on Kafka's *intéreurs* (1947, n. 218); while Ballo, Dorfles, Malipiero and Solmi treated themes connected with Surrealism, Cocteau, Honegger, concrete art, Sartre. Within the

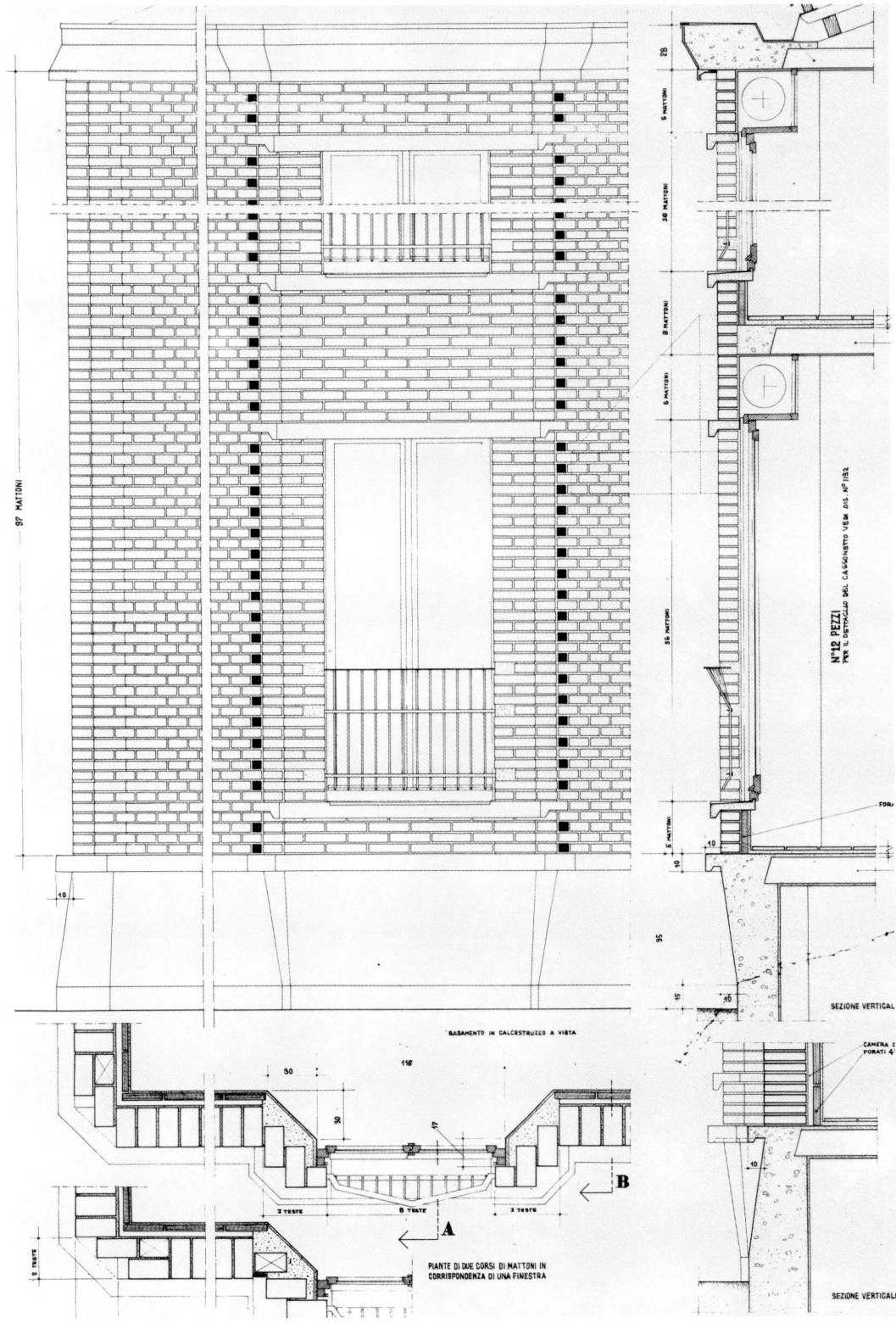

Residential nucleus for employees of Bossi spa, Cameri (Novara), 1956 (V. Gregotti, L. Meneghetti and G. Stoppino). Constructional details.

Competition for the new University of Calabria, Cosenza, 1973. Sketch for the south elevation of the Department of Structures.

architecture of the BPR, the complex heterogeneousness of European culture, tending towards the construction of *languages of uncertainty*, found attentive listeners. There is no other explanation of the surreal and subversive vein lurking in the projects as early as the completion of Palazzo Venier dei Leoni in Venice (1951), or the monument to Camillo Olivetti in Ivrea, or the pavilion in the Stupinigi park (1953), or the "Children's maze" at the Tenth Triennale.

Following a line parallel to the "language of silent things" adopted by Asnago and Vender, the BPR relied in those years on a language made up of half-uttered allusions, of aversions, of evocative figures: it was, ultimately, a quest whose starting-point lay in the *vortex of significances*.

But a vortex which theory tended to placate. The question mark hanging over the mainline of the tradition of the new was thus left as a sort of sword of Damocles over the head of whoever felt inclined to adopt and give continuity to the difficult teaching of the masters.

It was in the sector of design that some sort of shape began to appear in the manifold impulses absorbed by Gregotti and the younger Milanese in the early 1950s. The single object, in which the new generations of architects in Northern Italy took refuge, summed up in itself that will to create form that aimed directly at the recovery of representative values. In this way, a whole universe of certainties was placed in crisis. The dissolution of the object and its replacement by a process, with varying degrees of richness in metaphorical valences, at the centre of the entire range of avant-garde themes, was now called into question: not as a "return to order" but as part of a new mimesis. The subject to be represented, however, proved elusive. In the card table of solid curved timbers (1955) or the "Cavour" armchair (1959), what emerges is above all the will to come to a showdown with the Utopias of contemporary design, to denounce the ineffectiveness of any simulation tending towards the construction of short-lived socialized models, to speak "to the present." And that present, unavoidably, was dominated by a bourgeoisie which seemed never to have completed its "liberal revolution." So all one could offer them was a "Cavour armchair:" an armchair to sit "and weep in," as was said at the time, with an irony no less inferior to that which prompted the choice of the conservative statesman's name to denote the object. There's nothing heroic about Gregotti's Cavour; sentimentalism caustically directed at an élite public replaces the asceticism underlying the disenchantment (judged as too negative) of the cold steel of Mies or Breuer. Gregotti, like Canella, Gae Aulenti and in general the whole group that came to be described as "neoliberty," was aware that the recovery of the representative had already been taken up, even in the field of design, by Le Corbusier and Charlotte Perriand in the thirties, with Surrealistic inflexions, and that the "social portraiture" of furnishings in curved timber had its bordering referent in Aalto's work for Artek.

In reality, the neoliberty episode represented, in relation to Italian culture, the revelation of the ambiguous relation between autobiography and a projection towards images of redemption. The entire phenomenon of neorealism had existed by virtue of this oscillatory relationship. The "gentle revisions" of the Turinese and Milanese intelligentsia had accentuated its subjectivist polarities. The autobiographical vein was at work in those who felt they had lost their bearings in the real and hoped to find them in *le temps perdu*: and never mind if instead of living in a house one dwelt in a labyrinth with its entrances and exits concealed. The game – a perverse one – was to pause on the threshold, reached so laboriously, blinking at the outside world. With good reason, Gregotti attempted to draw up a balance sheet of that experience, saying: "The architect had by this time discovered the nature of his compromise, of one compelled *to do* without really *being*: he had discovered that the screen of one's own subjectivity was the cruel mirror of this compromise; and the sharper and more penetrating the image, the more completely did it reflect the impossibility of an entire culture." (V. Gregotti, *Orientamenti nuovi dell'architettura italiana*, Electa, Milan, 1969.)

If, however, we pass on to consideration of the results of this flirtation with the heyday of the European bourgeoisie in the output of Gregotti, Meneghetti and Stoppino, we immediately realize that the revival of Art Nouveau currents, of the weave of materials, of the allusive detail, is incredibly reticent. The polemic with the "modern" tradition appears conditioned by an ill-concealed Oedipus complex. Incest – Jocasta being inevitably the figurative culture of Symbolism – is out, except in the form of a little cautious petting, within the bounds of decency. Returning after almost thirty years to works like the Tadini Lambertenghi store in Novara (1955), the residential nucleus for Bossi at Cameri (1956) and the tower blocks for offices, residences and hotels in Novara (1955), they look much more restrained than the building which was the manifesto of neoliberty, the "Bottega d'Erasmo" by Gabetti and Isola, and only marginally affected by the poetics of nostalgia. Instead, it is possible to describe them as buildings without a city, outsized pieces of furniture: even subjectivism becomes a state of mind compromised by a "condition of impossibility." And yet, if we look into it closely, we see that there is also subjectivism in Gregotti's return to Antonelli in an essay, written in collaboration with Aldo Rossi, published in *Casabella* (1957, no. 214, pp. 62-82): its scientific tone does not completely conceal the true purpose of the "recherche" it contains.

The twofold significance of Alessandro Antonelli in Gregotti's eyes is clear. On the one hand, he was an architect who conformed to traditional technology but through an excess of realism miraculously transfigured it. On the other, he was a figure whom Gregotti, when very young, might have come across in the family album, and so a part of private memories that he put surreptitiously into circulation through subtle intellectual expedients. Moreover, if the new technical experiments of 19th century "functionalism" underlay the origins of the "modern," Antonelli had already taken up a "revisionist" position, and one that was hence capable of implementation. In opposition to Labrouste and Le Baron Jenney, the architect of the over-elaborate structure of the "mole" in Turin and the cupola of S. Gaudenzio in Novara appeared as an "alternative father." What's more, a father who seemed unlikely to induce any castration complex.

Among all these motives, one stands out, especially as we read between the lines of Gregotti's essay on Antonelli. In the latter's architecture – especially his civil architecture – the technology is realistically adapted to the productive level of Piedmont under the Savoy monarchy and is not separated from a quest for representativeness in the created object and its social, as well as urban, characterization. The "house of columns" or the Villa Caccia at Romagnano Sesia are nothing less than "portraits" of the Piedmontese bourgeoisie: from the restraint and gloomy reserve of those buildings it now seems legitimate to deduce an admonition addressed to the local heirs of that particular social stock. This speaks volumes about the significance that not only Gregotti but also many of Rogers' pupils ascribed to history: looking back across the years at the quarrel with the master, it now seems to have been motivated by matters of detail rather than radically different positions. A great reservoir, from which conjuring hands are ready to pluck "wonderful mandarins," the discontinuity of the flow of history appears at the same time as a disquietingly inclined surface, rich in the unexpected: the encounter with it was destined to be all the more fruitful the more its oneiric dimension was preserved.

But this presupposes an initial familiarity with the signs, if not the languages, of dreams. The event extracted from its historic series will function by itself: called upon to legitimate present choices, the phantom conjured up might even lead towards forms of automatic writing – architectural discipline permitting. But architecture – like it or not – is embedded in the era of technical reproducibility, which sets a limit to temptations of this sort – the essays by Rosenberg and Benjamin were either still unwritten or untranslated in the fifties, but this made no difference to the outcome. The encounter between history and design failed to take on surreal features, stranded on the threshold of the hybrid.

Nostalgia, moreover, is all the more eloquent the more it is restrained, the more it is glimpsed in the interstices of the non-committal. This makes it difficult, however, to imagine

*Missoni retail centre in Milan, 1976.
Axonometric.*

the object of Gregotti's nostalgia. Melancholy may be turned into material for designs, whereas the system of references beckons to the reader but leaves him bewildered. While the workers' housing estate in Novara (1956) contains the expected reference to Antonelli, the rental home (1957) also in Novara mingles with the 19th century sources – the need to re-evoke the magical sadness of a Piedmont seen through intimistic eyes – a reminiscence of Perret's *esprit de géometrie*. So, from Antonelli to Perret: no consistency of the technological sort underlies this juxtaposition. Gregotti's Perret is not the Perret so dear to the fable of the "modern movement," nor the Perret that emerges from the pages of the 1955 volume devoted to the French master by Ernesto Nathan Rogers. In fact, Gregotti's article in *Casabella* (1959, no. 229, pp. 6-11; review of Champigneulle's monograph) took issue with Rogers' canonical reading and stressed the Romantic valences of both Perret's architecture and much of the French "retour à l'ordre" in our century. The rational asserts itself at the same time as it declares itself an unattainable objective: to such an extent are Perret's self-limitations shot through with nostalgia (in Gregotti's interpretation), with the real protagonist, the unspoken, seeping out from it.

Yet Gregotti's dwellings in Novara don't take this tack. Here everything says too much. As in the office block in Via San Gaudenzio in Novara (1959-1960), but not so peremptorily, in the rental dwellings (1957) the reiteration of the structures is drowned in a proliferation of detail: its recital seems deliberately created to throw the reader off the track, to draw him into a game of pretence and dissimulation. So Gregotti's historicism is deceptive: nor can one call it properly speaking an instrumental use of history, since the subtlety of the references seems more essential than any polemical reflection upon it. Again: the dwellings that belong to '57, such as the residential nucleus for Bossi, try desperately to preserve their character as objects. This too is a motive of recovery, obligatory, in the revisionist climate of Italian architecture in the fifties. In this respect it may be observed that this accentuation of the object follows as a consequence essentially from the relegation of the urban dimension to a parenthesis. Gregotti, Meneghetti and Stoppino were wholly skeptical about the mythology of urbanistics: they approached the city only as a stage backdrop. The offices in Via San Gaudenzio, Novara, rhythmically marked by the bow windows evocative of "Chicago Functionalism" and terminated by an allusive deep-folded entablature, even go so far as to flaunt their qualities of design; but their overt connection with "environmental pre-existences" makes the work exemplary in this respect.

Be that as it may, the themes connected with a recovery of the *mémoire involontaire* met with a crisis in the early sixties. The Milan exhibition, *Nuovi disegni per il mobile italiano* (March 1960), marked a borderline beyond which there extended the distinct territories of the neo-avant-garde and the new Italian reality seen, as occasion demanded, through phenomenological or autobiographical lenses. It was no accident that these were the years when Enzo Paci compelled Italian culture to come to terms with Husserl while Rome and Milan were being transformed through the viewfinders of Fellini and Antonioni.

The concern with "the object alone," which had led Gregotti to "rediscover" the architecture of Expressionism in an essay for *Casabella* (1961, no. 254) was now found wanting. Eager to grapple with the issues where they arose, Gregotti seemed inclined to accept conditionally the invitation from Vittorini's *Menabò* to switch allegiance to the neo-avant-garde. The result was symptomatic: the entry to the '64 Triennale. It's clear Gregotti saw that work as a manifesto. The reflections of the gruppo '63, the renewed concern with control over techniques of communication, the discovery of a range of meanings inherent not only in learned languages but also in behavioural ones, the experimentalism through which the neo-avant-gardes renewed the ethics of transgression, all created a vortex of themes from which there emerged reviews like *Edilizia moderna, Il Verri* and *Quindici*, adopting different attitudes, often satisfied with their own incoherency. But coherency wasn't the theme linking Eco's brilliant semiological exegeses and

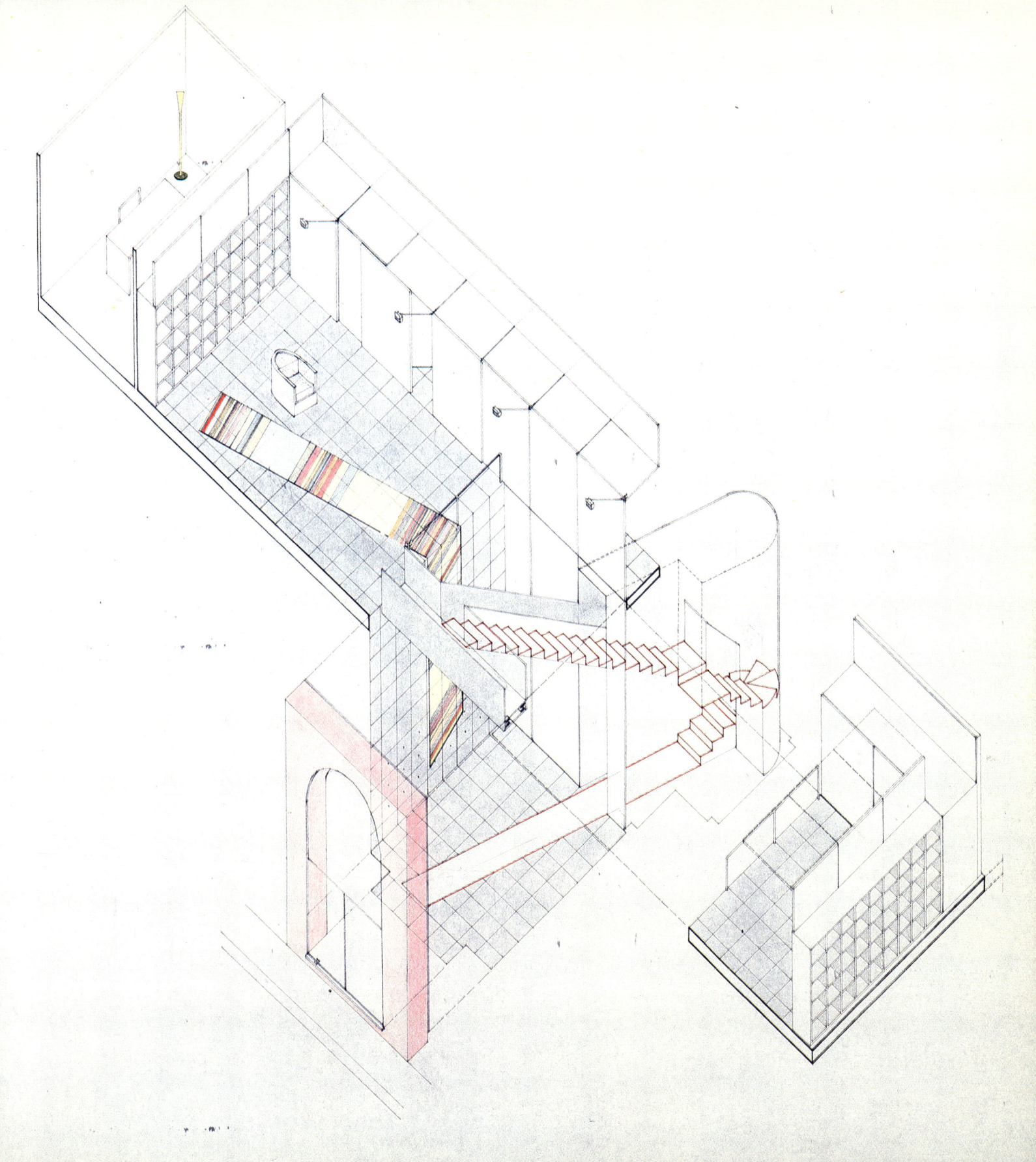

Balestrini's poetry or Gregotti's questing after new fields of architecture. The problem of language, especially in the case of the last-named, was now under a compulsion to emerge from the closed ground of superstructuralism. Measuring itself against a mass public and resting on control of the quanta of information, the visual rhetoric exploded outside its proper limits, hybridizing with the most varied techniques of communication, denying itself the privilege of "possessing objects." In consequence, in the '64 Triennale, primacy was accorded to the randomness of *relations*. Only the random – but weren't those the years when Eco's "open work" was the standard of reference? – could recompose the shattered codes within the single disciplines; only the transitoriness of "relations" gave coherence to the bombardment of multiple shocks – visual, acoustic, sensorial, literary – that the designers of the Triennale subjected their public to.

The public was bombarded – therefore violated. It should be added that the sadism that appears in the operation reveals an ambiguous attitude towards both the emitters and the users. In some ways, it's the same ambivalence that had characterized the work of Le Corbusier, Xenakis and Varèse in '58, in the Philips pavilion at Brussels. But is it only an accident that Corbu left this particular work out of his *Oeuvre complète?* Yet the Kaleidoscope of the 13th Triennale, despite the accentuated scenic quality that typified it, was in contradiction to Gregotti's previous works. Calling into question the concept of "leisure" itself, it tended to awaken radical doubts in the visitor, over his own position in time and space before anything else. From the "decompression chamber" one passed to the "vacant-time room," to the alternative routes of the room filled with Luciano Berio's "Homage to Joyce," to the final prism on which two films by Tinto Brass ran simultaneously, reflected six times by mirrors. The technique of the montage was combined with the technique of distortion: a sound track composed by Balestrini and a succession of coloured images composed by Achille Perilli, at the end of Brass's films, burst on the scene in twenty-four combinations, destabilizing the role (as detached observer, because of an excess of stimuli, or as an irretrievably other-directed presence) of the spectator, whom the mirrors of prismatic space forced to view himself reflected six times, involuntarily integrated into the film images.

The magical caverns of the '64 Triennale were thick with grim forebodings, but architecture did not look like the discipline best suited to fulfil them. The artificial disorientation that dominated those rooms projected into the sphere of the imagination some of the pivotal issues of "Italy of the economic miracle:" it wasn't the metropolis that was the subject of the implosion, but a magnetic field of behaviour perpetually being metamorphosed. Control had to be exercised over that fluid ground, those quicksands, whose dangerous fascination was clearly noted: it was no accident that the instruments were those of a "frozen avant-garde."

It was highly symptomatic, this attempt to control the aleatory flow of information emitted by a range of technological media. In '64, it is evidence of a notable effort on the part of visual culture to check its instruments in the light of processes that by then had elaborated spreading strategies in magmatic form. The new languages disrupted any remaining coherence in the argument, making dualistic oppositions illusory, demolishing and recreating currents of discourse against which the arms of classical rationality seemed ineffective. At the '64 Triennale, the work of architects, of semiologists and of visual operators attempted an *intercodal* operation: essentially an attempt to dominate and possess in its entirety the metamorphic mechanism of the technological transmitters, to construct a language of plurality and the ephemeral, to manoeuvre the *multiversum* devoid of centres of communications. The "slaves of Hephaestus" – to use an expression of Ferruccio Masini – felt obliged to measure their own capacities of configuration in relation to the snares of the media analyzed by McLuhan. These were responses from intellectuals discovering just to what extent that *multiversum* had made the old groupings untenable, how far *being spoken* conditions the formation of knowledge and representations of the real.

Gregotti, for his part, moved through the experimental regions of the neo-avant-gardes with an eye to investigation of the structures of communication. What and why should one communicate, if one is confronted with the disappearance of the subject? What part is played by the solidity of the architectural sign within the fluid field of relations surrounding it? What materials are still able to produce some effect in this field? By working on these questions, Gregotti made a methodological advance which amounted to a breakthrough when compared with his previous work.

Meanwhile, a new issue had been emerging in the formal configuration of the region-territory. The theme of the dialogue between geography and the architectural sign came to the fore in the course of the INU conference in Trieste (1965), in the volume *Il territorio dell'architettura*, published by Gregotti in '66, and in a monographic issue of *Edilizia moderna*, also in '66.

Gregotti's conflict-ridden relation with history was directed wholly onto the geographical scale. Modernity, he wrote in the volume referred to, is proceeding towards a "radical revision of historical time," in which "phenomena are standardized into a formal concreteness which one has to dig one's way into, worming one's way inside until one breaks through the thick layer of things and events to reach a new state of awareness." Yet this same revision leads to conditions of "quasi-suspension of historical time:" towards history conceived as a series of successive and discontinuous configurations, awaiting a significance. Significance is conferred by the voyeur who worms his way into the thick layer of things and events: the disenchanted eye that views the extent of geographical space, identifying in it, mute and mysterious, the signs that render it historic, of culture that has taken over nature and nature that seems to be advancing to challenge new cultures and further acts of possession. This means reading the territory, in its physical concretization, as an archaeological structure, which does not however seek either restoration or completion. The city is no longer the privileged site of memory, the built is no longer a sea in which to dive for wonderful fish. The theme of "environmental pre-existences" has taken a leap forward in scale, which involves an entire methodology of planning and the poetics underlying this.

In some way, however, for Gregotti the geographical theme in the mid-1960s constituted a polemical response to the theme of the "great dimension," which had been disturbing the repose of Italian architectural culture ever since 1960. And, in the first place, because Gregotti saw no validity in the ideological afflatus of the hopes accompanying studies of business centres or territorial infrastructures in those years: this is borne out by, among other things, his increasingly isolated position in the editorial team of *Casabella continuità*, which from '62 down to its demise (1964) acted as the mouthpiece of dreams of renewal directly bound up with the discovery of "the mass" and indirectly with a changed political frame of reference.

Gregotti, basically, has been very careful to avoid frustrations. The disenchantment with which he had participated in the brief "neo-Proustian" phase was erected by him into a barrier against the optimism of theoreticians of the city-territory and against the Utopianism of inventors of facile megastructures. The geography-architecture relationship did not, in Gregotti's eyes, begin and end in a new administration of the existing, nor in a strategy based on the infinite redesignability of the environment. Instead, the aim was to identify "a strategy of the discontinuous and of the circuit... based on diversification," as he was to write in an article in 1977 (in *Casabella*, no. 421, p. 60). This identification presupposes the possibility of concrete verification, hence of a different professional commitment, to ensure that the new theme introduced would not also be exhausted – as with so many in recent Italian experience – before it could be tried out.

This is why the designs from the years 1964-69 do not indulge in any forecasts – futurology must necessarily be alien to one who, despite himself, is an adept in the *école du regard* – nor push into the side tracks of experimentalism. The three blocks for the cooperative "*un tetto*" in Via Cassoni, Milan (1968), articulate and enrich the development

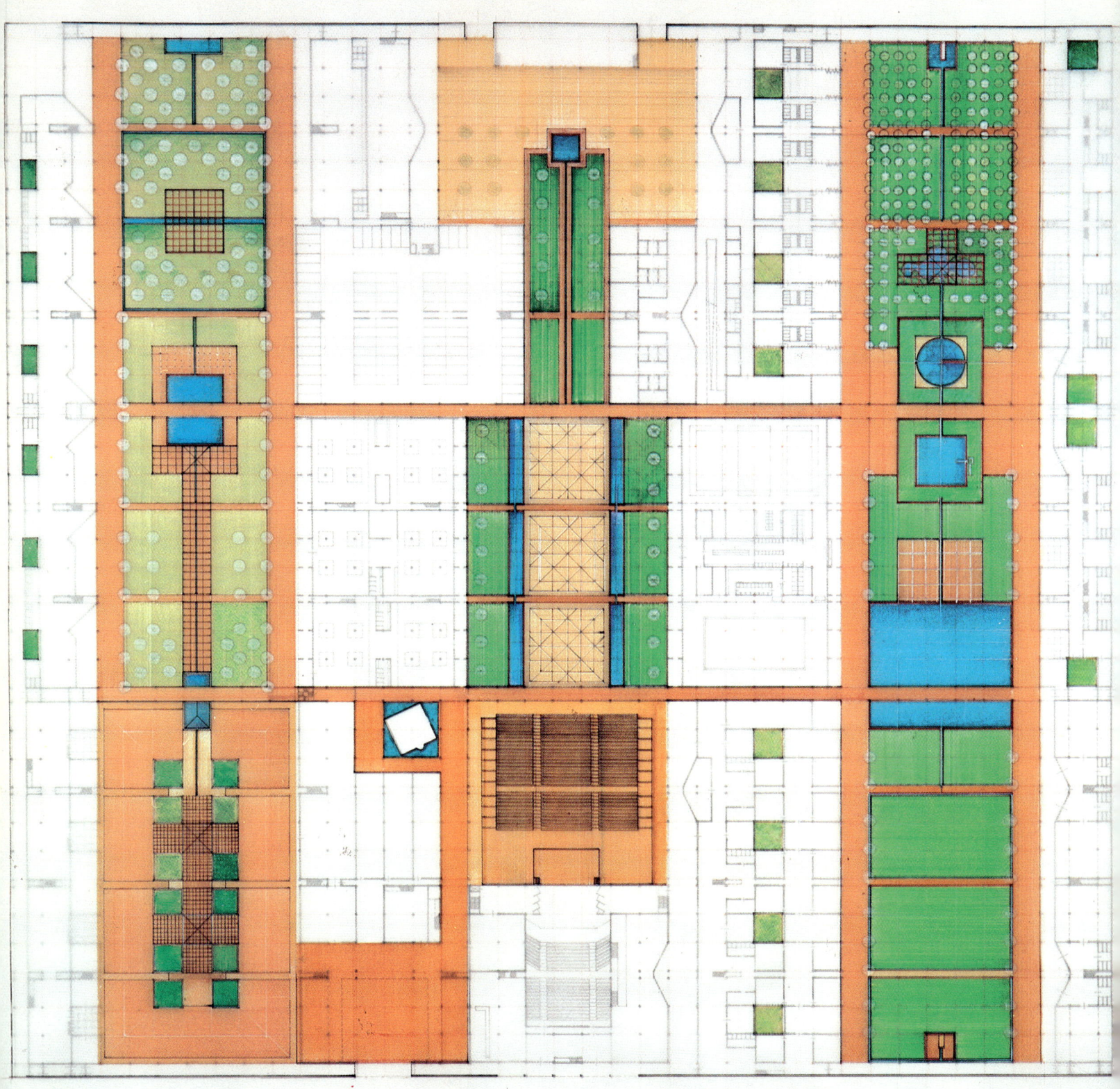

Dar Al Hanan School, project for a school for 2,000 girls, Jeddah (Saudi Arabia), 1978. Layout of the inner gardens.

started with the Milanese buildings in Via Palmanova (1963): with the top two stories set so they jut out, an artificial horizon stands out boldly as if to assert, together with the cylindrical hinge-links of the staircase blocks, a desire for form intended to resist the engulfing formlessness of the metropolitan outskirts. Yet the three buildings do not renounce volumetric articulation; but what has disappeared is the playing with metaphors, which reappears instead in the Filatura Bossi building in Novara (1968) together with a theme that Gregotti was to repeat in the Gabel textile factory and offices in Como (1972): the industrial building is proclaimed in the landscape as an exception, becoming charged with allusions.

It is possible to establish some faint relationship between Gregotti's excursion into the areas of production and the practice of Gino Valle: the remoteness from the productive world is still too marked to prevent it from being recreated with mysterious suggestions. This explains, in the case of the Filatura Bossi factory, the way the great air intakes and vents project from the homogeneous texture of the grit panels forming the wall-screen: the sequence of cylindrical and semicylindrical volumes not only creates breaks and "surprises," but also arouses visual expectations which it in some way frustrates. The industrial reality is modulated with the modes of the surreal; and yet the exception remains geometrically delimited and fixed, in its role as superstructure. This is repeated in the Gabel factory with emphasis laid on the design of the top, where the vaulted roofing and the underlying prismatic volume seem to be seeking to liberate themselves from the restriction of the standardized outer shell. It should, however, be borne in mind that the buildings in Via Cassoni and the Bossi company headquarters constituted the last achievements of the Gregotti, Meneghetti and Stoppino partnership, dissolved in the autumn of '67 after fifteen years activity.

Like many of the professional choices made in the period around '68, this was rich in symptomatic significances. A whole era of Milanese architectural culture is contained between '64 and '69 – between the ousting of Rogers from the editorship of *Casabella continuità*, a traumatic experience for the younger generation, and the disappearance of the master, after the *déluge* of '68, in search of new fields. The *koiné* of the early sixties now stood revealed in the full extent of its falsity; particularly so to architects like Aldo Rossi and Guido Canella, possessing divergent but still solid linguistic foundations, or like Gregotti, for whom language remained as a problem.

Two significant events for Gregotti in '68: the start of his work as lecturer at the Palermo architecture faculty and the encounter with Franco Purini. So here was a partial break with the Milanese milieu, essential for someone like Gregotti, architecturally a voyager, and a compulsion to collaborate with one of the most promising hopes of the Roman school, engaged on experiments with the primary elements of architectural language. The plan for the new science departments of Palermo University (1969-72), on the site of the Parco d'Orléans, which Gregotti worked on together with Pollini, presents a new unity of form. Behind the outer facade-wall 3.60 metres thick, traversed by communication trenches that cause them to resemble the earthworks of fortresses, there are arranged the "insulae:" the blocks designated for the various departments, subdivided into two modular organisms, set out compactly, clearly displaying their earthquake-proof, prefabricated and precompressed structure, whose joins form the underlying design of the facades. The allusion in this design to industrial architecture has been seen as a symbolical response to the paradoxical situation of a university culture within the chronic absence of any future prospects that still characterizes the unproductive and parasitic cities of southern Italy. (Cf. P. L. Nicolin, in *Casabella*, 1974, no. 394, p. 18).

But was it really legitimate to hold that the autobiographical valences no longer acted on Gregotti, because he had chosen to embrace the "grand manner?" At the immediate level, one tends to think of a dialectic between extroversion and introversion. It is unquestionably more fruitful to compare two modes of approaching the southern reality which are so remote in time and different from each

Comprehensive project for access studies and detailed plan of the Isola del Tronchetto, Venice, 1980. View from the north-west.

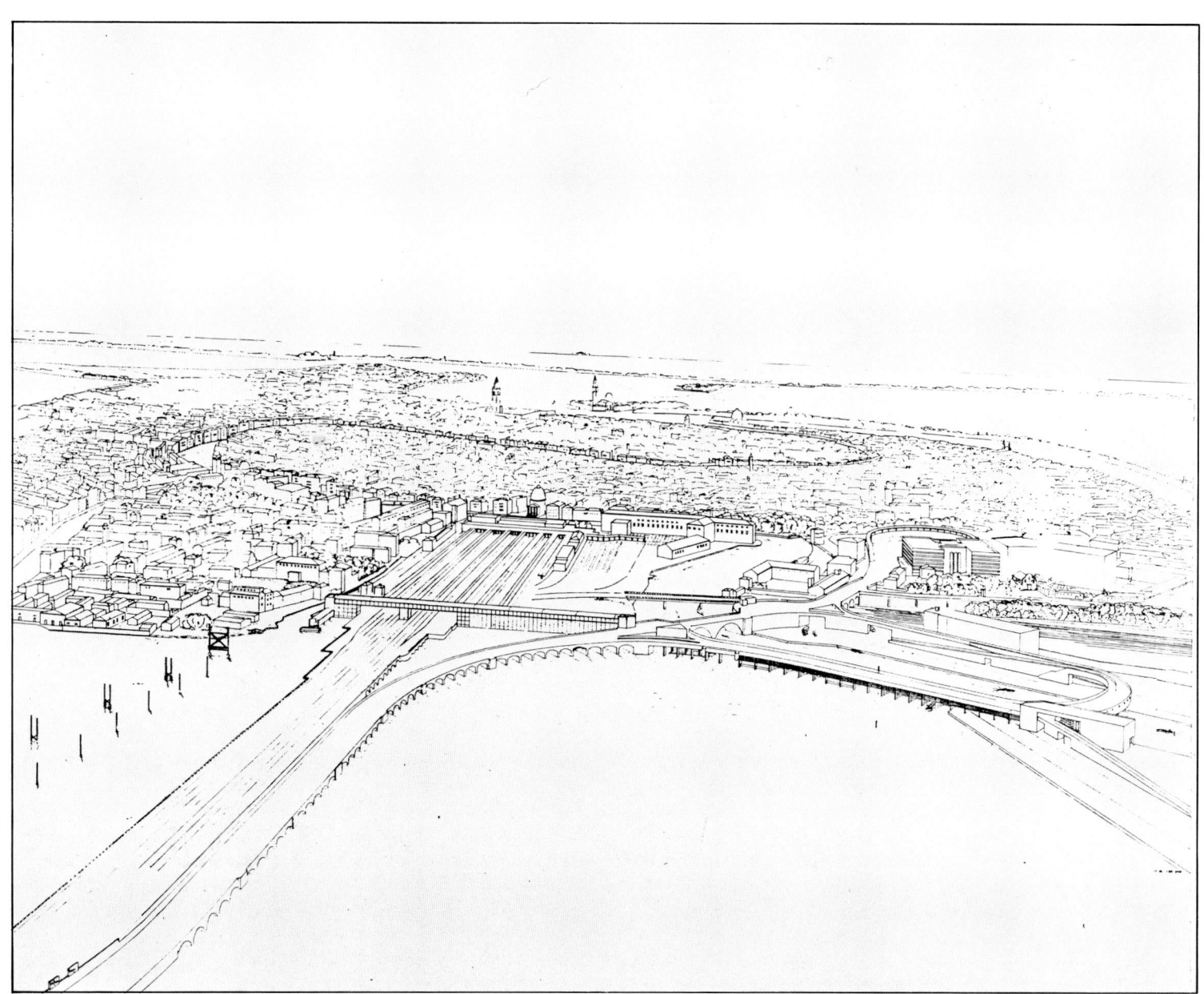

other as to acquire a historic significance. The "discovery of the south" came about, in the case of upper middle-class intellectuals originally extraneous to it (such as Vittorini, Carlo Levi or Quaroni) in the form of the sort of anguish felt by a helpess bystander who feels the need to take upon himself collective guilt of obscure origins; and this gave rise to the *poiesis* of *Cristo si è fermato a Eboli* or the heartfelt homage to the "eternal peasant" in the dwellings of Martella.

At the start of the seventies, it was only with feelings of disillusionment that one could go to Palermo or Gibellina – where Gregotti, together with Samonà, shared in the design of the new centre (1971): it was now essential to defend oneself from the dangerous glamour that had conditioned intellectuals in their vein of "realism." Gregotti's Sicilian projects express this "defence:" hence, self-defence. The reference, in the science departments in Palermo, to an "Arab-Norman" morality has this significance: by proposing mechanisms of defence, the "colonizer" – who comes from the "other" Italy – stifles his own guilt complexes.

The design for "La Rinascente" in Palermo (1968-69), worked out in collaboration with Purini and Hiromichi Matsui, is a further sign of the choices made by Gregotti. Sited in the "four nooks of countryside," between the mediaeval centre and the 19th century expansion towards the north, everything in this project expresses the theme of the "hinge." A many-sided metaphor, a hinge is something that links and yet separates, that enables spaces to open into one another but also stresses their independence, that asserts their presence but simultaneously disguises itself as an ambiguous element. The design thus splits into two independent organisms: the first with a rectangular layout and a regular iron structure; the second a triangular concrete arrangement, disrupted by the vertical blocks of services left unfaced. Commenting on this design, Massimo Scolari related it to the poetic of James Stirling and the Schocken department stores by Mendelsohn (cf. *Controspazio*, 1971, no. 3). But the chain of associations could be extended. In fact it is hard to ignore the reminiscences of Poelzig and Quaroni present respectively in the sequence of panelled bands in Via Ruggero Settimo and Via Mariano Stabile and in the packed volumetric collage of the rear; while there is a smack of constructivism about the triangular prism of piping jutting out at the top, serving the functions of publicity.

Besides, in Gregotti's case architecture grows out of other works of architecture; the multiplicity of references present in the design for "La Rinascente" in Palermo should not cause us to lose sight of the subject of the work. A unitary form, solid, wrapped up in itself: the myriads of objects washing around it stress its quality as *Reklamearchitektur*. Poelzig and Mendelsohn are not evoked just accidentally, and in the same way there is nothing accidental about the suggestion of Quaroni in the rear elevation. There is no synthesis between unity and multiplicity: the instability of this dialogue is appropriate to the metropolitan formlessness which the "hinge" absorbs, introjects and displays.

This same formlessness may, however, be sifted, reordered, analyzed and recomposed: it can be used to make a language devoid of the expressionist residues present in the design for Palermo. This is what has happened in the design for "La Rinascente" in Turin (1969). Here it is no longer an object but a system of directions and relationships, and what is more, a dialogue with the city made up of assonances and distortions. The subject of the organism is the irregular rotation of the axis that directs the long inner gallery: the law of the orthogonal is broken by following the impulse provided by the features of the site, calling to mind the urban and commercial features of the Parisian *passages*, making the new element a link with the Turin grid, taking Via Po as a pattern of geometrical "deviancy" within a rigidly regular network. The concept of form itself – especially when compared with the design for "La Rinascente" in Palermo – undergoes a profound scaling down in Turin. It is not what appears as an image but the fruit of a re-elaboration of that chain of relationships, which here acts as the protagonist: on an outsize scale, the gigantic cavern compels one to measure the gap between the new organism,

Plan for the new A.C.T.V. boat yards on the Giudecca, Venice, 1980. Preliminary sketch of the facade of the building for Naviglio Minore.

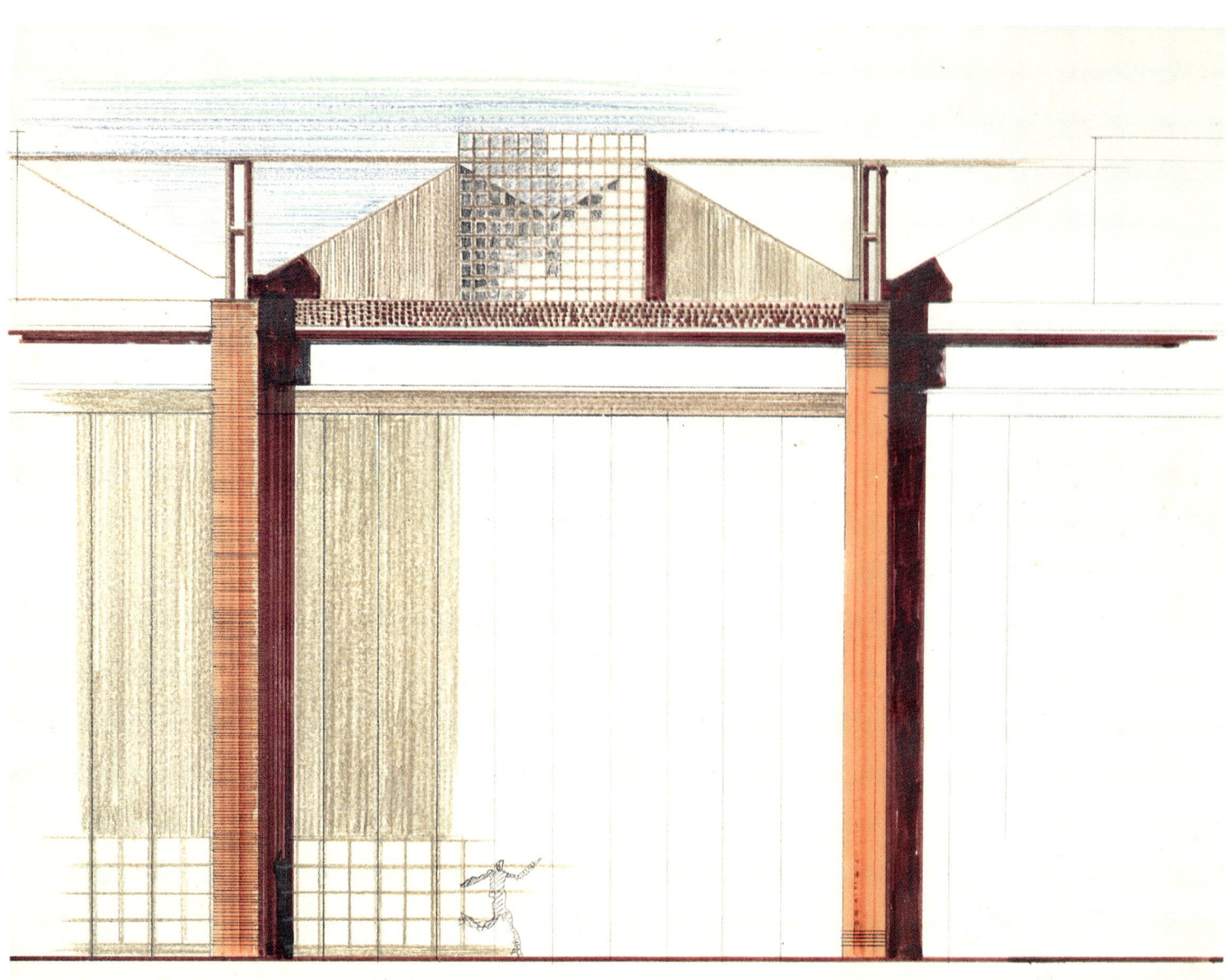

in its hermetic oscillation between solid and hollow, and the continuous web of buildings enveloping it. In this way, the arcade that runs between Via Lagrange and Via Carlo Alberto introduces an element of *hazard* into the grid it so blatantly violates. The great full-height portals, revealing the richness of the interior, bespeak this violence, which actually multiplies the semantic qualities of the grid itself, and even – thanks to the alienation effect played off against the urban scale – brings out its infinite potentialities. The block cut across at the corner and suspended on Via Carlo Alberto and Via Giolitti stresses, through its hieratic quality, the primacy of the inner space, a telescope that makes it possible to rediscover the images of the city gradually and from unexpected angles: the "machine à vendre" does not, now, act as publicity for itself but for the fragment of the city planned by Carlo di Castellamonte, relating to a tradition in which the space for merchandise is identified with the space of the metropolis. What counts is however the carefully calculated theatricality achieved by this break inserted in the monotony of Turin's fabric. The art of "creating relationships" no longer necessitates fabulation and this strengthens the ability to handle the logic of the unexpected.

The collaboration between Gregotti and Purini has turned out to be qualitatively productive: the "determinate abstractions" of the young Roman architect and his "classifications through types of formal element" are not without their effects on a work like this one, which in many ways opens out into the subsequent large-scale projects, in particular the IACP estate (state housing) in Palermo – the ZEN estate – which won the competition held in 1970.

In justifying the choices determining the composition of the ZEN estate, the Gregotti group adduced, firstly, the particular nature of the site, located on the borderland between an urban zone and the territorial dimension, the bridgehead of the development of Palermo along the axis of Via Maqueda-Via Libertà. A demand for "consolidation" would therefore seem to emerge from the context itself; but also the need for protection against natural presences felt as "too expressive." An urban structure contracting upon itself, rigorously related to a grid which gives coherence to the elementary system of subdivision of the site and hence able to provide a commentary upon a local tradition based on the pre-eminence of the walled-defensive aspect. The design of the ZEN estate adheres even too didactically to this underlying choice. The eighteen "insulae" (blocks) arranged on three different levels, taking advantage of a natural slope of the ground, are huddled together, linked through the towers at the head ground of each building, which taken together act as the large-scale *principium individuationis* for the whole complex. The *insula*, however, is the determining typological unit of the estate. Forthright, it stands out as a finished structure, yet one that is articulated internally by "incidents" and thoroughfares: as antecedents, one could invoke Michiel Brinkman's complex at Spangen or Ehn's Lindenhof, but taking care to avoid direct references. What is really important is that this forthright typological absoluteness cuts itself free from the "poetic of repetition." The towers, the stepped profiles and the multiple thoroughfares form chains of events: the mechanism guiding the overall morphology is that of a geometry astonished at the results of its own rigour. For this reason, the centre of the collective services, arranged in a band, necessarily assumes the form of a "variation" in relation to the grid of reference established by the aggregation of *insulae*, while the median space that breaks crossways into the homogeneous web of buildings takes on the quality of a rhetorical expedient.

Hence a "too-built-up area," projected like a meteor detached from the body of the city and huddling in on itself under the brooding menace of the landscape: this is how the design of the ZEN estate appears, aimed to stand forth as a great territorial marker but also stressing that not even on this scale is it legitimate to abandon the instrument of allegory. Its defensive compactness is, in fact, allegorical: the geometrical excess dominating it sets up a dialogue with its skyline – here there is a suggestion, between the lines, of the Viennese designs of "stepped" dwellings by Behrens

Project for A.C.T.V., Venice, 1980. Section of the basins for Naviglio Maggiore and section in perspective of the workshops.

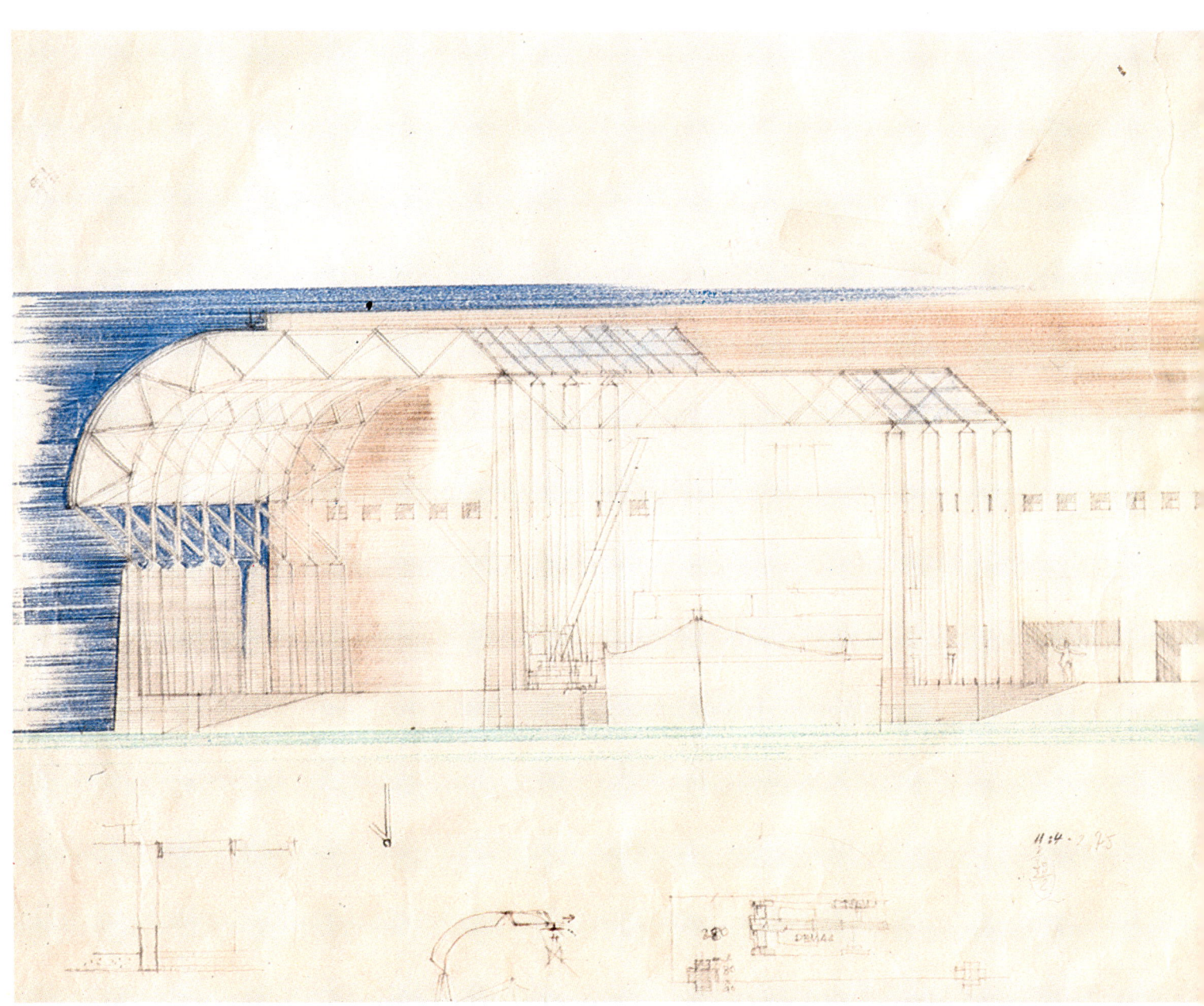

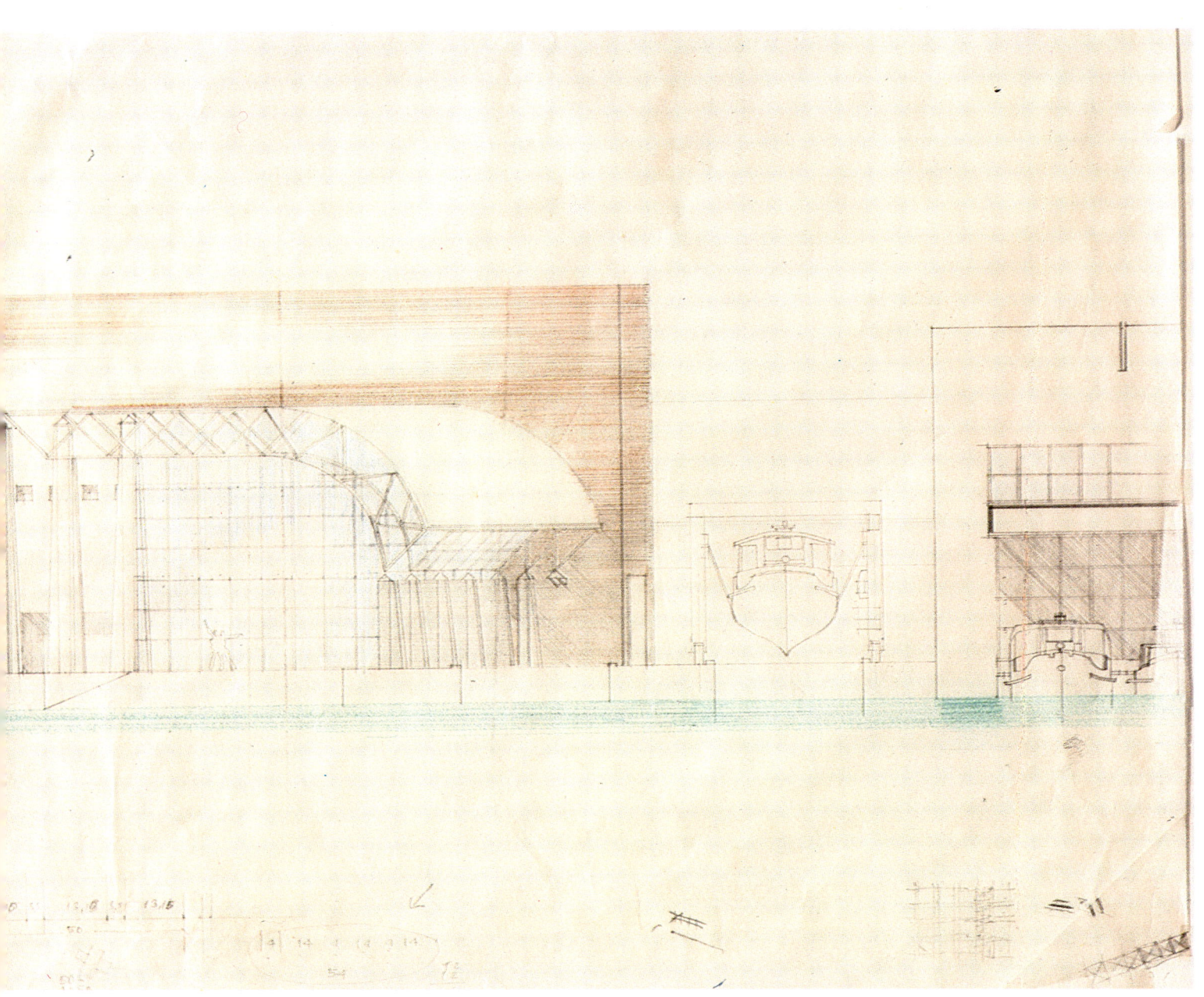

and Popp – in opposition to the excess of an environment that is geographically and historically too expressive.

The "carefully calculated ambiguities" mentioned in the project report (in *Controspazio,* 1971, no. 3), relate to what is also there described as a "catalogue of negations of current ideas about the dwelling," revealing the wisdom of a composition that is capable of subduing and controlling ambiguities and negations.

After the carefully calculated distortions of "La Rinascente" in Turin, and developing to its extreme the concept of an object resolved into a multiple system of relationships, the design of the ZEN estate is a response, four years later, to the requirements put forward in the monographic issue of *Edilizia moderna* devoted to the form of the territory. It was impossible to satisfy those requirements theoretically: from this point on, the significance of the nature-culture relationship is made concrete in a chain of designs, rather than in Gregotti's writings. The compactness of the ZEN estate is also that of a syntagm enclosed on itself in order to endow itself with an identity, to be recognisable as a structured system, whose signs form part of a new and still experimental alphabet. In the same way, though less consistently, the Gregotti group produced a design for an estate housing 70,000 people in south Vienna which has a single overall image, interpreted by Oriol Bohigas as "an enormous *castillo* with a central patio." An image "invented" – still in the words of the Spanish critic (cf. "Arquitectura bis," November 1974, p. 21) – even before the architectural ins and outs had been entered upon; and this appears from the fact that: "... la voluntad de crear esa imagen es tan patente que e alla acude incluso la memoria de los elementos prestigiosos de la historia local, como las perspectivas inclinandas de Schönbrunn o la contundencia de recorrido del Ring." Be that as it may, the immense Hof uses the Vienna south project, its typological enhancement and the dimensions of the undertaking, as material for an astral montage. The natural/artificial interplay here falls into abeyance. But immediately the quest gets under way again, with one of the most significant projects worked out by the Italian architectural culture of the early seventies.

A system of dykes restraining the forces of the natural site or inserted on it like mysterious relics: this, at first view, might be the interpretation on the project by the Gregotti group for the new University of Florence (1971), in which the themes of the projects in Vienna and the ZEN estate reappear refined and subjected to a process of verification. The sureness with which the five long parallel blocks are set out and spaced at irregular intervals, to be the premises for teaching and research centres, is the outcome of an intention to make the nodal function of the new complex intelligible on a territorial scale, in relation to the historic nuclei of Florence, Prato and Pistoia. The town design seeks to give concreteness to the choices embodied in the master plan for Florence. Hence the importance ascribed to links with the business centre of the city, with the axis Florence-Prato and with the Castello station. The five blocks that rise up rhythmically spaced to mark the act of taking possession of the environmental space, have a gaunt and bare appearance, as if to go beyond their specific functions and assert their "sacral" character. The foundation of the university is a solemn act. Unintegrated, the new entity makes the territorial tract between Prato and Florence dissonant: the act of founding, underscored by the reiteration of the blocks, respects a ritual, follows a law. This explains the classical hieraticity of these "dykes." The simplicity of the signs is the consequence of the propitiatory-mystical character connected with the action by which a new urban entity comes into being: the parallel bodies, intersected by the metropolitan railway and regional road system, stand out unmoving in the landscape like figures in an abstract pantomime alluding to archaic tonalities. The unity of the aligned blocks conceals, in fact, a very high degree of typological and functional flexibility. The typical section of the block reveals two lateral containing walls used for the vertical and horizontal paths of communications, defined in this way, there is a light constructional system mainly of metal, achieving great flexibility and capable, of meeting a range of changing requirements. A twofold structure, therefore, in which the relation between fixed elements and mobile ones acts as a function of the unchangingness of the overall image.

Here, too, the references to historic precedents are clear, in particular to Le Corbusier's "plan Obus." But in the design for Florence University by the Gregotti group, there is no indulgence in any "riot of contradictions." The Apollonian immobility of the long blocks, which with their basic module of 7.20x7.20 metres, determine the multiples ordering the entire complex, is eloquent of the achieved mastery of multiplicity: a mastery that extends to the area contained between the basic structures of the site, measured in their turn by the sequence of vertical blocks with a square ground plan. The great dykes "contain" forces, within themselves as without. At the same time, the high-rise blocks, which progress in a series and are arranged at right angles to the linear blocks, have the task of connecting plainland with hills: the image of the new "heterotopia of culture" engages in a dialogue with the landscape that is made up of "pre-established disharmonies."

Great emphasis on form for the most formless of Italian institutions, one might comment moralistically. In reality, the occasion for producing a design is, for both Gregotti and Purini, a stimulus to raise discussion about architecture in itself. The experience of the plan for Florence University was to have a sequel in Purini's development: here one thinks of the competition entry for the business centre in Latina and the design for the Montericco quarries. Both the ZEN estate project and the one for Florence University present intensely introspective complexes. The universe of forms so arranged that they live as anthropological statements within the great containers of nature is matched by a universe of forms intent on preserving itself from any external contamination. Compared with the works of the fifties and sixties, the ingredients of the narration are plainly more mature, in accordance with changes in the instruments of design themselves. The old firm made up of friends from university days is replaced by "Gregotti Associati:" the trend is towards a managerial dimension of design in which qualitative valences are active at a level uncontaminated by uncontrolled states of feeling. Whatever remains of craftsmanship in the professional organization of the office in Via Bandello can easily be gathered by checking the individual designs and the vicissitudes of their construction. In a certain sense, even Gregotti Associates is the expression of not so much a reality as an impulse, an intention perhaps even a premise, knowing but dynamic, one in which a "workshop" where overalls are compulsory wear has very chancy prospects, to say the least. But, ultimately, that problematic is the nucleus which Gregotti would never be prepared to renounce. In permitting it to find expression, the danger of repetition is averted. Take, for instance, the way the dyke is again taken up, made explicit and varied in one of the most felicitous designs of Gregotti's latest work, the plan for a residential estates at Cefalù (1976). A system of bridges serving a residential function is sunk into a narrow valley, overturning every typological convention. The site is made part of the design materials. The succession of "dykes" compels nature to speak out, while the concision of the sign alludes to a dialectic whose synthesis has been made problematic.

This is a poetic and a method whose most successful outcome appears in the winning entry for the University of Calabria (1972-73). Once again a university structure and again the reality of southern Italy: but more important than either, again a dimension and a site that permit a further step forward in the quest for models of settlement, profoundly anchored in the particularities of places. The starting point is the system of hills descending towards the Crati valley from the Paola range. A longitudinal sequence of slopes and ridges, at right angles to the present axis of expansion and the layout of the city of Cosenza. To this geographical location, a twofold approach: a linear system of blocks having a square ground plan, to be used for departmental activities, is linked with a 3,200 meter bridge equipped with urban amenities, a slender but unmistakable fixed sign that connects the railway station with the state highway from Silana to Crotonese. Terraces of residential

IVI Chemical Research Centre at Quattordio di Alessandria. Detail of the facade on the side of the workshops.

constructions straggle along the northern slope, branching off from the ideal points of alignment between the linear structure and the hilltops along which run the local roads. In this way, the landscape becomes "recomposed," gradually being brought into syntony with a dissonant yet thread-like element.

Since the southern slopes are covered with olive-groves, this further helps to produce an alternating succession of low-rise residential units and natural spaces. The bridge-system, for its part, does not make an artificial horizon; at most it suggests one, while giving glimpses of the hills and the ruggedly varied terrain both above and below the connecting axis, which runs at a constant altitude. This altitude also acts as a guide to the height of the departmental blocks that are solid down to the ground, responding to the altimetric variations imposed by the local physical relief.

The conflict between the artificial, superimposed line of direction – the bridge – and the "natural" ones – the roads along the hilltops – is made explicit: at these nodal points the structure widens out, creating squares with an urban effect, intended as the location of the university's services, setting up hinge-links between the two systems that underlie the entire structure of the complex. This, as a linear system, lends itself admirably to construction in successive phases, until it reaches an envisaged ceiling of 12,000 students, after which student halls of residence will be located in the old centres of Cosenza and neighbouring towns. The open form of the whole complex also permits continuous adjustments in the organization of the departmental nuclei. Neither *Roadtown* nor *Ciudad lineal* underlie this composition: once again Gregotti excludes Utopia from his cultural equipment. It is significant that it is precisely from an anti-Utopian investigation typical of Gregotti that a design of this sort, for the University of Calabria, has grown up, one that will make it possible, once it has been completely executed, to check the strength of the efforts made by Italian architectural culture to involve the whole of the environmental space in its own renewed *Formfrage*. Here this is done, not by hieratic solemnity as in the blocks of the University of Florence, but by stretching Ariadne's thread across the void. Gregotti settles into the Crati valley. The ambition to achieve architecture made up of pure relationships seems to be satisfied here. What is left of the object does not "dwell" in the natural environment: it is "astray" in its setting, feeling compelled to cluster about the only point of reference, which is received in this setting like the solidified echo of a word uttered everlastingly by the chorus of hills and vallies: the confident and indifferent line that overrides every natural incident and takes strength in its own consistency as pure sign.

So, from the fetish of the object to the crisis of the object: the trajectory of Gregotti's quest revisits the stages in a process that is historically marked out and experiments with various formal organisations, depending on whether it is the design for the Manilva tourist centre in Malaga (1974, with Bohigas, Martorell and Mackay), the new headquarters of the Istituto Feltrinelli in Milan (1974), or the Montedison research centre at Portici (1978), rich in ideas in the manner of Stirling and reminiscences of Terragni.

An exceptionally confident handling emerges, from this complex of studies. Any attempt to limit Gregotti's contribution by belittling its characteristics and speaking of neo-rationalism, completely misses his main goal: Gregotti entrusts his impulses not to tried and tested syntax nor to collages gloating over their own indulgences, nor the revival of cathartic ideologies, but to a skilled working and reworking.

In this handling there emerges no apology for technique: if anything, it contains a suspension of judgement, rendered apparent by the fixity of the forms. The hieraticity that shapes the projects analyzed above takes on different characteristics in the new centre for the Istituto Italiano in Tokyo (1980), or in the designs for the new IVI research centre and the terminal of S. Marino (1981), demonstrating that the process of stylistic reduction is not an end in itself nor the vehicle of a minimal poetic, but is the instrument of a free interplay of articulation in relation to contents. Thus, while the design for Tokyo pays homage to the pioneers of the modern Japanese tradition, the S. Marino terminal fits into the city as a finished place, a machine for mediation, a "stairway" placed like a hinge between the centre and the open spaces, an urban sculpture concentrated in its great L-shaped slabs and in the squares that they enclose. In this way, the process of reduction achieved by the signs is transformed into eloquence: the profile of the slabs emphasizes and concludes the profile of the walls that descend from the castle, but also produce a polyvalent and multifunctional city gate linked with the buildings (restructured) of the old mills and ceramics factory.

Just as in the Cefalù project, stylistic rarefaction in the S. Marino terminal becomes charged with surreal valences: the "sewing up" operation achieved by the architecture displays its own ambiguity. It is no accident that in the description of the design presented with the competition entry for the restructuring of the south Tiergarten area in Berlin (1980), Gregotti and his collaborators declared their wish to "maintain, through the idea of urban unity, an ambiguous relationship, of incomplete tension, of broken memory." Berlin, therefore, as the metropolis of laceration, a living body taken as the symbol of the modern sense of bewilderment. A bewilderment that is incurable, but which admits of representation: the fragment itself can be consecrated as the new *idolum*, but it can also lend itself to lay "constructions."

It is precisely by fixing a fragment of Berlin's urban history that Gregotti proceeds in the south Tiergarten district: the handling makes a direct approach to the historical sense of disquiet, becoming pervaded with the "Berlin dialects" of the twenties. The system of relations set up by the project takes as its coordinates the environmental qualities of the Landwehrkanal, the chimney of the "Pumpwerk," the industrial buildings on the Genthinerstrasse; the new district appears as a cementation of the area, a painful comment on the dialectics that had animated Berlin in the Weimar period.

"The Berlin childhood" to which Gregotti's *mémoire volontaire* refers is not Bruno Taut's or Mendelsohn's. In the five articulated blocks with their corner towers, in the great access portals and throughways, in the texture and variations of materials – klinker facing with two colour-tones, from yellowy-grey to brick red, and greyish-blue metal structures – as well as in the succession of types, other memories surface: the rehandling turns insistently to texts by Behrens, by Max Taut, by Erwin Gutkind. And in the body of the building, isolated and at right angles to the Lützowuferstrasse, the tribute to Scharoun is explicit. Berlin as reconsidered by Gregotti is the Berlin of exceptions, or rather of the tensions between aspiration to the norm and the primacy of the breakaway, the distortion, the deviation. Gregotti's "Berliner dodecaphonie" is the commentary of a Grossstadt that had been capable of staging the pantomime of angst in expressionist cabarets.

In Berlin, Gregotti imposed the measure of composition on the chosen dialects of feelings; but in Venice, the city that represents an incessant challenge to the concept of the "modern," it is not possible to make arbitrary choices amongst the many languages that intermingle in the labyrinth of the lagoon. While the Berlin project was able to take the form of an essay, the three designs Gregotti worked on for Venice favoured pure composition. Besides, a recovered rigour of composition emerges clearly from the designs of Gregotti's latest period. Composition is opposed to the mutability of design, geometrical arrangements are opposed to the technique of *bricolage*, a method of indirect control is opposed to the methods of direct control. Gregotti is certainly not the first to have subjected the relationship of rule-exception to such parameters: from Louis Kahn to Giorgio Grassi, the idea of "regularity" has a history all its own. But he is unquestionably the most coherent and least dogmatic among the "composers". It is precisely by recourse to a method capable of securing definite fields for variations that Gregotti is able to tackle the delicate subject of the urban threshold in Venice – the edges of the Giudecca and rio del Ponte Lungo for the ACTV dockyards, the island of Tronchetto for the new tertiary centre – and the restructuring of a sector of Cannaregio (the Saffa site). As far as can be deduced from the state of progress on the three projects mentioned here, Gregotti is aiming at codifying a method of intervention that can be generalized on the lagoon: the detachment implicit in the conceptual grids adopted permits a dialogue with the settings that is based on the shapes of their "difference."

Gregotti's compositional conceptualism displays an undoubted ability to bring into question once again the theme of the border between water and land, the result of an age-old study in the Venetian environment, not excluding the intrusion of "inventions:" hence, in the Cannaregio project, the aggregational interplay of types; in the Giudecca plan, the variations on the ground plan and structure; in the Tronchetto project, the rhythmically staggered fronts, the projection of the glazed prism, the differentiated network of the commercial streets.

In this way Gregotti's syntheticism deposits its subdued signs within the contexts taken as subjects with which to establish "civilized conversations:" an increasingly refined sense of craftsmanship sustains the tone of this conversation, which includes among its merits the banishment of any temptation to turn the design into an occasion for "carnivals of the intellect."

One is tempted to relate this sort of study to the work of Rogers' other two pupils, protagonists with Gregotti of the new cultural climate of the sixties: Guido Canella and Aldo Rossi. The art of composition, the dramaturgy of decomposition, the adventures of memory: the disquiets of the fifties lead to separate lines of study without communication between them, yet all flowing into the "great game" of current Italian architecture. It is, in fact, in contact with Canella's civil invective and the suspended atmospheres of Rossi that Gregotti's "severity of style" becomes even more expressive. Besides, the metaphor of the dyke, that we have found resurfacing so often in his latest designs, also seems a good way to denote emblematically a personal stand being made in relation to a context that renders itself comically busy in order to disguise its own bankruptcy.

Having concluded his task of extenuation involving the "diseased material" inherited from the generation of the "disquieting Muses," Gregotti also seems inclined to call it quits with architecture as "essay." Always ready to question his own bearings yet sure of his route, Gregotti's journey into the territory of architecture appears as the trail of an inquirer continuously being compelled, almost despite himself, to abandon the *jeu* in favour of the *sérieux*. His optimism in design is also the symptom of an epoch, of a cultural condition, of a gamble directed towards the present: essentially the fruit of his stubborn will to be present in a "citadel devoid of banners."

Ten projects 1964-1981

13th Triennale (1964): Introductory section to the theme of leisure time

This project was made by Beppe Brivio, Umberto Eco, Vittorio Gregotti, Lodovico Meneghetti, Giotto Stoppino and Massimo Vignelli.

A theme of the sort presented by the Triennale, "A Critique of the Ecology of Leisure," presented complex problems of communication. We have taken account of four basic principles: the introduction of "scenic time" into the route to be followed; reduction of captions to a minimum, with the greatest possible emphasis on elements of pictorial, graphic, and scenic evocativeness; introduction of alternative choices along the route; the placing of the various significances on different levels to secure the visitor's attention, which is diverted at the Triennale to the most varied range of interests.

On entering, the visitor finds himself immersed in a multicoloured and opalescent milieu (the "Terminal of Exaltation"), the walls lined with a modular series of shining images, flashing on and off, accompanied by a sound track on which are superimposed simultaneously invitations to enjoy leisure time (marvellous trips, radio announcements of shows, invitations to gatherings, sports events, dances, parties), all presenting opportunities which the leisure industry offers consumers. Since the graphics and figurative materials are taken from real adverts, this sort of "paradise" of escapism has all the appearance of something attainable and concrete and prompts the visitor into a mood of euphoria. This euphoria is then destined to be symbolically deflated when he enters the second room through the cinema doors ("Decompression Chamber": painter, Aurelio Caminati): squalid and empty, with a series of large dusty inscriptions. This is meant to represent the reality of the "vacant time" which we end up having to organize after an exhausting day's work and with only limited time available, hindered by money problems, traffic jams and the essential emptiness of the choices offered. In this second room the visitor finds a series of five machines: aluminium cubes measuring 90x90x90 cms., in style somewhere between a juke-box and a washing machine, with Lichtenstein's big pointing hand plastered across the front. The tops of these machines light up alternately with a series of press-buttons corresponding to a set of definitions of the visitor (age, profession, sex, favourite pastimes). When the data have been fed into the machine, it issues a ticket containing the explanations of the first two rooms and indications how to choose one of the four routes through the next room. The relation between the data fed into the machine and the information it issues is of course quite false, just as it is false to believe, in our present circumstances, that we have made a free choice about the use of our leisure time. A fundamental and labyrinthine illusion is symbolized in the next room. Here the material, of a silvery metallic appearance (walls, floor, ceiling), is completely unified: the steps we walk up are reproduced on the ceiling, multiplied by a series of transverse mirrors, doubled by a symmetry which places us in the position of mirrors and also alters the essential isotropism of the whole space, setting it at right angles to the route, leading to a loss of the sense of geometrical position and dimensional relations.

A stacked series of containers, tubular in shape and square in cross-section, sheared lengthwise at random, forms the structure of the four routes to be followed. As a whole they are vaguely reminiscent architecturally of a cross between an underground station and the service conduits of a future metropolis. The interiors of these conduits, eight in number, develop four leading themes handled by different painters, and at their heads they bear symbols of four cross-sections through the history of the four types of dialectical relationships found in leisure: the same symbols appeared earlier on the tickets issued by the machines in the previous rooms. The first theme (Techniques: painter Enrico Baj) involves the connections between leisure time and technological development in their negative and positive aspects; the second theme (Illusions: painter Lucio Del Pezzo) is a casebook of historical situations which we traditionally see as a life of blissful idleness, whereas in reality the leisure celebrated in them was never the privilege of the whole of society, or only in some equivocal sense; the third theme (Utopias: painters Lucio Fontana and Nanda Vigo) is connected with hopes and conjectures connected with future societies where all of mankind's possibilities of spiritual and physical development will be recognized; the fourth theme (Integration: painters Roberto Crippa and Fabio Mauri), finally, refers to historical situations, from the medieval church to the modern cinema, where leisure has been celebrated as the passive reception of messages handed down from above, instruction of the masses.

The four paths through the eight square-sectioned conduits are arranged so as to form a series of alternative routes, each developing a fully self-contained topic, so that visits can differ in length while the spectator is also forced continually towards choices which give him a feeling both of exclusion and of a continually eluded alternative. (The sound track of the container is music by Luciano Berio, "Homage to Joyce", over-recorded with the singing voice of Cathy Barberian Berio).

On emerging from the four-track container, the "Corridor of Captions" projects the theme onto the present, preparing for the final room. The "Corridor of Captions" is based on the principle of symmetry, implemented through a diagonal cross-section.

The visitor is invited to sit on a long divan that runs across the whole room. Opposite and behind him there are two compositions consisting of coloured signs. On one side he will read the caption constituting the central thesis of the section: "One of the dangers of industrial civilization is that leisure is organized by the same centres of power as control work. In this case, leisure time is consumed at the same rate as work time. Enjoying oneself means becoming integrated."

On the other side, a series of alternating

1. Corridor of Captions.

flashing lights appears at first sight as a composition of normal publicity signs. In reality it turns out to be a composition of clichés and commonplaces about leisure, playing on underlying connections with well-known features of publicity at the level of graphics.

At this point the lights on the signs go out while two sets of spotlights come on and light up the seated spectators and also a series of dummies sitting on a divan placed symmetrically opposite them and tilted up towards the ceiling, revealing to the spectators their own helplessness.

On emerging from this corridor, one enters the final "Kaleidoscope." The rectangular space of the room of honour in the Triennale is visible and painted completely black. Inside it there is an enormous silvery object consisting of two triangular prisms, each of which is placed symmetrically to the other and fitted together along their longitudinal edges.

A triangular door leads into the head of one of the prisms, and inside it is like a large cinema auditorium, its cross-section that of an equilateral triangle. The inner walls of the prism, 24 metres long and 10.30 high, are entirely clad in mirrors, and while the two ends reflect and multiply the interior in infinite images, the side walls create the illusion that the spectator is inside an enormous hexagonal prism 18 metres high. Two films (directed by Tinto Brass) are projected onto the white floor of this room and simultaneously reflected six times in the mirrors: the subject of one is leisure and of the other work. The films last nine minutes and consist of a collage of repertory pieces. A special montage technique makes it possible to make the two themes coincide rhythmically and at the same time to develop several themes in one film, creating a complex series of presentation.

The spectator sees himself projected onto the walls six times, in the middle of the cinema screen, participating and physically involved in the performance. One ends up feeling strangely crushed and helpless after the rosy promises offered so glibly in the opening room.

At the films' end, a sound track by Nanni Balestrini and a series of coloured collages by the painter Achille Perilli overwhelm the scene in twenty-four combinations, in a sort of pile-up of the final ruins of our leisure-time. A voice announces the end of this first section and issues an invitation to move on to the next room.

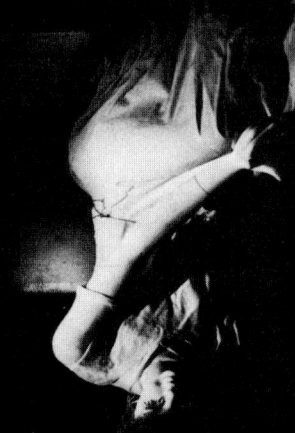

Uno dei pericoli della CIVILTA' INDUSTRIALE è che il *Tempo Libero* SIA ORGANIZZATO DAGLI STESSI CENTRI DI POTERE CHE CONTROLLANO IL TEMPO DEL LAVORO IN QUESTO CASO il *Tempo Libero* E' CONSUMATO SECONDO LO STESSO RITMO DEL TEMPO LAVORATIVO DIVERTIRSI SIGNIFICA FARSI INTEGRARE

2. Container with four routes.

3. Longitudinal section of the large Room of Containers.

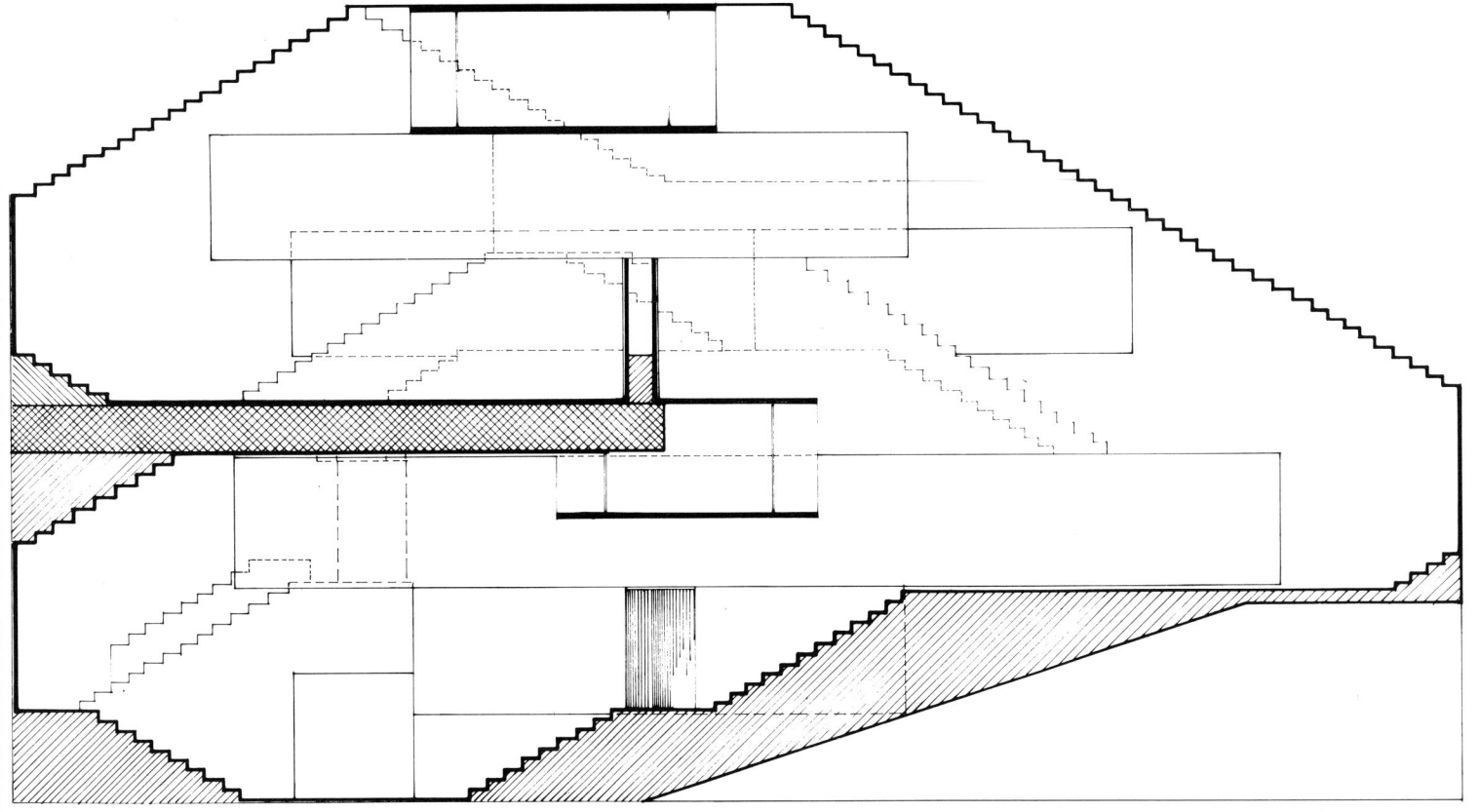

4. Section of Kaleidoscope room.

5,6. Views of Kaleidoscope during projection of films.

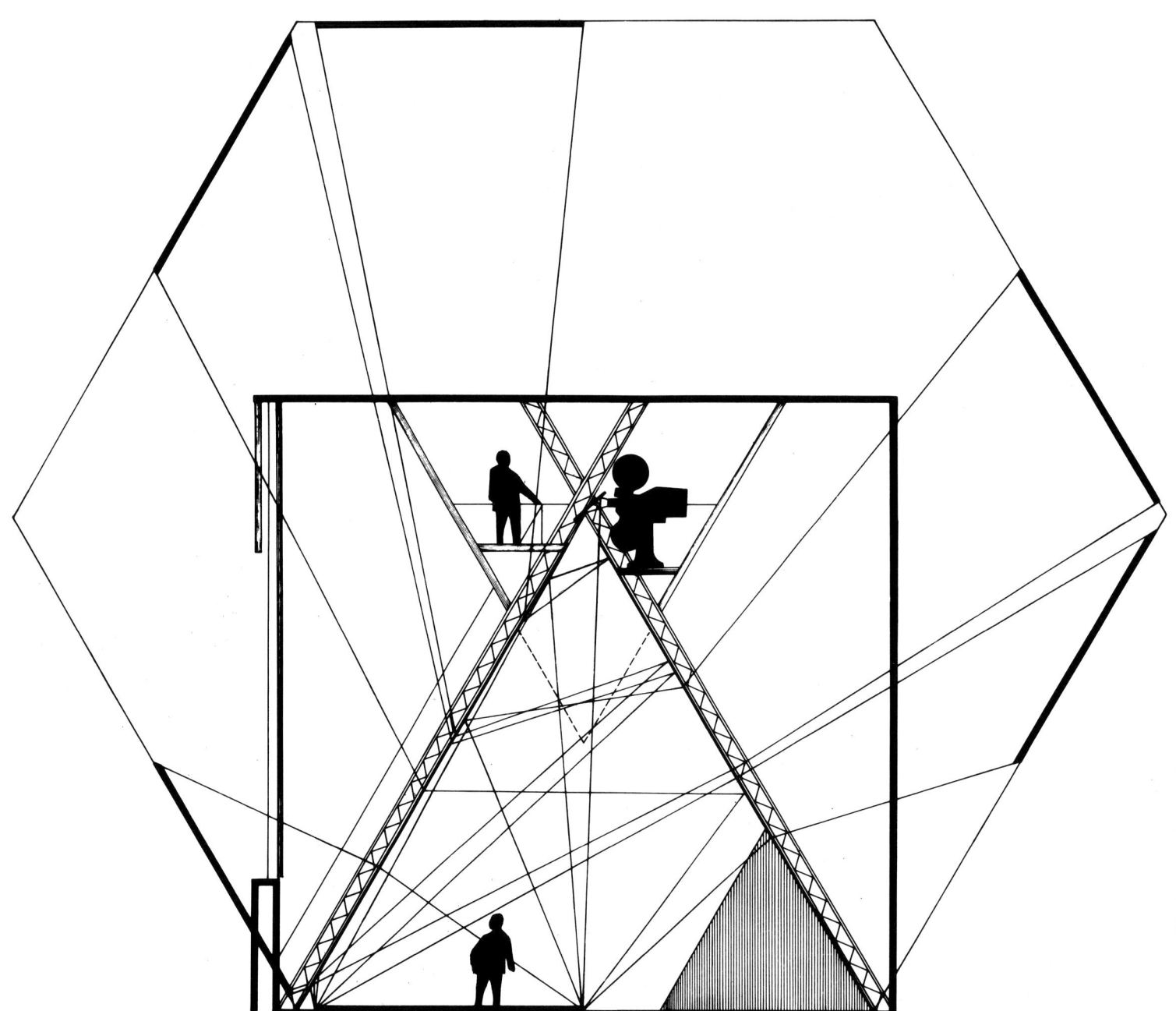

New Science Departments at Parco d'Orleans (University of Palermo)

1. *Chemistry Department: central bay.*

This project was made with the collaboration of Gino Pollini.

The group of new Science Departments is located in a site in the Parco d'Orleans which abuts directly onto the historic centre of Palermo, between Via Brasa, Via Altofonti and the buildings already erected for the university departments of the faculties of Arts and Philosophy, Agriculture, Economics and Commerce, and the Polytechnic. The project as a whole involves the construction of departments of Chemistry, Physics, Biology and, in a later phase, Mathematics and Geology, with a maximum scope for expansion of up to 235,000 sq. metres. To this should be added 65,000 sq. meters of general service buildings and student accommodation, a total of 10,000 sq. metres of connecting elements (parking spaces, squares etc.). In addition there are to be linked sports facilities, mostly outdoors but including a reserve of 10,000 sq. metres for indoor facilities.

The complex of Science departments is arranged on the axis of the present Viale delle Scienze and laid out around a set of three elongated pedestrian precincts of different levels, with all the science departments abutting onto them and the collective services for the student residences aligned along them. The squares are orientated to exploit the geographical lie of the land, which will be left unchanged as far as possible, with the sports facilities to be developed on the far side.

The three squares are arranged at three different levels which follow the natural rise of the land. The first is at 54 metres above sea-level, with more numerous connections with the collective services and entrance ways. The second is at 59 metres and designed as a hanging garden, connected with the first square by an outdoor theatre whose arrangement follows the natural shape of the terrain. The third is set at 61 metres and is envisaged as having a pond in front of the entrances to the departments of Mathematics and Geology, to be constructed in the future.

Wheeled traffic will run along a level lower than the pedestrian level of the squares, following the route of Viale delle Scienze and joining the new Via Brasa after completing the circuit of the whole system. This will serve the departmental system at every point from below, and also preserves the precious natural setting of the area.

Each department consists of two connected blocks, one essentially intended for teaching preliminary courses and the other for advanced courses and research.

Each of these blocks will be developed on two floors, and also have a basement level for parking and services. The basic module for both construction and installations of each block is 7.20x7.20 metres.

In addition to its research block, the Physics Department will have a workshop building located along the axis of the research block once the second phase of construction is complete.

The vertical bearing elements are composed of a prefabricated double pillar (with an interaxis of 7.20 metres both ways) which will permit vertical passage of the conduits and utilities (electric power lines, compressed air, gas, water pipes, distilled water supply, ventilation shafts etc.). These can run horizontally and open to inspection under the prefabricated ceilings which are so shaped as to permit the continuous horizontal arrangement of the conduits in both directions.

This is the first earthquake-proof prefabricated and precompressed structure of any importance to be put up in Italy.

2. *Aerial photomontage: location of new Science Departments.*
3. *Central bay of Chemistry Department.*

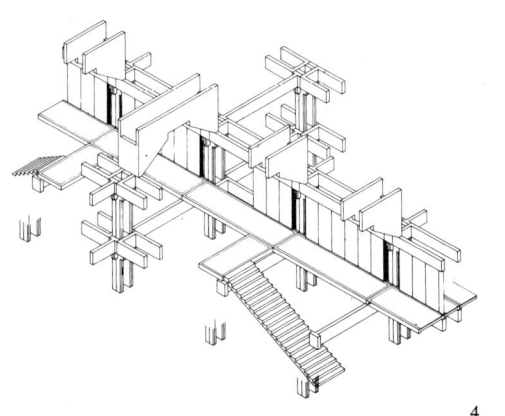

4

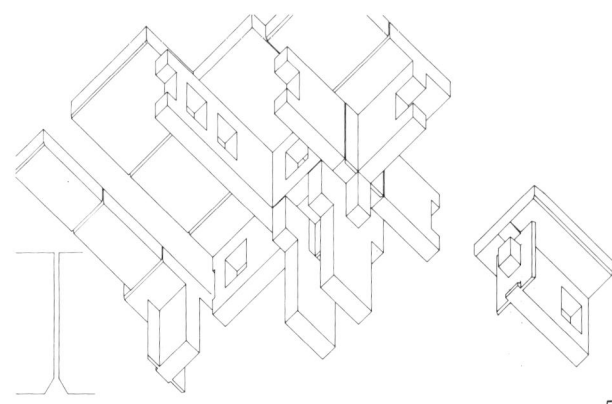

5

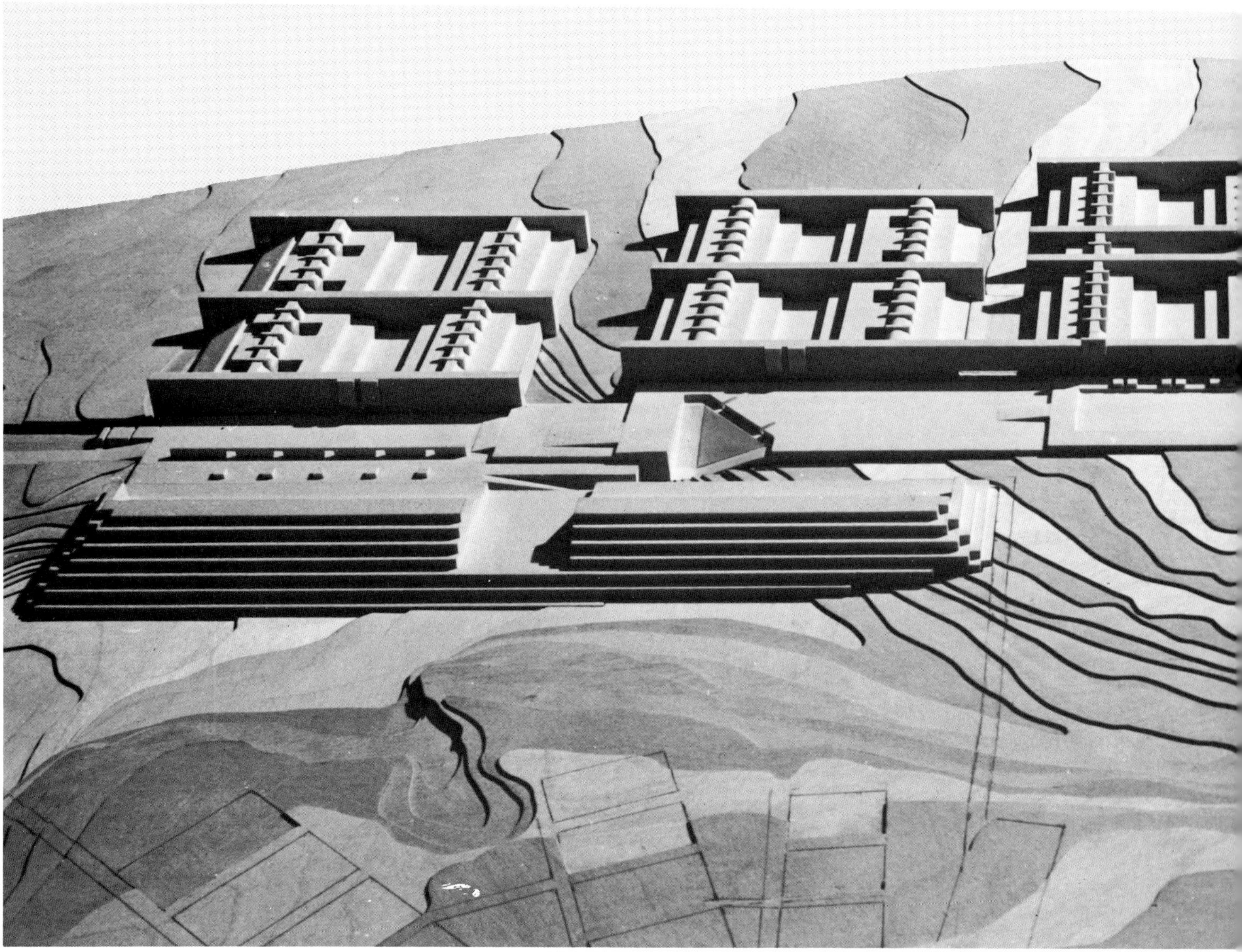

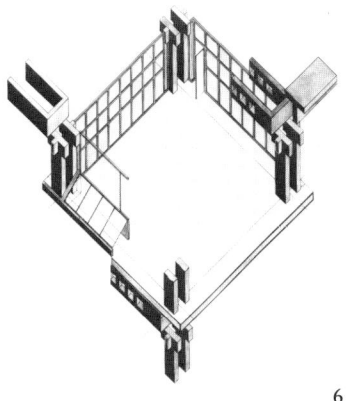
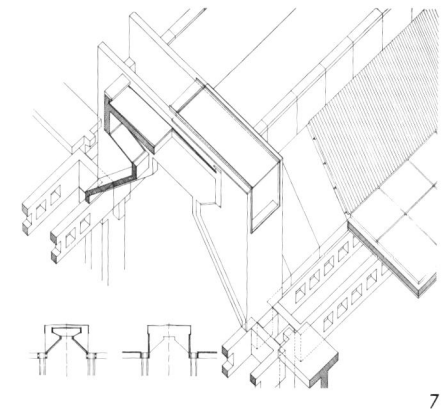

4. Axonometric of central bay of Physics Department.
5. Axonometric of structural nexus.
6. Axonometric of internal modular system.
7. Axonometric of detail of skylight in Physics Department.
8. Model of project.

9. *General plan.*
10. *Prospect of three departments.*
11. *Longitudinal section.*

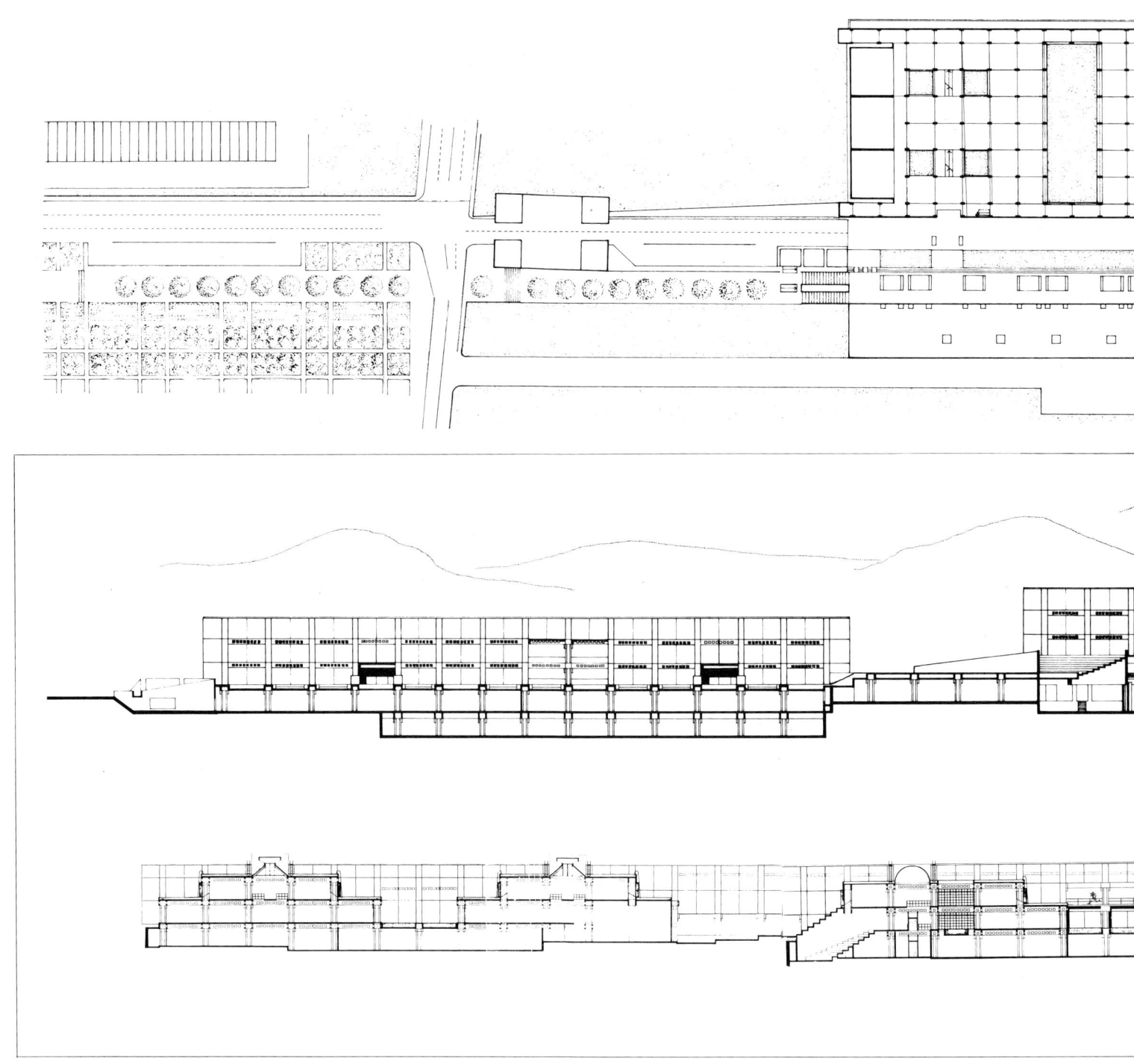

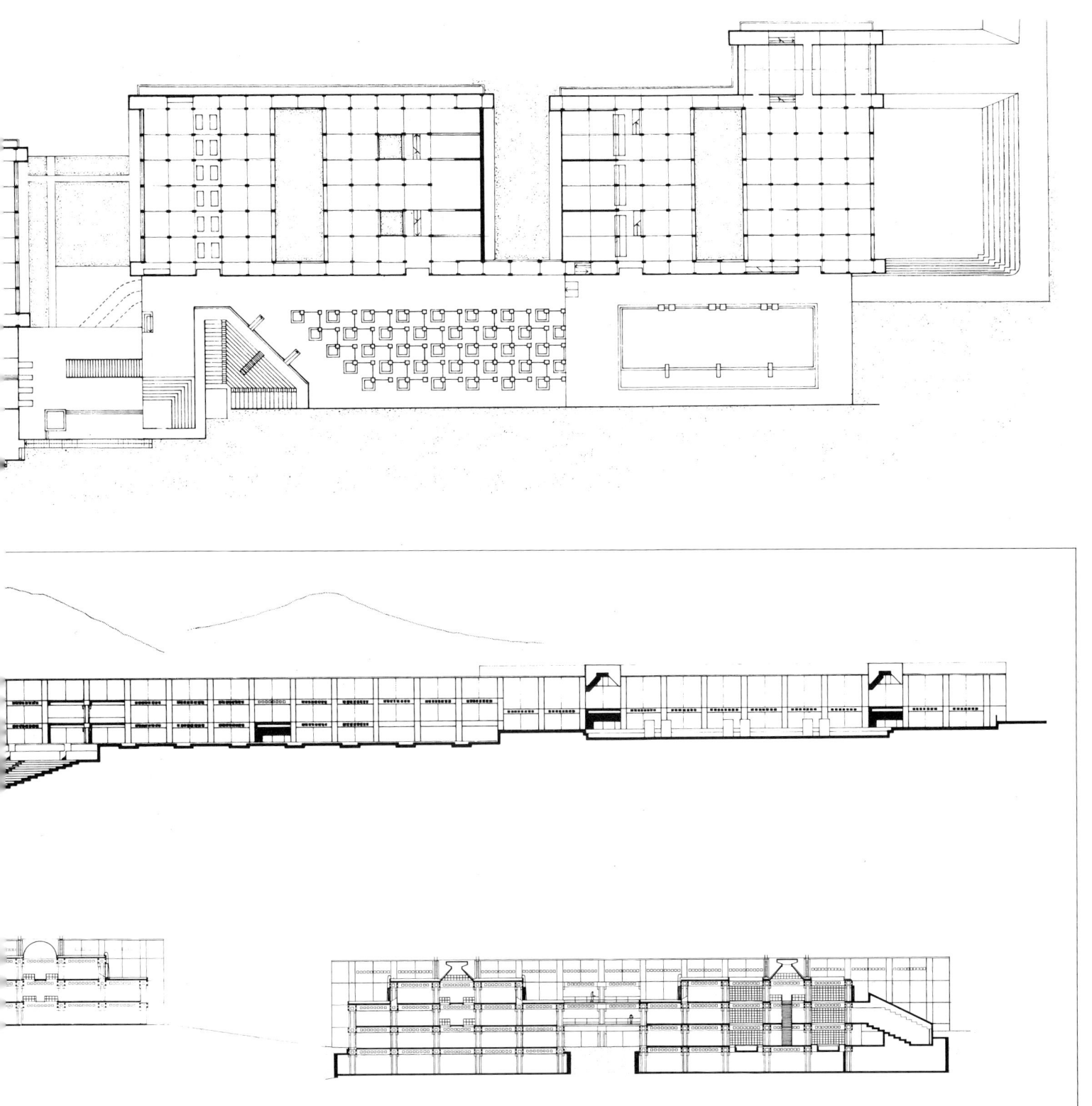

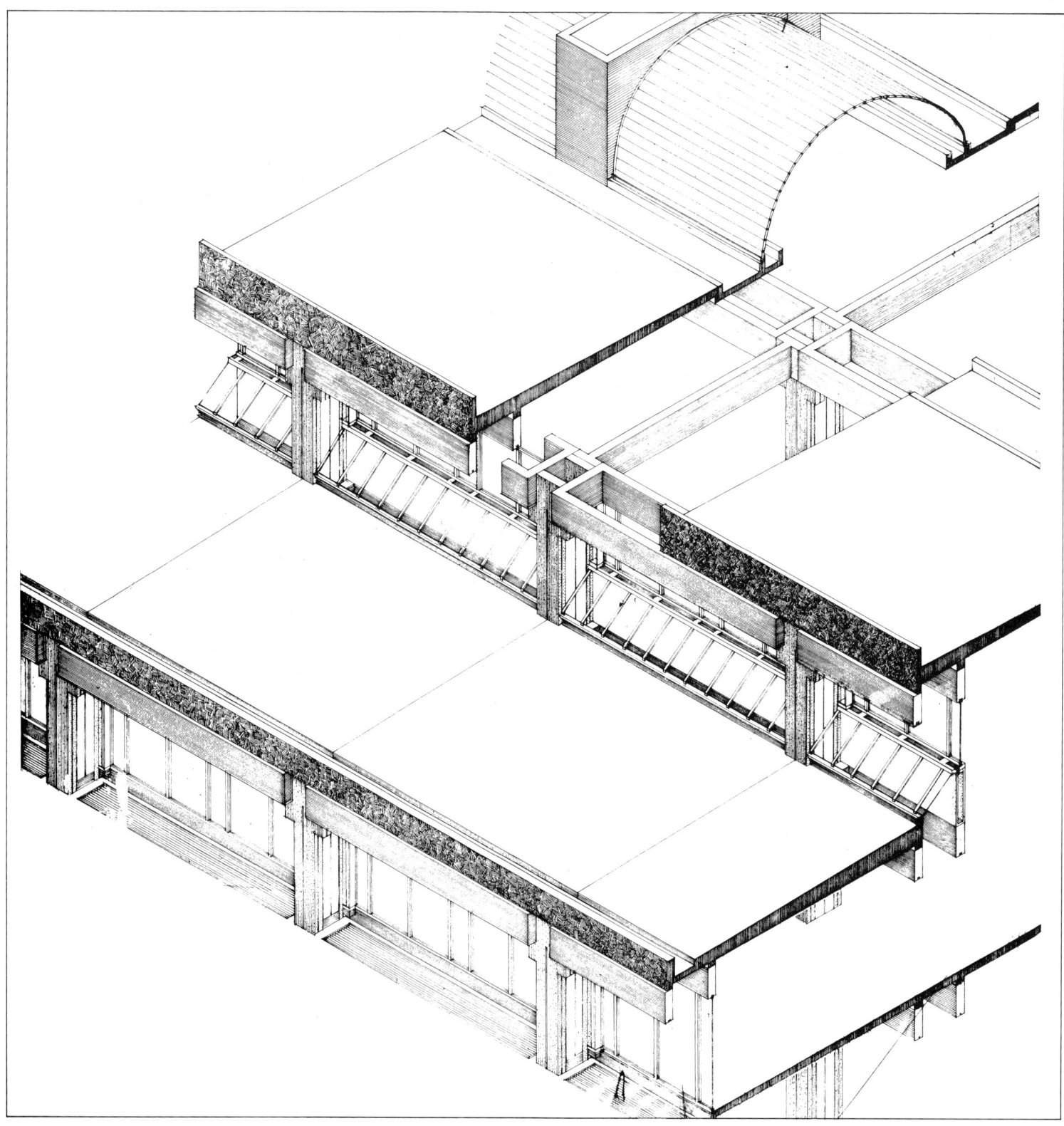

12. Axonometric section of front of Chemical Research building.
13. View of building site.

14. *Inner front of Chemistry Department.*

New campus of University of Calabria, Rende di Cosenza

The design for the Università della Calabria was the award-winner in a competition in 1974. The design team consisted of E. Battisti, V. Gregotti, H. Matsui, P. Nicolin, F. Purini, C. Rusconi Clerici and B. Viganò.

Our plan aims firstly to direct construction of the new University of Calabria towards a principle of settlement. This principle is based on a discontinuous alignment and its relation with the rolling relief of the landscape as a way of regulating and giving a recognisable identity to a large-scale pattern, as well as a method of measuring features of the landscape itself. Alignment and discontinuity are, moreover, ancient and characteristic modes of regulating settlement in Calabria. The plan creates an interaction between two different morphological and functional systems. The first of these systems consists of the linear sequence of buildings for the various departments crossing the chain of hills that slope down to the Crati river in the plain beneath the Paolana range.

The blocks with their square layouts to house departmental activities are connected with the varying ground levels below them by a fixed-level structure and are arranged along the axis of a landbridge equipped with urban amenities.

The second system takes into account the morphology of the outcroppings of hills in their longitudinal succession of slopes and ridges, with local roadways running along the heights and down into the valley and a network of low residential buildings set on terraces along the northern slope. Since the southern slopes are planted with olive trees, this creates an alternating sequence of residential units and natural spaces. The University's services, opening out towards the exterior, are placed at the point of junction between the landbridge system and the network of hilltop roads. At this point the structure spreads out to create squares with fully urbanised features so as to satisfy the need to connect the residential units with the teaching spaces, and also guarantee easy access from outside for the non-university population, as well as continuous use and vitality of the entire complex at all times. As a criterion of settlement, the principle may well prove valid and act as a criterion for other types of settlement.

The University complex, when fully functional, will house 20,000 people (counting students, teachers and non-teaching staff with their families) as a stable nucleus that will be one of the biggest communities in Calabria, excluding the provincial capitals. It will also be equipped with the finest public amenities in the region. The strategy underlying the plan aims at making the University settlement act as a structure that will redress the equilibrium of the whole of the upper Crati valley and provide it with services. So its relation with the city of Cosenza (which will act as a support in the early phase) will not be consolidated as the only favoured relationship: instead, the connections with the whole of the territory, studded with a series of settlements, will eventually become dominant.

The University's linear structure stems from its need to develop both its extremities, precisely individuated as privileged territorial points. At one end there is the crossing of the two motorways, running north-south and east-west, at the other is the railway line, where it emerges from the Paolana tunnel: it will be the main trunk-line connecting with the south between the Tyrrhenian and Adriatic mountain ridges. This creates a system which underscores the regional character of the university and the way it opens up the territory to new and valuable services.

In the first phase, the departmental buildings will traverse in linear succession the tract of the hill system lying between the four squares. The three valleys involved will house the sites of the twenty-one departments in such a way as to enable students to attend all the degree courses envisaged within the boundaries of the pedestrian precinct. The upper thoroughfare on the urban landbridge (width 7 metres) will be used for the public transport system and goods vehicles. The lower thoroughfare, for pedestrians, will be for internal circulation of the student population. Between the two, in a conduit with a triangular cross-section and easy access, will run the channels of technical plant. The high-rise departmental blocks are linked to the landbridge by a narrow vertical service block arranged either at right angles or parallel to the bridge, depending on the type of cube. The layout of the departments as a whole is arranged on a grid measuring 25.20x25.20 metres extending for two modules on either side of the axis and creating a band of settlement 110 metres wide. The high-rise buildings vary from 2 to 5 stories (each story is 5.40 metres high) in relation to the changes in altitude between the constant upper height of 232.40 metres above sea-level and its projection onto the line of cross-section through the underlying valley. These buildings are enclosed by reinforced concrete bearing walls with elements measuring 21.60x25.20 metres each side and set 3.60 metres apart. The horizontal structures are supported by metal girders with a span of 19.60 metres to allow access to internal communications. On these it is possible to arrange the structures of the interplanes and substories as gaps and solids. In the second type, the internal structures are also made of reinforced concrete and the pillars divide the interior into two different spaces which can be articulated in variable ways. On one side there may be small spaces for offices and studies, on the other large collective spaces for laboratories, lecture rooms, libraries etc. Natural lighting inside is provided by large apertures in the perimetral wall and transparent roofing with anti-glare elements. The view of the natural and architectural landscape outside is strategically arranged. The external modules of the grid are occupied by extensions at ground level of the high-rise blocks to form a sort of supporting base and house the heavier technical installations. The lecture rooms are established in single or double elements with seating for 250 people, contained in metal structures and suspended between the volumes of two lateral blocks so as not to interrupt the continuity of the slope and freedom of

1. *General view of the Valle del Crati.*

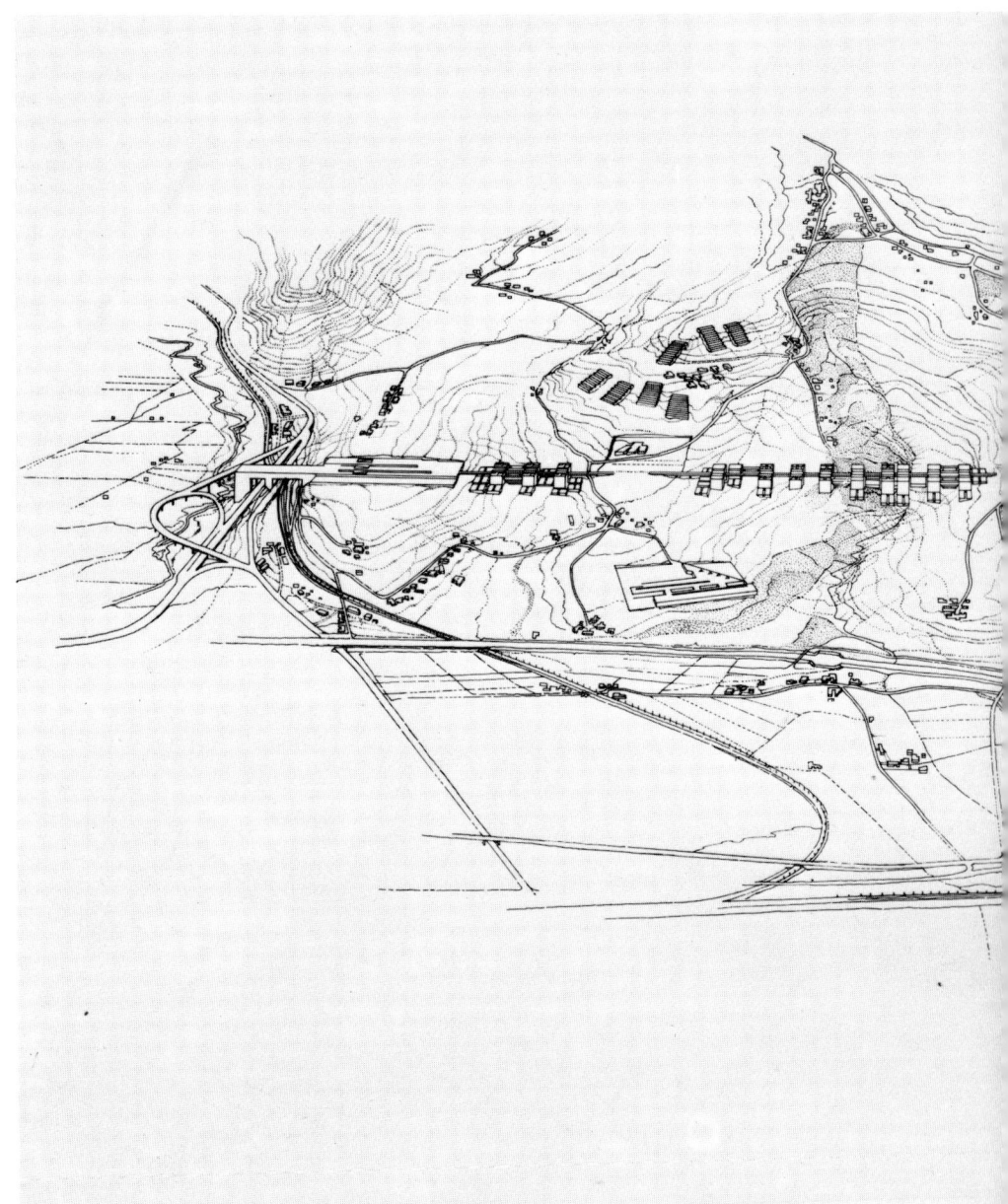

movement below the terraced intrados. The blocks are the basic elements for the grouping of the various departments, since they can house the whole range of teaching and research work and establish a morphologically significant criterion for expanding or altering the layout of the University's activities.

The final phase, with 12,000 students, is represented in the plan by a hypothesis which envisages the doubling of the departmental spaces. In this projection, a rapid communications system of the urbanized landbridge will be established, continuing at ground level as far as the two extremities of the new station with a car park at the entrance to the tunnel for Paola in the north and the link with the Silana-Crotonese road and car park at the end towards Cosenza. In the plains of the northern area there will be the structures of the big regional sports centre and the laboratories of the national research centre with their related reserve areas. When it has reached this state of development, the university complex will make full use of the two access systems which will grow out of the underlying principle of settlement: the two extremities of the alignment will be linked by a rapid-transit system and the hilltop roads will continue to fulfill the same function as in phase one.

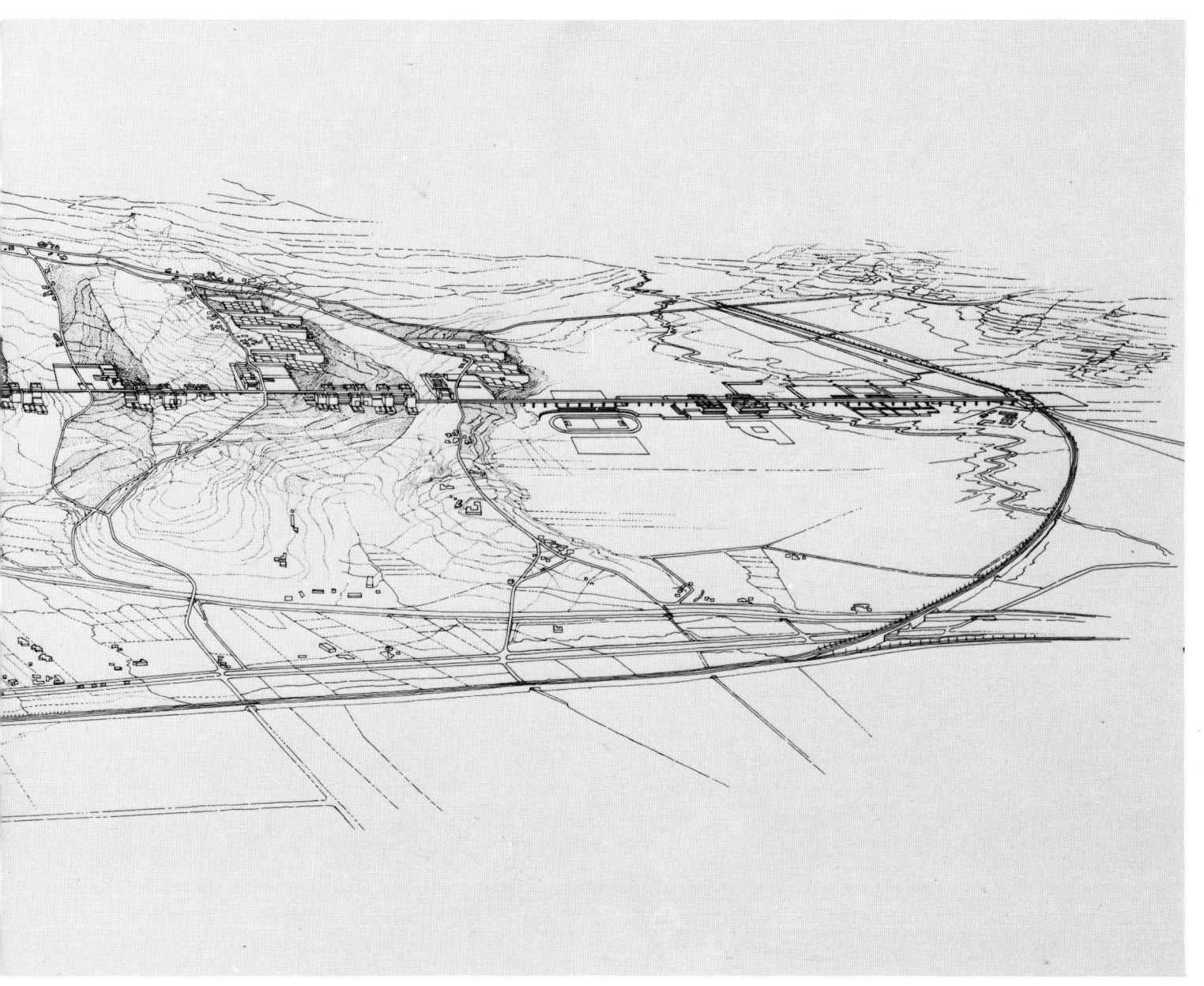

2. *Modular scheme of system of settlement.*

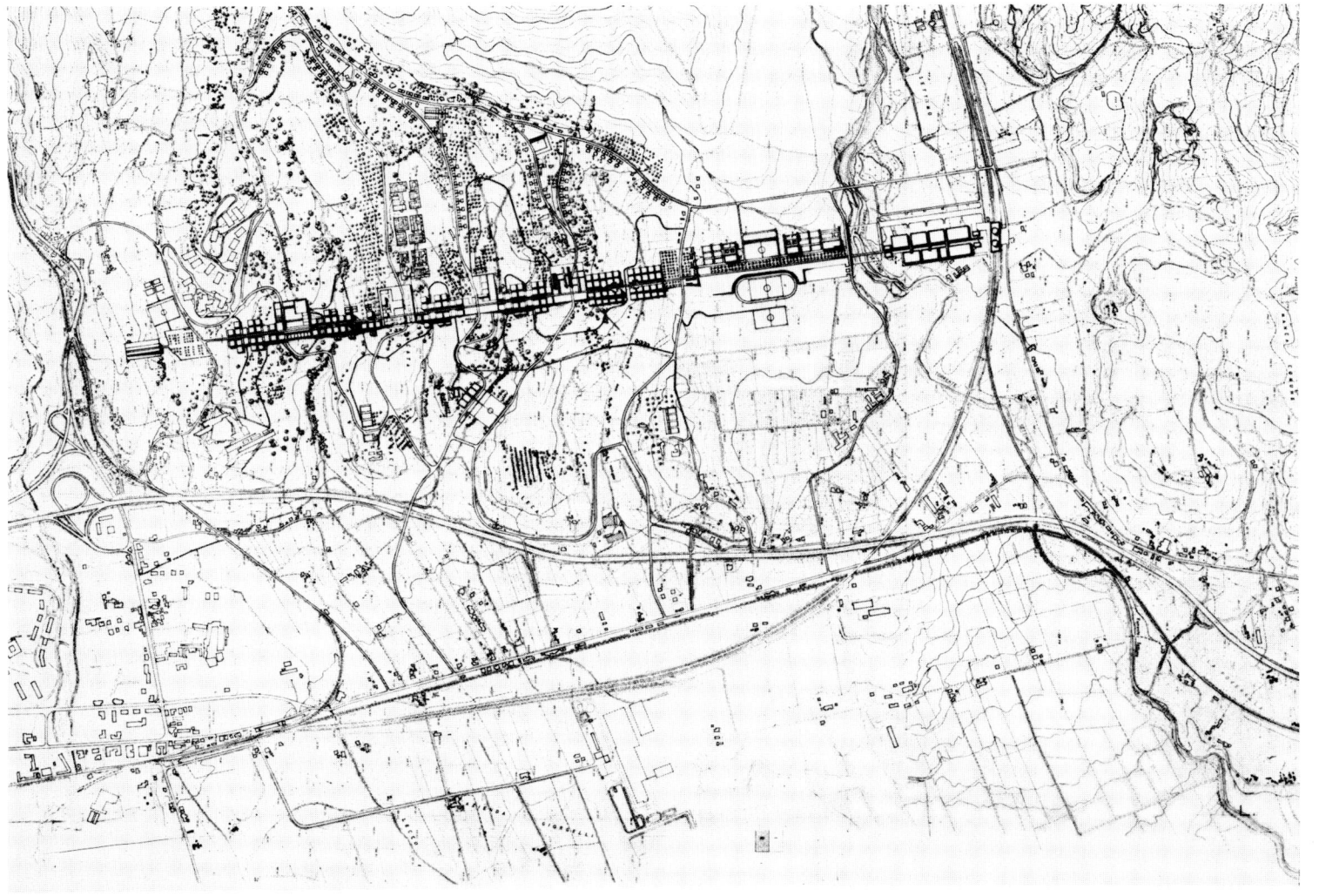

3. General plan of the project.

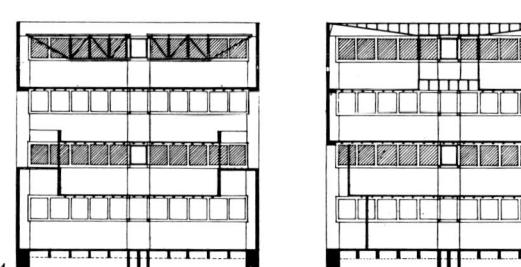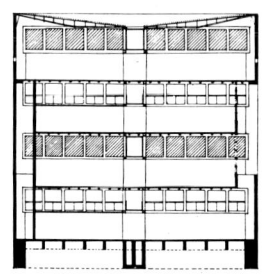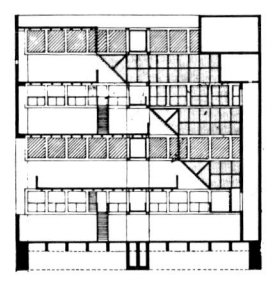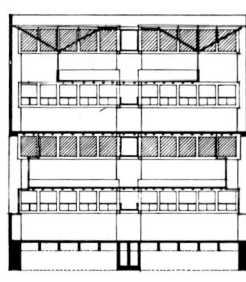

4

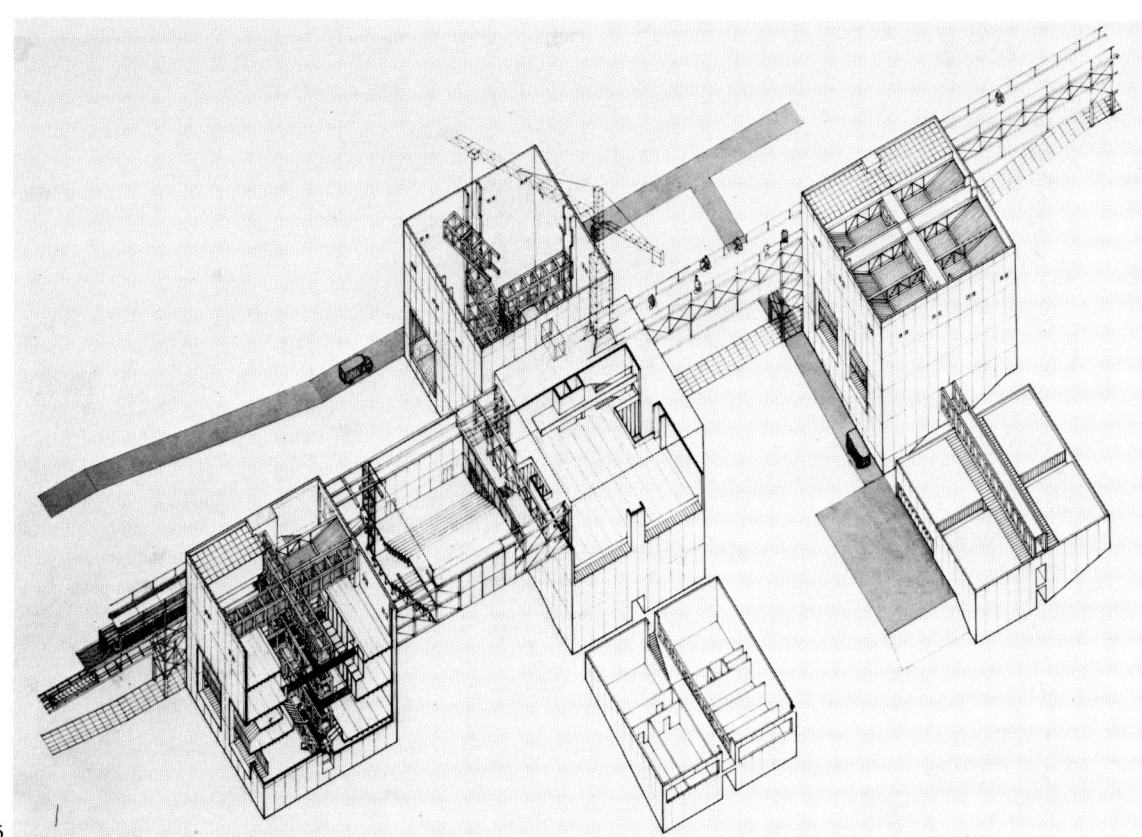

5

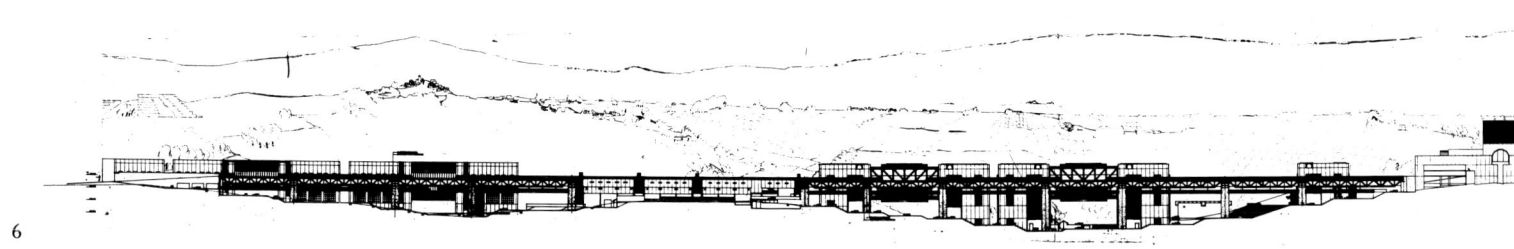

6

56

4. *Analytic study of sections of the high-rise cube.*
5. *Axonometric projection of component elements: bridges, high-rise cubes, low-rise cubes and consolidated lecture room.*
6. *General elevation, view-east side.*
7. *Axonometric section of the bridge.*
8. *Transverse section of consolidated lecture rooms.*

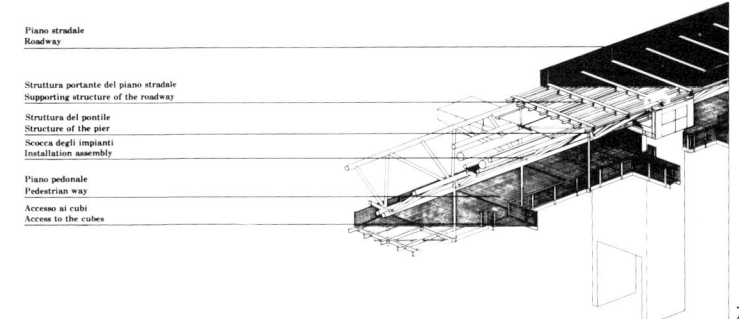

Piano stradale
Roadway

Struttura portante del piano stradale
Supporting structure of the roadway

Struttura del pontile
Structure of the pier

Scocca degli impianti
Installation assembly

Piano pedonale
Pedestrian way

Accesso ai cubi
Access to the cubes

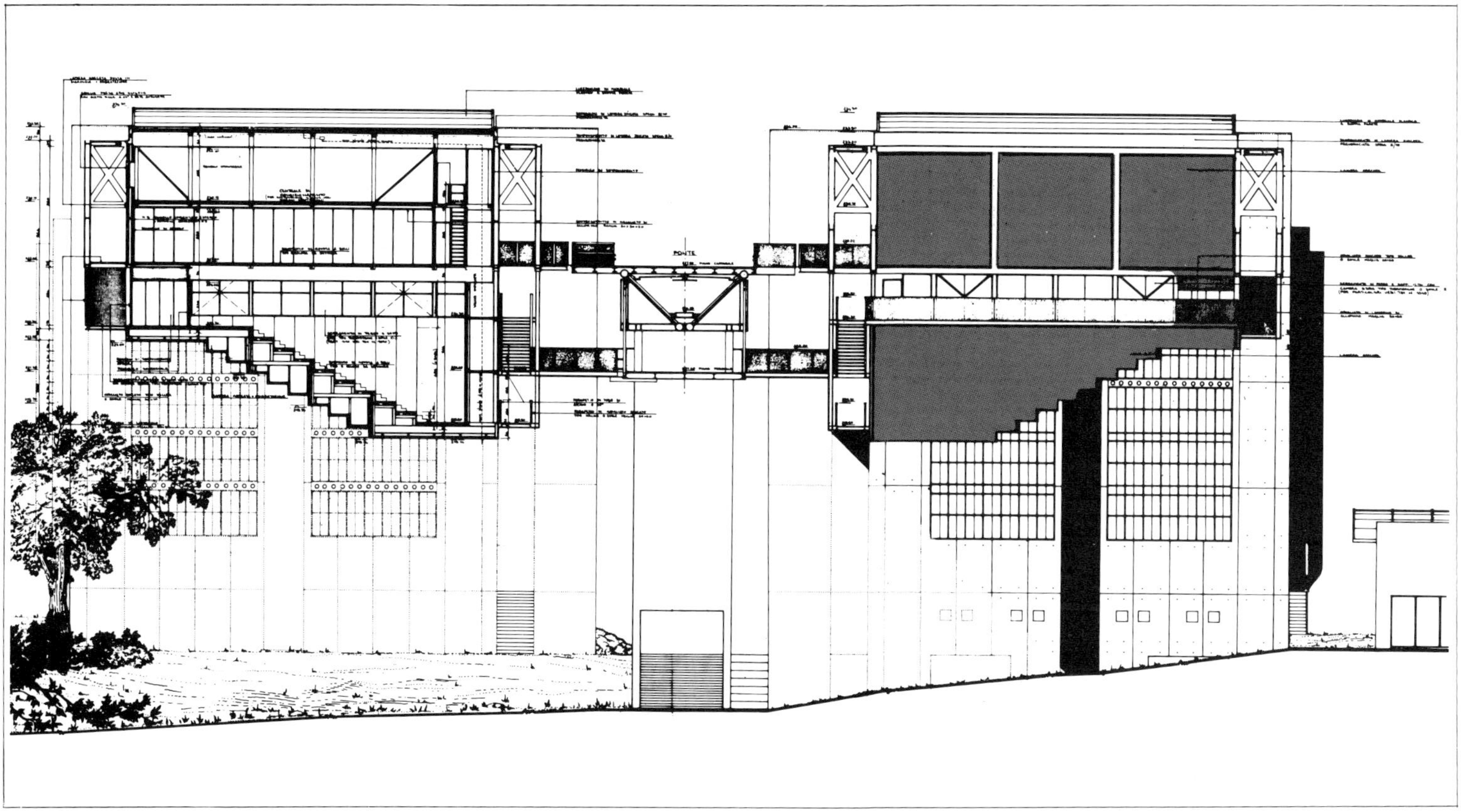

9. General plan of Departments of Chemistry and Humanities.
10. View of outdoor theatre.
11. View of consolidated lecture room of Humanities Department.
12. View of consolidated lecture room of Chemistry Department.

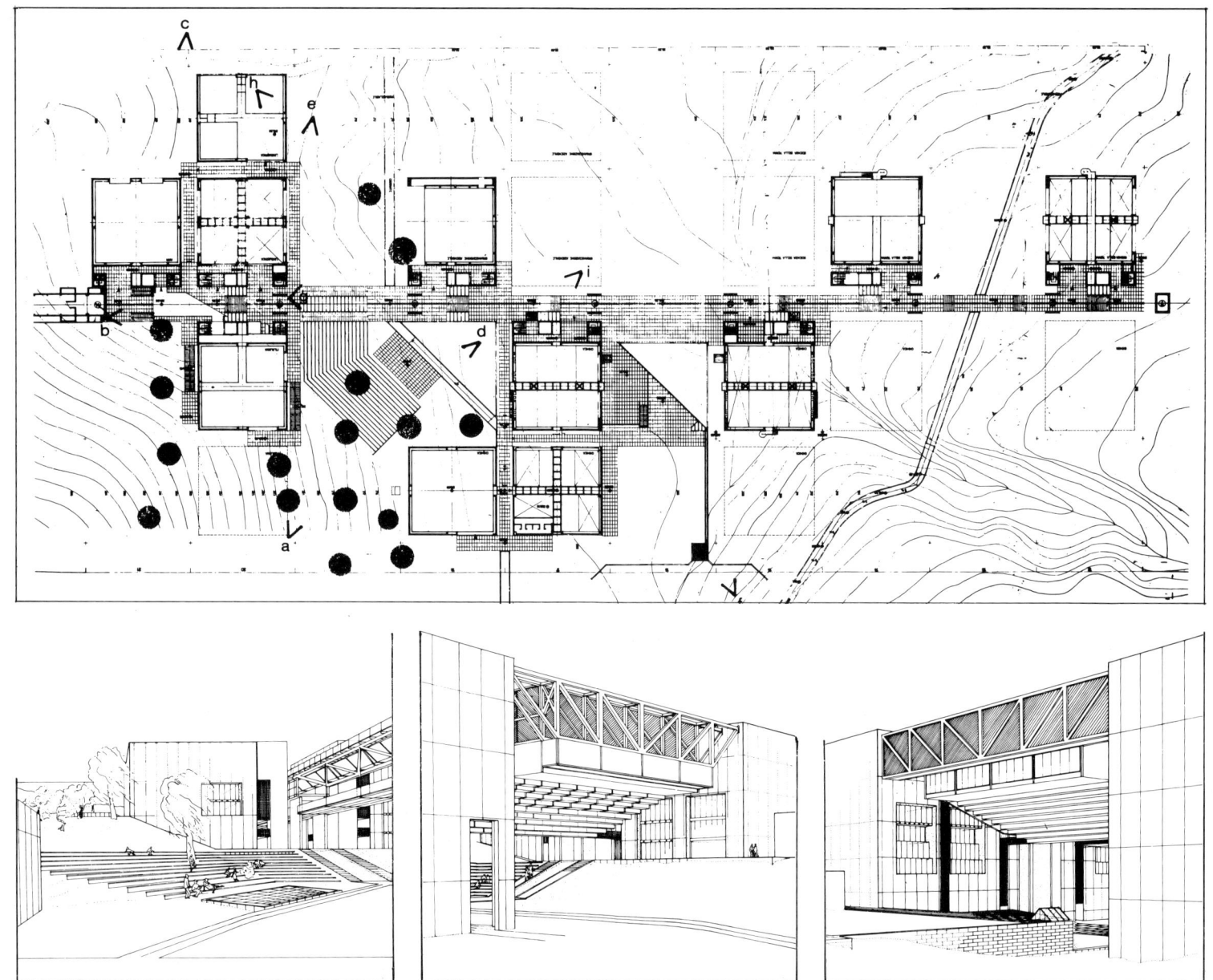

13. *General view of Departments of Chemistry and Humanities.*
14. *View towards Humanities Department.*
15. *View of passage under the bridge.*
16. *View of Structures Department.*

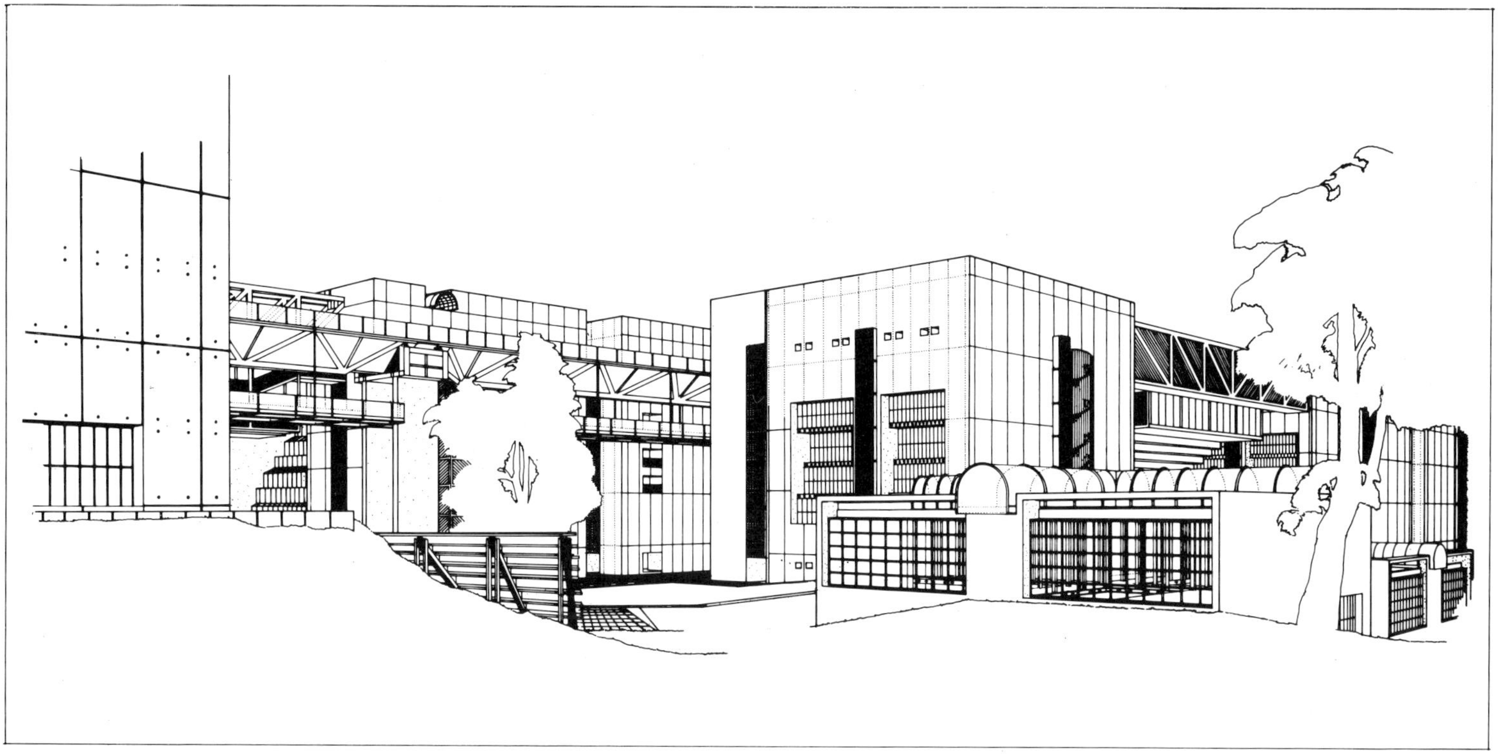

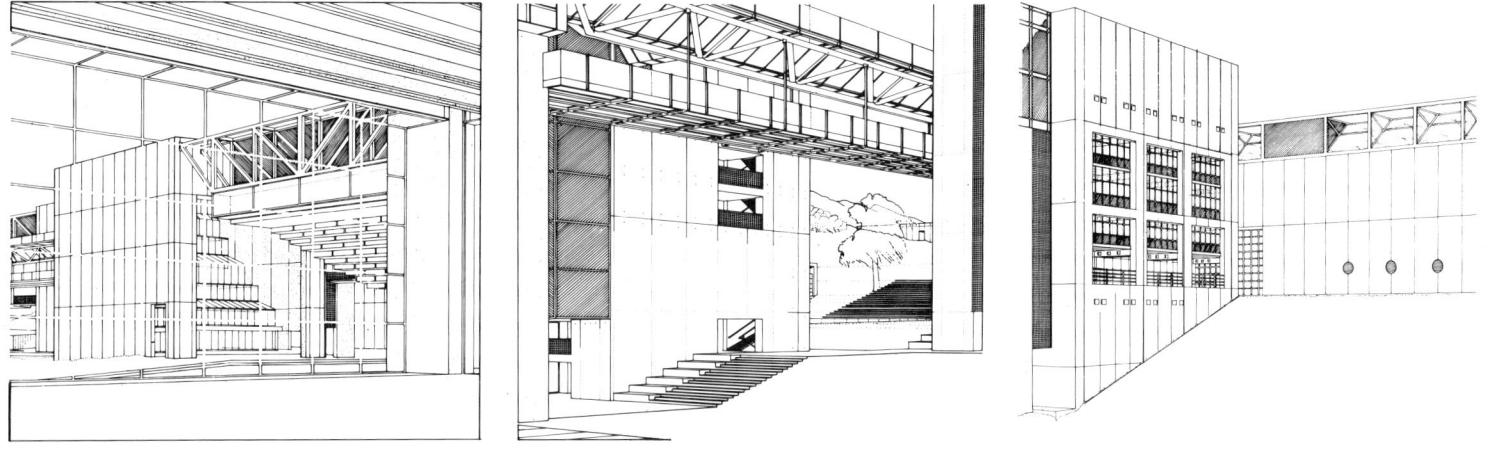

17. *Solution B: high-rise cube, elevation.*
18. *Solution B: high-rise cube, plan.*
19. *Solution A: high-rise cube, section.*
20. *Solution A: high-rise cube, plan.*

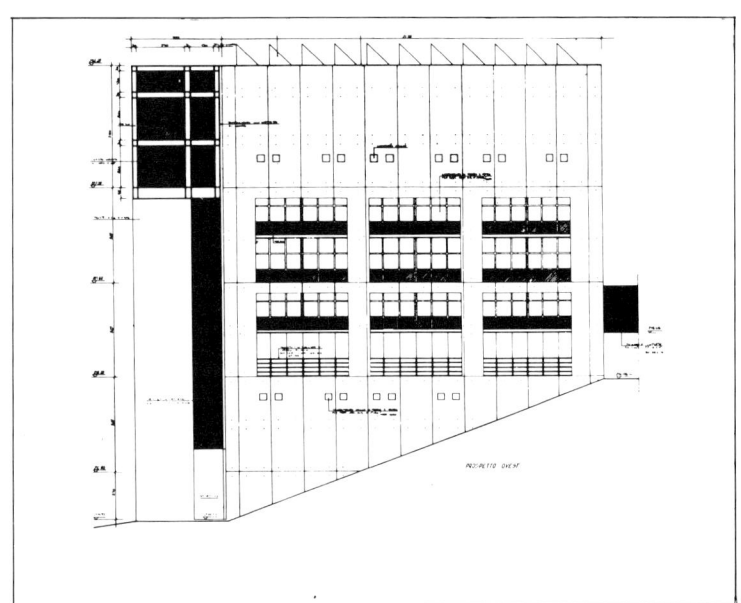
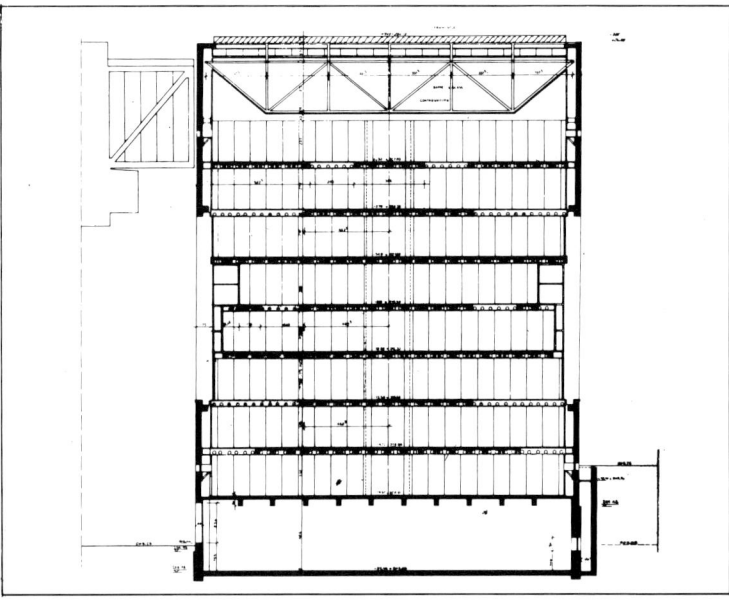
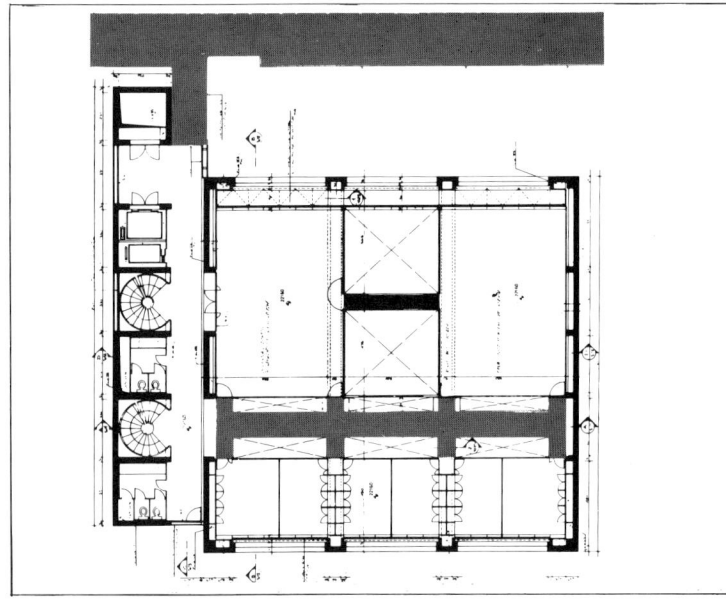
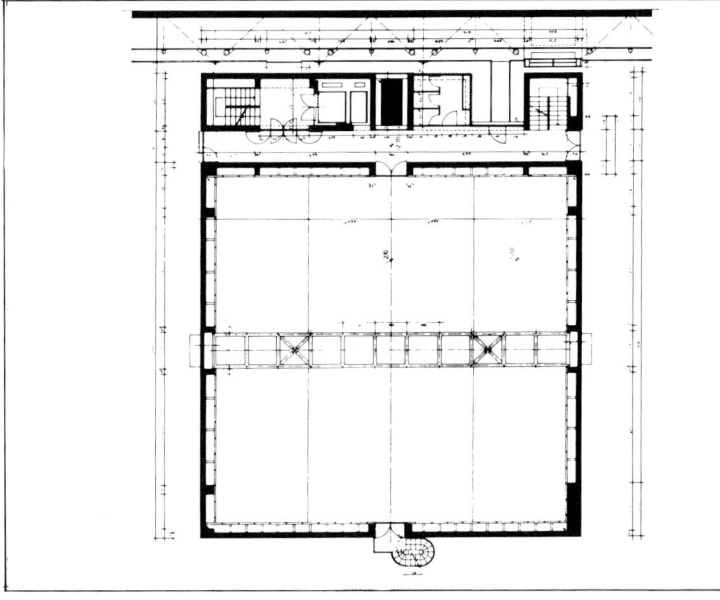

21. *Pillars of bridge.*
22. *Side of bridge.*
23. *Relation between morphology of terrain and plan of settlement.*
24. *Consolidated lecture hall between two high-rise cubes.*

25. *Low-rise and high-rise cube.*
26. *Side of high-rise cube.*

27. *Inner structure of Chemistry Department.*
28. *Inner structure of Chemistry Department.*

Research Centre at Naples, Portici

The Portici Research Centre has been designed to carry out research of a strategic nature and will give employment to 200-250 staff in its first phase and 350-400 in its final phase.

The main sectors of activity envisaged, mostly organized into departments, will be: a) Science of materials (polymers), b) Solar energy, c) Marine biology (algae), d) Agriculture, e) Defence of the environment, f) Corrosion (especially in a marine environment), g) Treatment of water. In the ambit of the centre and having departmental status, there will be a laboratory of Technical Applications with the aim of assisting the transformational industry of plastics.

The land available presents a series of difficulties typical of the area. Firstly there is the location of the site in relation to existing (and future) communications, imposing access to the centre "head-on." Then there is the markedly elongated shape of the site, which prompted a mainly linear development of the Research Centre, and the presence of the railway along the upper side of the site, creating problems of noise and vibration. Finally, there was its location on the sea-front, a positive element but involving delicate problems in the insertion of its bulk on a coast already defaced by large-scale, ill-designed buildings. The centre, to be constructed in successive phases, has been articulated into a set of functional zones grafted onto the main inner-communications system, laid out along the perimeter of the constructed section (except for the sea-front road) and is completed by a central axis for secondary transit to be used by service traffic. The zone immediately adjoining the access points contains: car park for staff cars and visitors, on three levels, two of them underground, with a total surface area of about 6,000 sq. metres and capacity of about 200 autos; porter's lodge and guest-rooms above; social amenities (canteen, company social club, sick bay, as well as meeting-rooms for the shop-stewards' council). All these services are located on a "plate" whose roof is set at 7 metres above sea-level and serves as a parking lot and communications link, since the access points are set at the same level. In particular, the social services exploit the existing depression in the ground to look out onto a green area in front placed at an altitude of 3 metres above sea-level and measuring about 5,000 sq. metres. Apart from this space, the Centre's ground level is fixed at a level of 5.50 metres above sea-level, corresponding to the present level of the terrain. Towards the railway line, and parallel to Via Nuovo Macello, the technological buildings have been placed (storehouses, workshops, areas for technological applications, small scale pilot plants etc.) to constitute a useful barrier between the scientific research laboratories and the railway. Towards the sea, but at right angles to the main axis of the terrain, there are the office blocks/science laboratories on three stories jacked above ground level, detached from the technological buildings but communicating with them by means of transverse bridging structures passing over the service axis. The detached research sections are arranged in very deep constructions with a central zenithal span, while the external facades at right angles to the sea are made up of a triple system: the plane of the screen-walls which contains the verticals of the special service installations, open to inspection from outside; the metal safety catwalks; the web of sunscreens made of reinforced concrete. Along the upper edge of this facade is the system of inspectionable ventilation outlets. The big doorways towards the sea light up the collective areas, and the fire escape stairs are fitted into their double thickness.

All the blocks are connected lengthwise at the level of their first story with the bridging buildings, where the libraries and other communal spaces are located. At the far end of the terrain, towards the present council abattoir, an area of about 6,000 sq. metres has been set aside, equipped with the main lines of plant and fluids and fitted up for open-air experiments and temporary erection of pilot installations. Adjoining this area the plan envisages closed or simply covered structures for storing inflammable or otherwise dangerous substances and technological installations. The structures are to be of reinforced concrete, partially prefabricated and suitably painted, and of steel for the "bridging" buildings linking the laboratories. The lightweight accessory elements (roofing shells) are made of panels of layered plastic materials (PVC and/or PRFV), suitably shaped in a limited range of sizes.

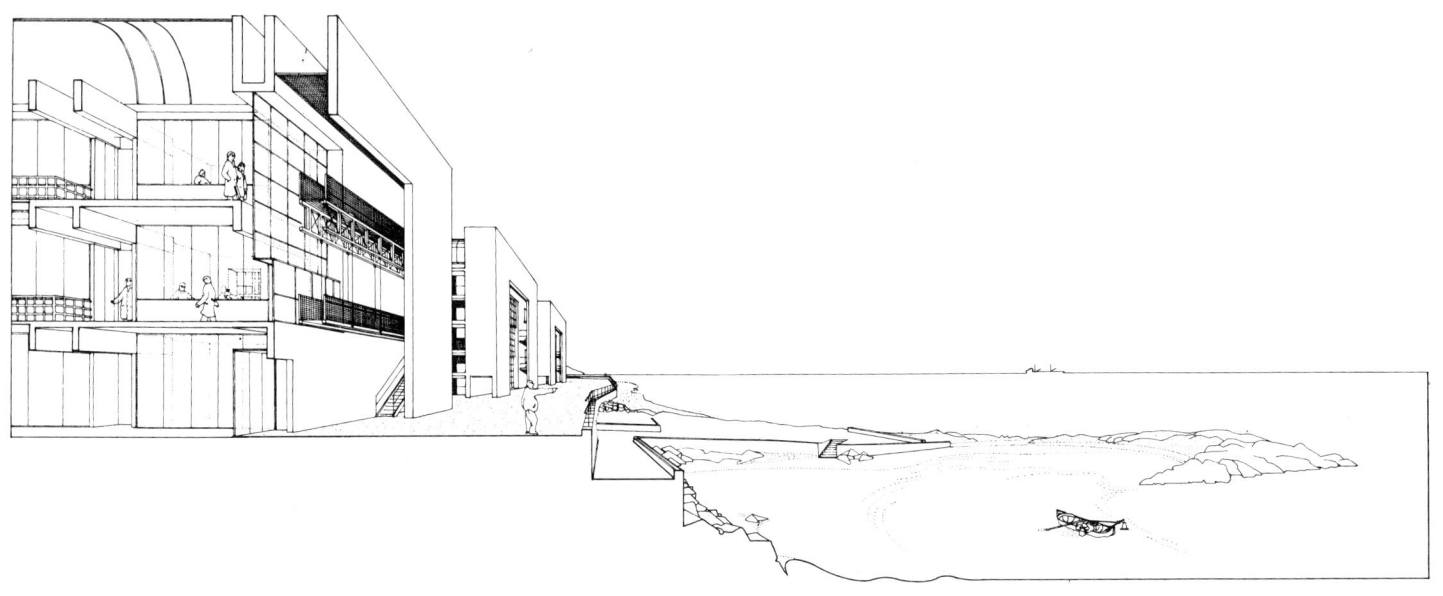

1. *Portals of Scientific Research facing the sea with the section through the first Research block.*
2. *Photo-montage from the sea.*

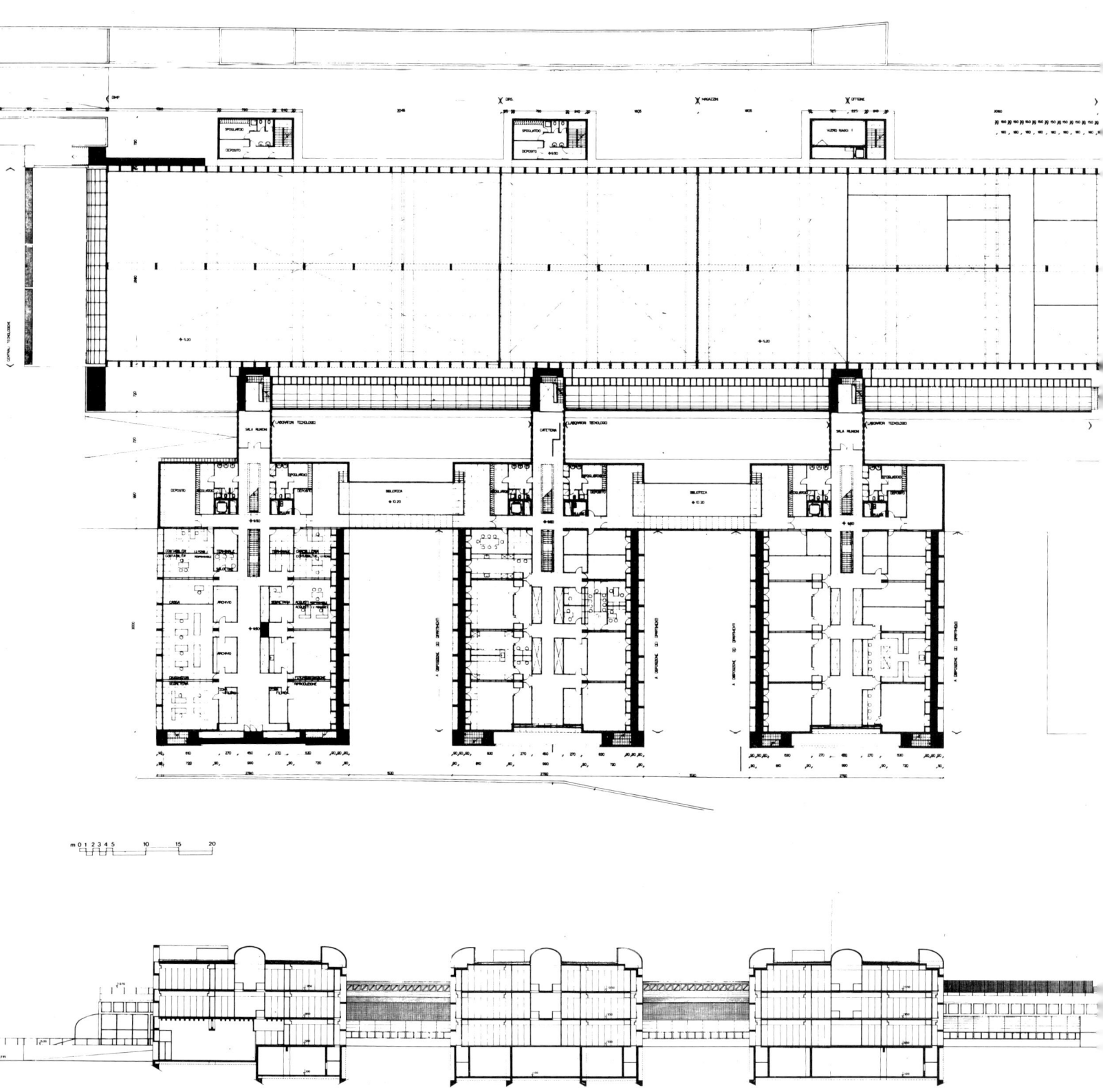

3. First floor plan.
4. Longitudinal section of Research blocks.
5. Photo of model.

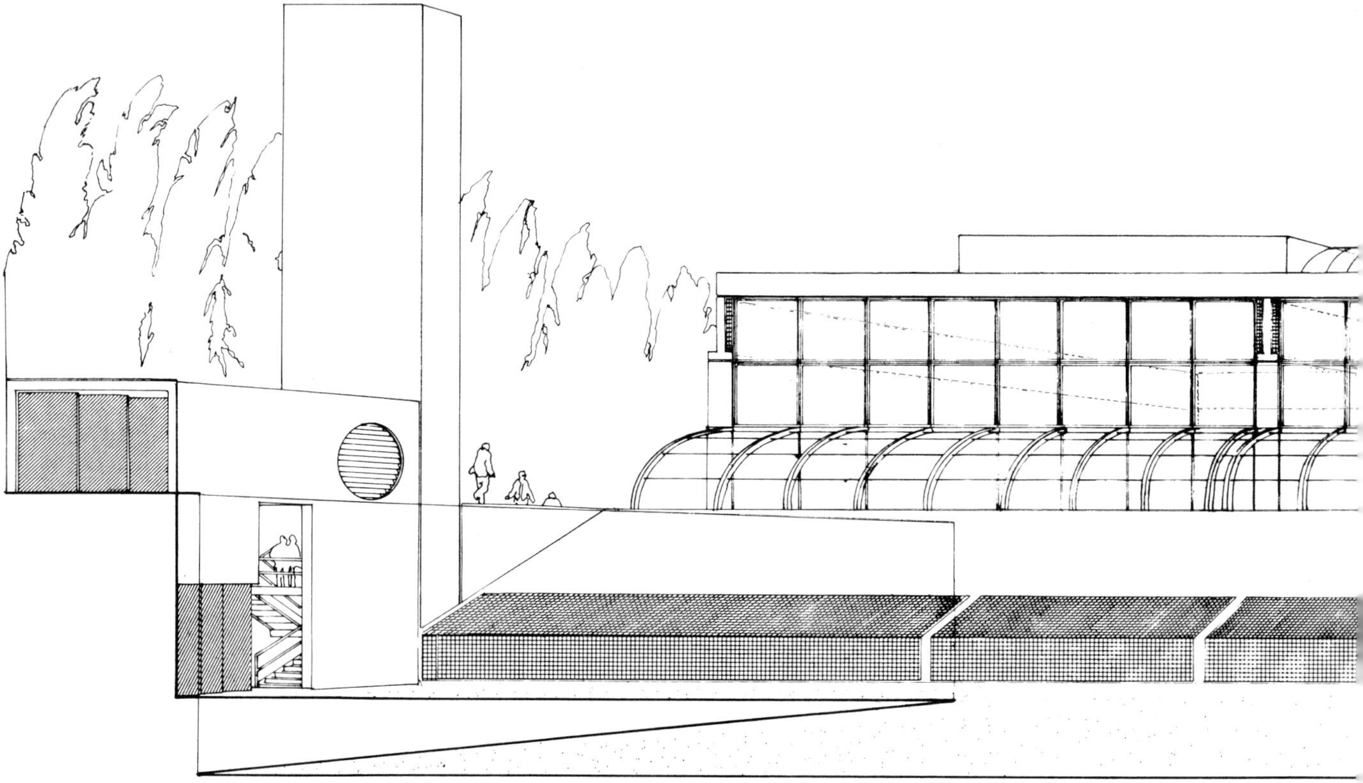

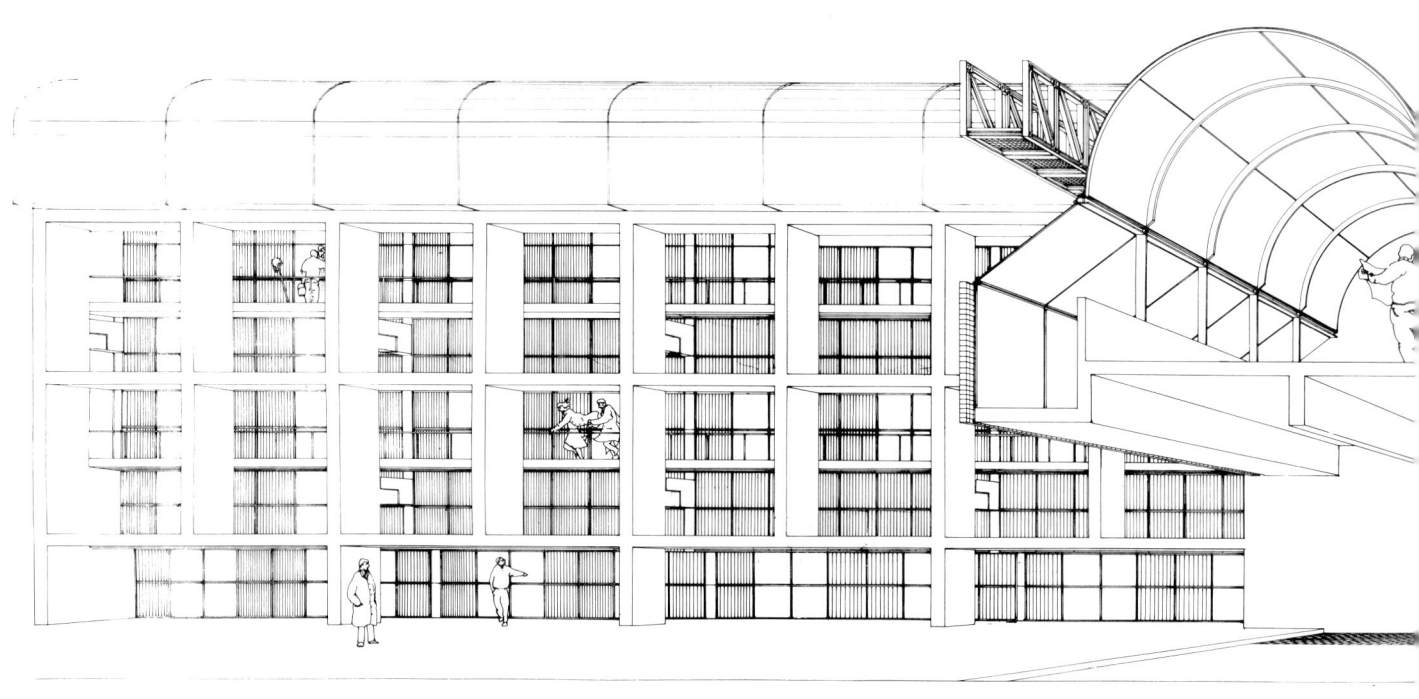

6. *View onto the south-west head of Technological halls.*
7. *Perspective section onto internal road.*

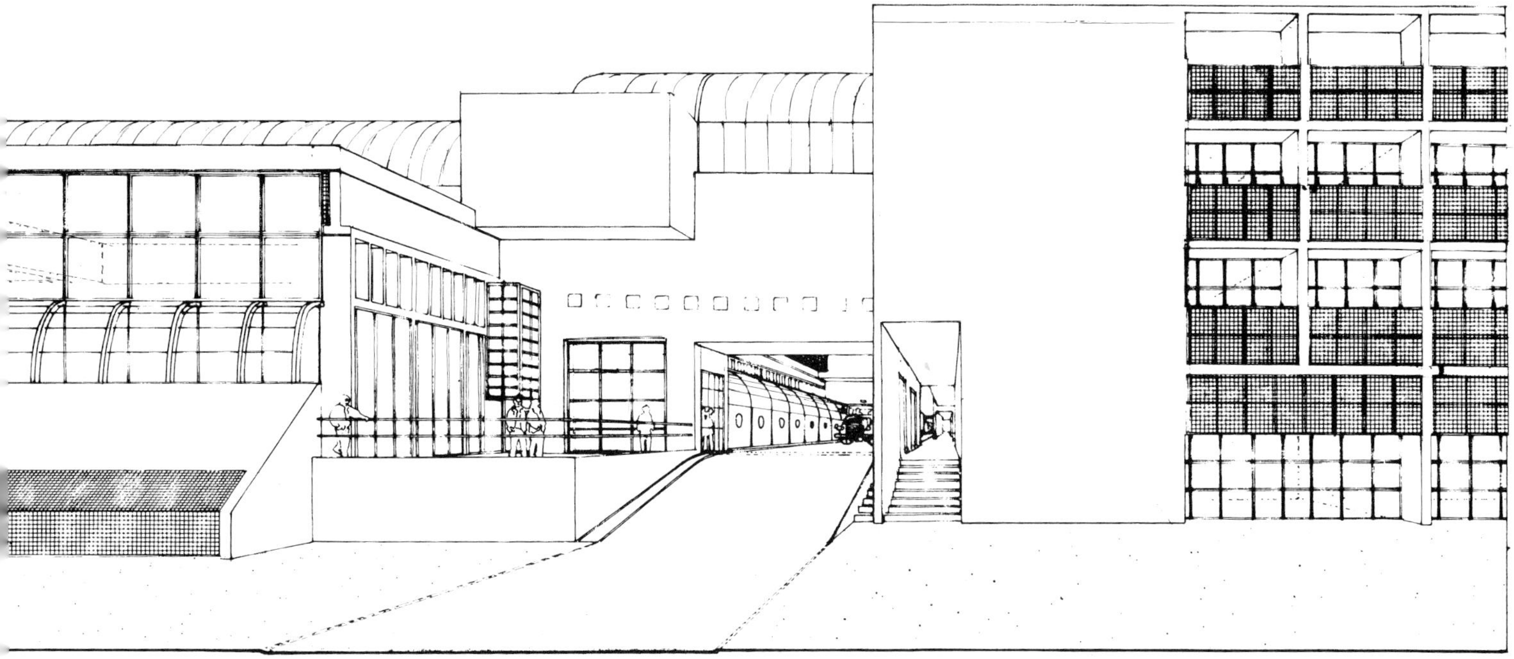

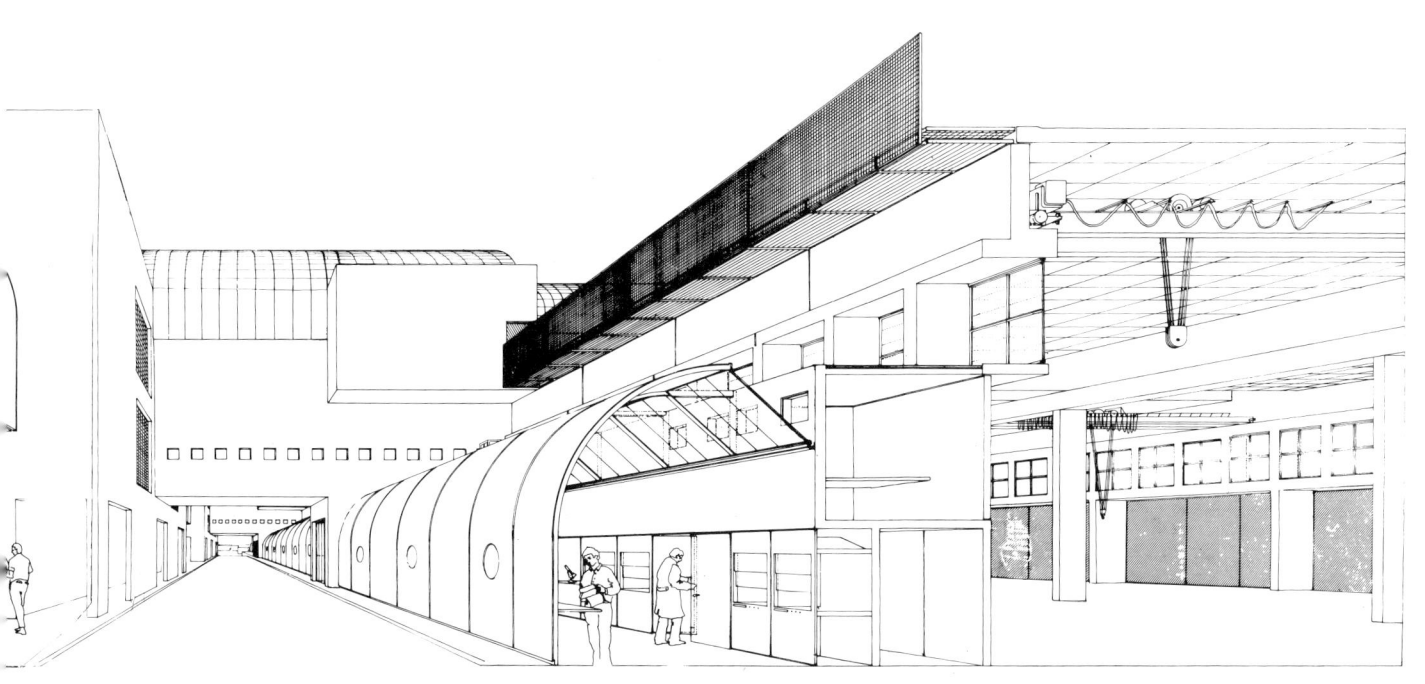

8. *South-east elevation of third Research block.*
9. *North-east elevation.*

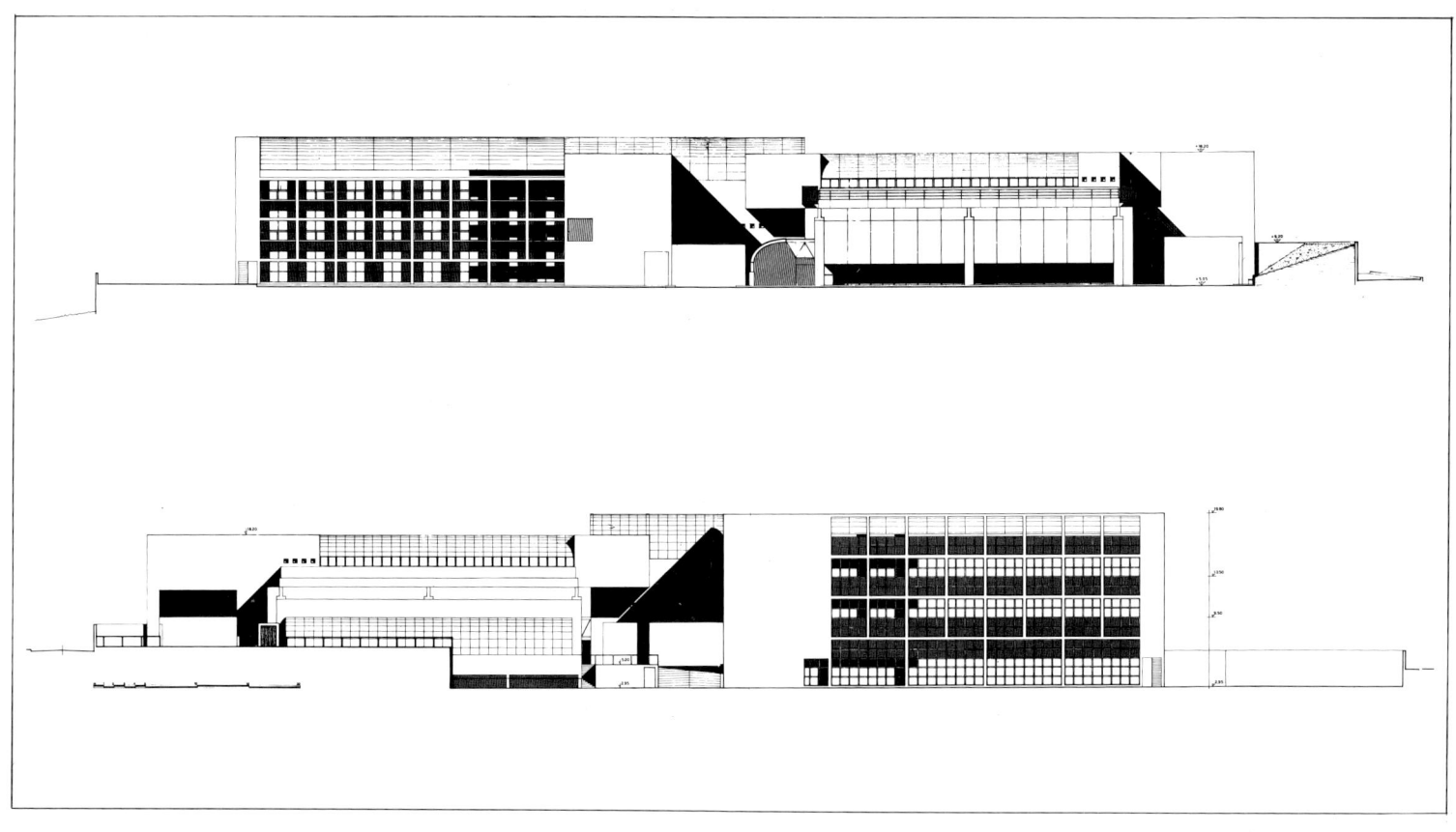

New A.C.T.V. boat yards on the island of the Giudecca in Venice

This project makes use of the specific conditions of the site, achieving integration of an architectural solution with rational functional requirements.

The theme of the "transverse" site, one that crosses the island of the Giudecca in its full width, was one of the main points of reflection underlying the plan. This point, which grew out of the original formative principle of the island (particularly because of the large monastic and productive structures sited there), was taken as the guiding principle of the plan of the layout. Parallel to this was the aim to preserve as many as possible of the existing buildings, not from the principle of conservation for its own sake but because the alignment of the buildings on the northern edge of the Giudecca is a manifestation of continuous construction which, apart from any architectural merit in individual buildings, is of the greatest value on the urban scale as a whole. The uses for which they have been earmarked (entrance, changing rooms, canteen, welfare, offices) can be realized perfectly well merely by restructuring the interior.

At the junction of the two buildings (along the front) there is the opening for the main entrance to the boat yard with its vault set at a double height and ridged with a wooden frame.

This provides the yardstick, measured from the foundations, for the boat yard as a whole and its new organizational principles. On the Rio del Ponte Lungo the existing buildings are retained and reclaimed. The front along the lagoon is identified by the presence of the whole system of wharfs and docks for repairs in or out of the water.

The alignment of the waterfront has been slightly modified along the alignment of the previous wharf to the east of the boat yard, which makes it possible to give greater definition and compactness to the front itself, both functionally and architecturally.

A wooden floating framework moored to buoys about 80 metres from the waterfront and parallel to it serves as a depôt for the boats (*vaporetti*) and a parking place while they are awaiting repairs. The overall organization of the boat yard is achieved architecturally by two complex systems of construction whose ground plan is related in one case to parallel alignment with the Rio del Ponte Lungo, and in the other case set at right angles to the shore of the lagoon. The first of these is the sequence of depôts which have been organized through restructuring of the existing building on its east side. It is interrupted in the centre by areas for painting and sanding that replace the part of this long building which had already been altered for technical reasons in the fifties.

The second system of buildings is defined by a long structure laid out along the west side. It is 33 metres deep and will be used for repairs to small craft out of the water. The structural span is 11 metres, with lightweight metal roofing.

The workshop building defines the part towards the lagoon of this more recent section. It is organized on a square two-story module which provides a uniform solution to the problem of the relation between the workshops and the docks for smaller craft. Each element is structurally independent and enables the whole complex to have service canals for the movement of men and machines from one end to the other. These spaces also provide the optimum location for stairways and service hoists. At the centre there are two courtyards providing ideal light, while the workshops, whose functional lines are at right angles to the waterfront, permit good working conditions with easy internal/external access. The front along the lagoon is defined by interaction of the square module which covers the section for maintenance work afloat and is equipped with a system of mobile wooden pontoons. In this case, too, natural lighting is provided from the shed roof overhead.

The workshop building is sited along the median line of the work route and this is a further point in its favour; in addition, the major movements of traffic will take place under the roofed areas. Along the waterfront, the passage is covered by a framework of iron and glazing, while a wider passage than the other continues inside the body of the workshop building, emphasized by its greater height, leading with a break to the route behind the depôt for the *vaporetti*.

The concept of the non-parallel arrangement of these buildings, while retaining the service spaces needed for movement around the buildings themselves, has made it possible to create a large service yard in the centre, which facilitates the manoeuvres needed in carrying out work, especially the use of the mobile slip for transport and docking of the *vaporetti*. The diversified arrangement of the flooring should also prevent this space from taking on too large and indefinite dimensions. The relation between the materials used – iron, glass and untreated brickwork – stems from the traditional constructional materials of Venetian industrial buildings.

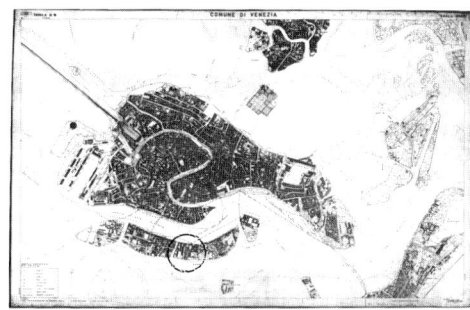

1. *Location of the project site.*

2. General plan at ground-floor level.   3. Layout and volumes.

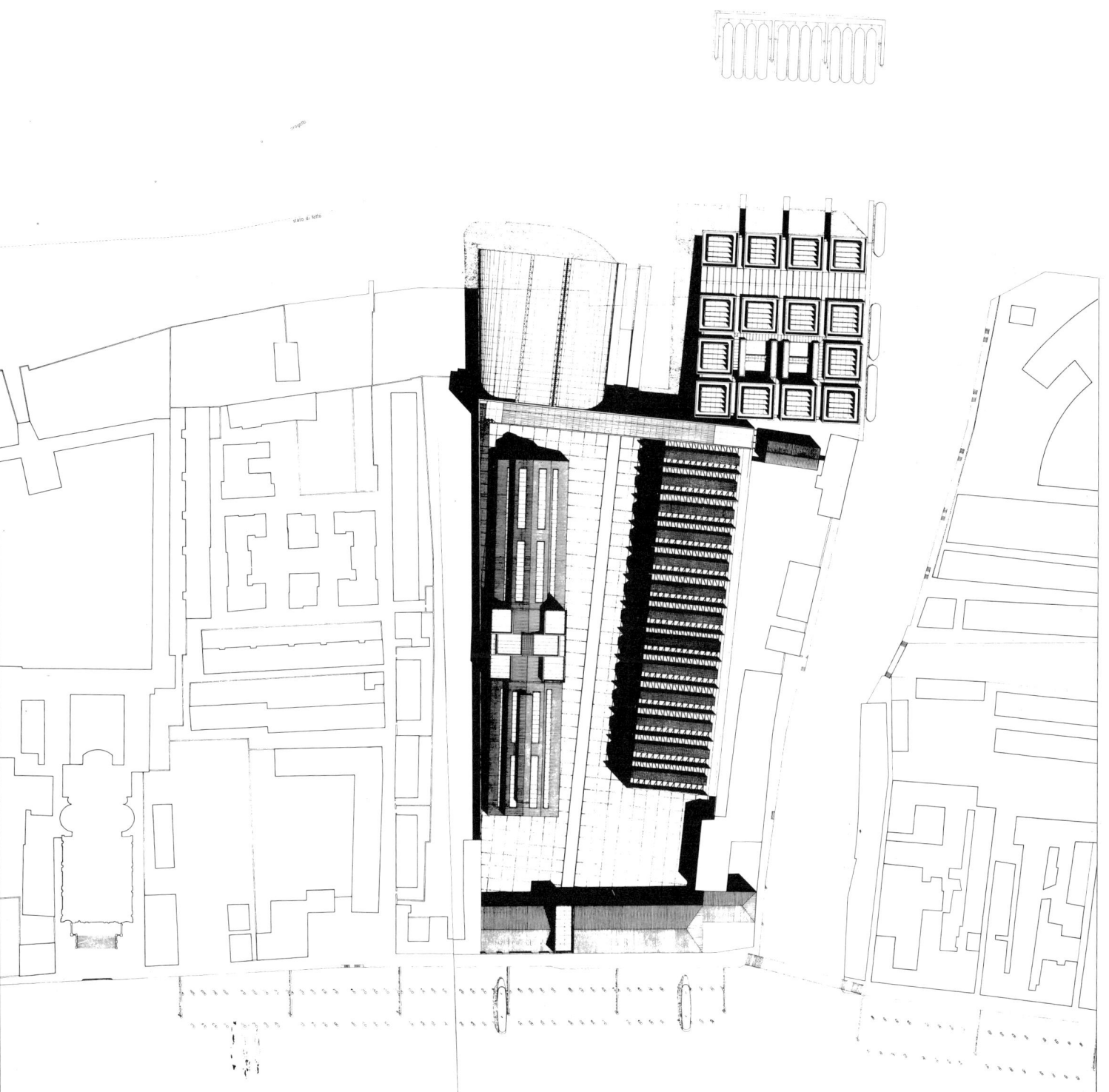

4. Profile along the canal of the Ponte Longo.
5. Inner elevation of the building for smaller craft.
6. Elevation along the canal behind the Giudecca.

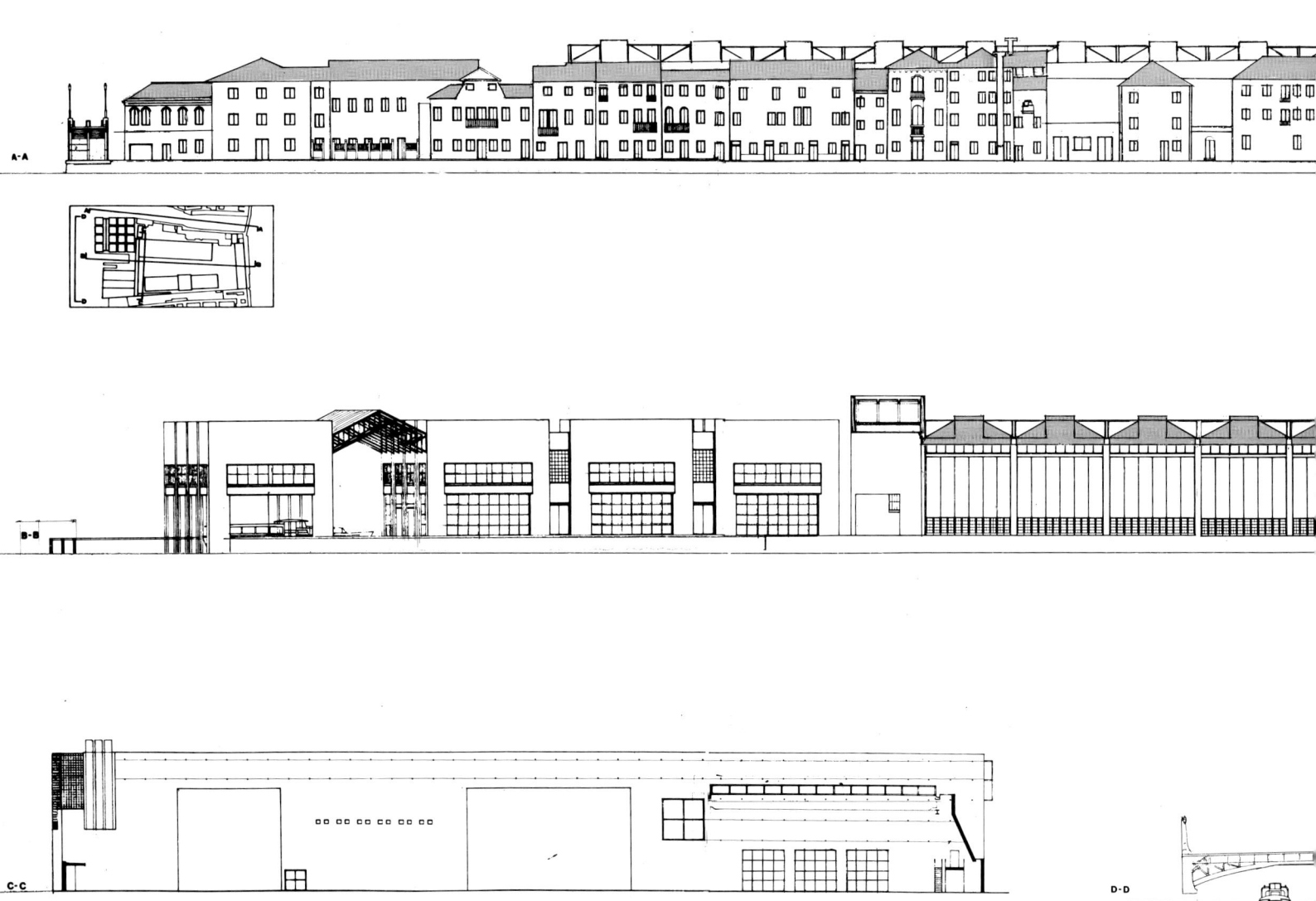

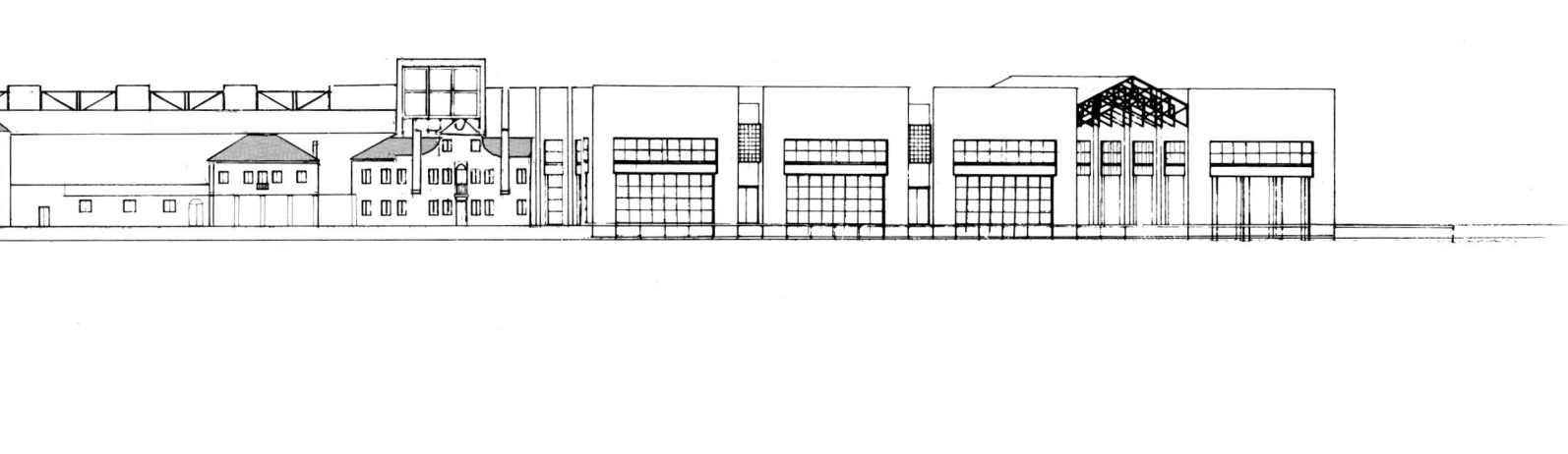
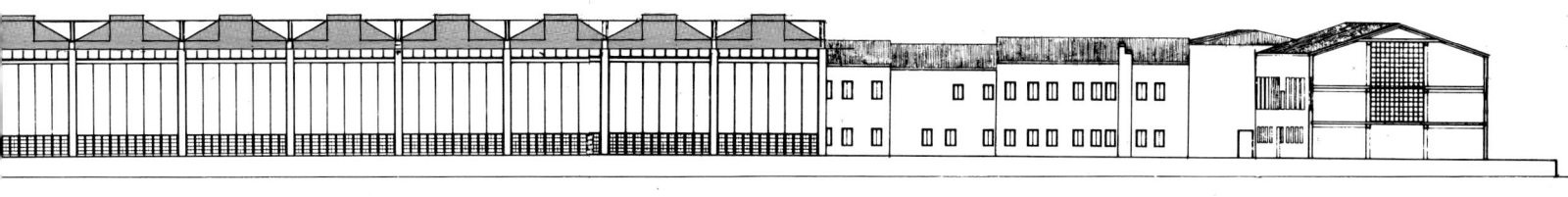
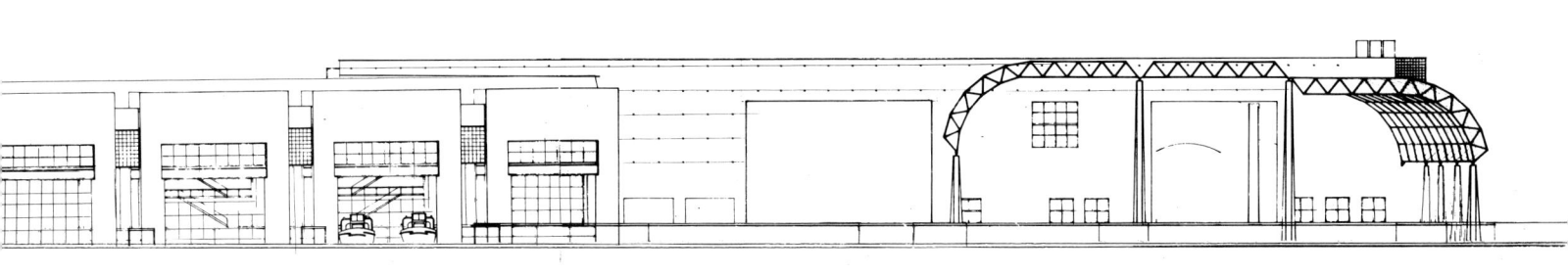

7. *Section in perspective of workshops on the front facing the lagoon.*

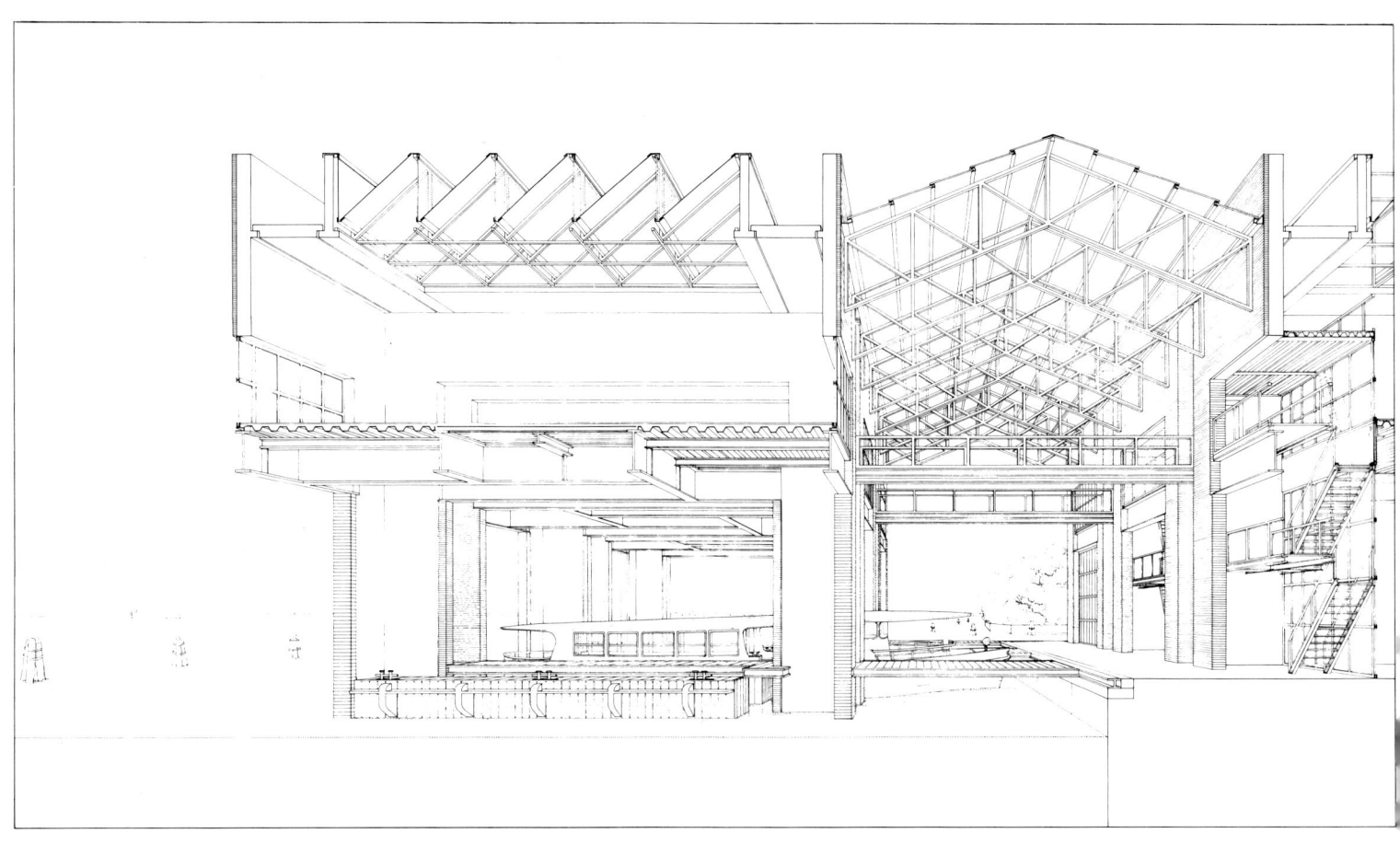

8. Elevation and section of the building for smaller craft.

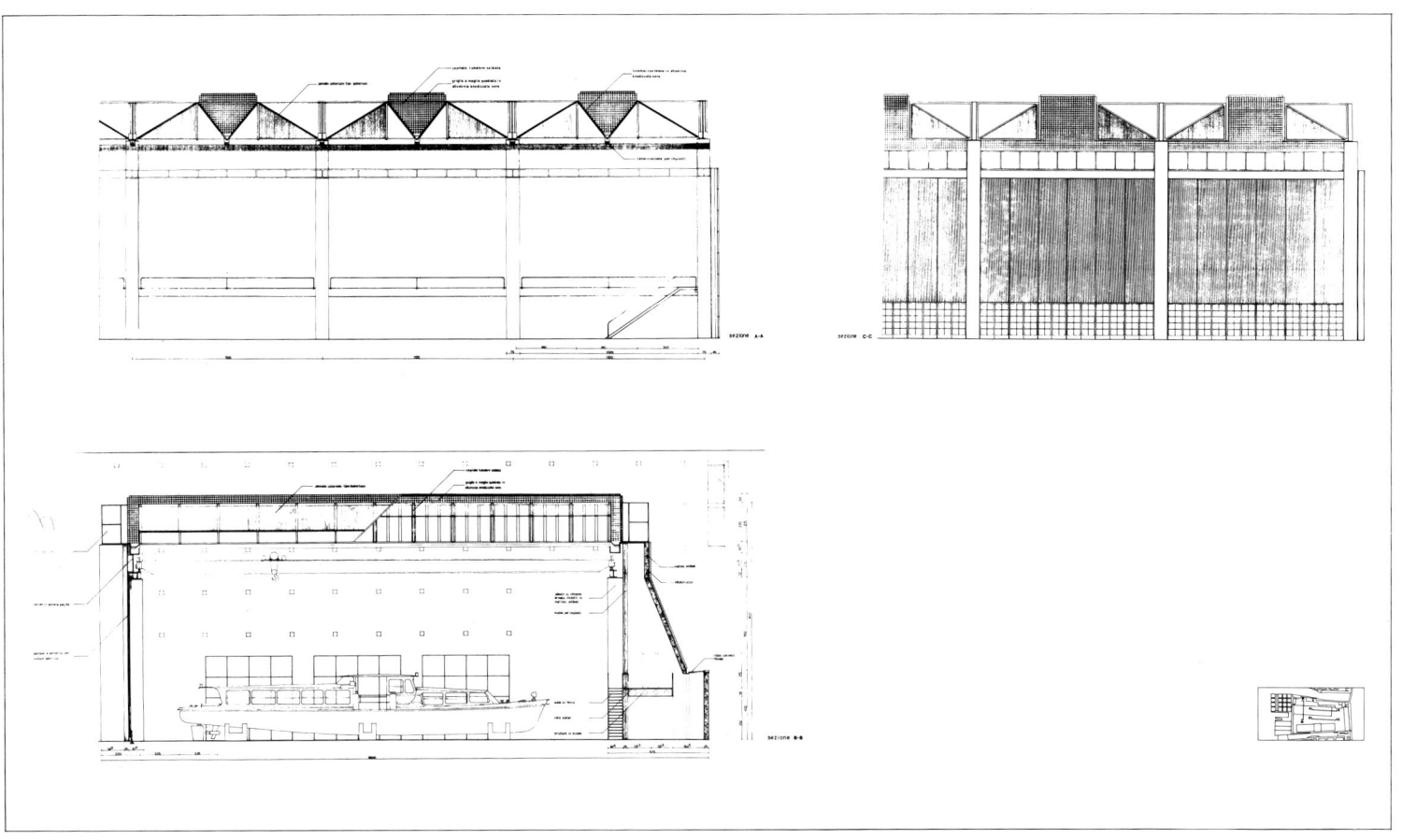

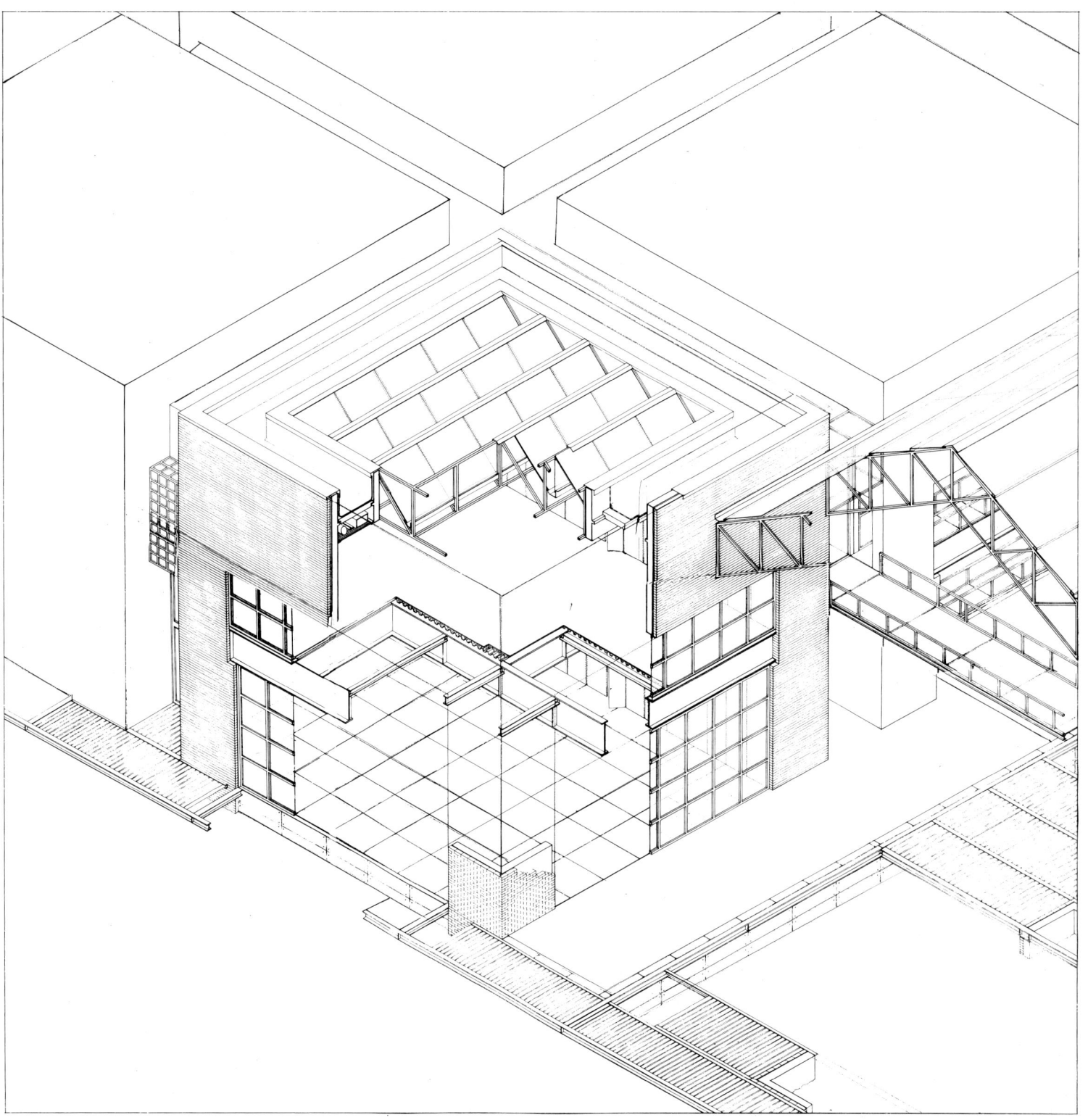

9. *Axometric section of the workshops.* 10. *View of the canal behind the Giudecca.*

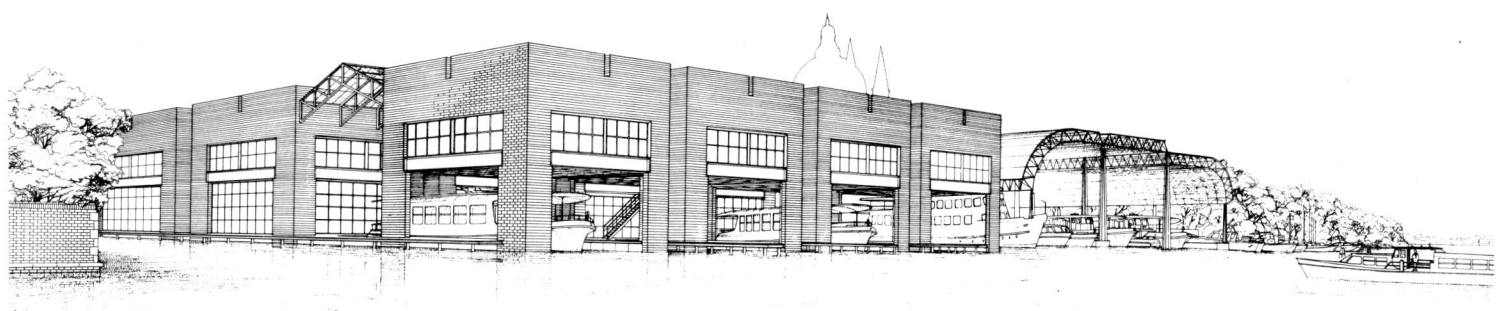

11. *Bird's-eye view.*

Residential nucleus at Sestiere di Cannaregio in Venice

The Cannaregio area consists of three islands with the *rio* (canal) forming their main connecting element. The ex-Saffa site, on the island of Cannaregio West, is virtually the only area for new buildings envisaged in Venice's town plan within the old built-up area.

The choices and main assumptions in planning this project are based on the solution of the problem stemming from the fact that this site is essentially comprised between two systems of buildings: the prong-shaped arrangement along the *fondamenta* of Cannaregio and the system on the Lista di Spagna.

The surrounding contexts, strengthened by two pre-existing systems of buildings, are very different in either case. The system abutting onto the Lista di Spagna is substantially external to the site and blocked off by the construction of new public Regional services, while the prong-shaped arrangement along the waterfront of Cannaregio is orientated towards the project site.

The articulation of the boundaries, the great differences in their structure between the systems of buildings and the canal, is hence the first element to be examined in order to achieve a twofold set of objectives. On the one hand, consolidation and completion of the existing structure of settlement, ensuring that the project will possess the qualities of an urban element by giving a final architectural solution to what is at present a simple random juxtaposition of different functions. On the other hand, adoption of the related dimensions of open spaces and thoroughfares, both within the new project and in its connections with the existing structures, as guidelines and scale elements underlying the principles of the plan.

The definition of the rules guiding the project is based on an examination of the general features of the context and the extent of the system of building. As a whole, what emerges is the unevenness and fragmentariness of the context, the heterogeneity of the buildings, heterogeneity and discontinuity which are also functional defects, in particular with regard to the part along the *rio* della Crea, while the buildings stretching away from the *rio* del Cannaregio are very inconsistent, with a clearly defined system of proportions and typologies only in the strip along the waterfront and becoming much less clearly defined in the buildings stretching behind. The choice of the elongated courtyard structure – though not exclusively, as we shall see – and the positioning of the new buildings are the means adopted in the project to achieve completion of the existing system of buildings and reorganization of access ways, establishing a hierarchy in the repetitive system of parallel *calli* (alleys), with each one identified and differentiated by varying their dimensions, planting them with trees (in some cases) or creating garden spaces, reinserting productive craft activities in existing structures of a proto-industrial nature, and locating public services in the end sections of the structures.

The complex system of relationships between the new project and the existing buildings is articulated by means of the introduction of further building units, whose uniqueness and individuality is stressed, as in the case of the small building in the form of triplex one-family homes, which is intended as the mediating element in the rotation of the two types with elongated courtyards, and in the case of the building set between the Testa building and the first of the two yards: here the typological and dimensional features of the building opposite are repeated; but, above all, it reflects the specific quality, in this area, of the relation between the buildings along the *fondamenta* and the buildings receding from it, completing this type of building with the renewal of the park behind and the construction of a building to act as the boundary of the park itself.

The architectural and building project itself, despite the fact that it is made up of a number of housing units, rejects seriality completely and creates a marked hierarchy, while it reinterprets the treatment of the facades along all the sides, reinforcing the significance of the individual element in relation to the individuality of its location.

The second of these fundamental questions arose in the project site, and involved the creation of relations between the two main existing systems of building and between these systems and the neighbouring islands (S. Giobbe etc.), which constitute this part of the city: this has been dealt with by creating the Campo Lungo, which makes it possible to organize pedestrian access towards the abattoir and sports facilities; but above all it acquires a role as the main element in the layout and connection of the two systems referred to above, as a public space *par excellence*.

It is in relation to this space that the other building units, which make up the project are defined, with the two elongated courtyards shaping the design of the ends of the buildings, and with the definition of the architectural and typological features of the S-shaped building on the edge of the site, as well as the variation in their height, not only in relation to the differences between the two fronts along the *calle* and the *campo*, but also in relation to the variation in spatial conditions and longitudinal connection with the ground, i.e. the front onto the Campo Lungo, and onto the raised green space that prolongs the open area of the field towards the entrance to *calle* Priuli.

The exceptional element constituted by the portico with its double height, supported on pilotis, marks the first variation in the orientation of the building and the meeting-point between the thoroughfare of Campo Lungo and the main transverse thoroughfare leading from the *fondamenta* of Cannaregio; the variation in the section and height of the building marks the second such element and also the termination of the building itself near the end of the *calle* Priuli.

The building which abuts onto the *rio* della Crea also derives its shape from its position between the two *campi* and from the fact that it is the only building facing onto the water. Hence the choice of a typological layout which is particularly deep, with staggered floors and the service block in the centre, the long boathouse orientated towards the main *campo* and the *cantinole* in the lower side opposite.

1. *Location of the project site.*   2. *General plan with the new project.*

3. *Photo of model: overhead view.*

4. *Ground floor plan.*

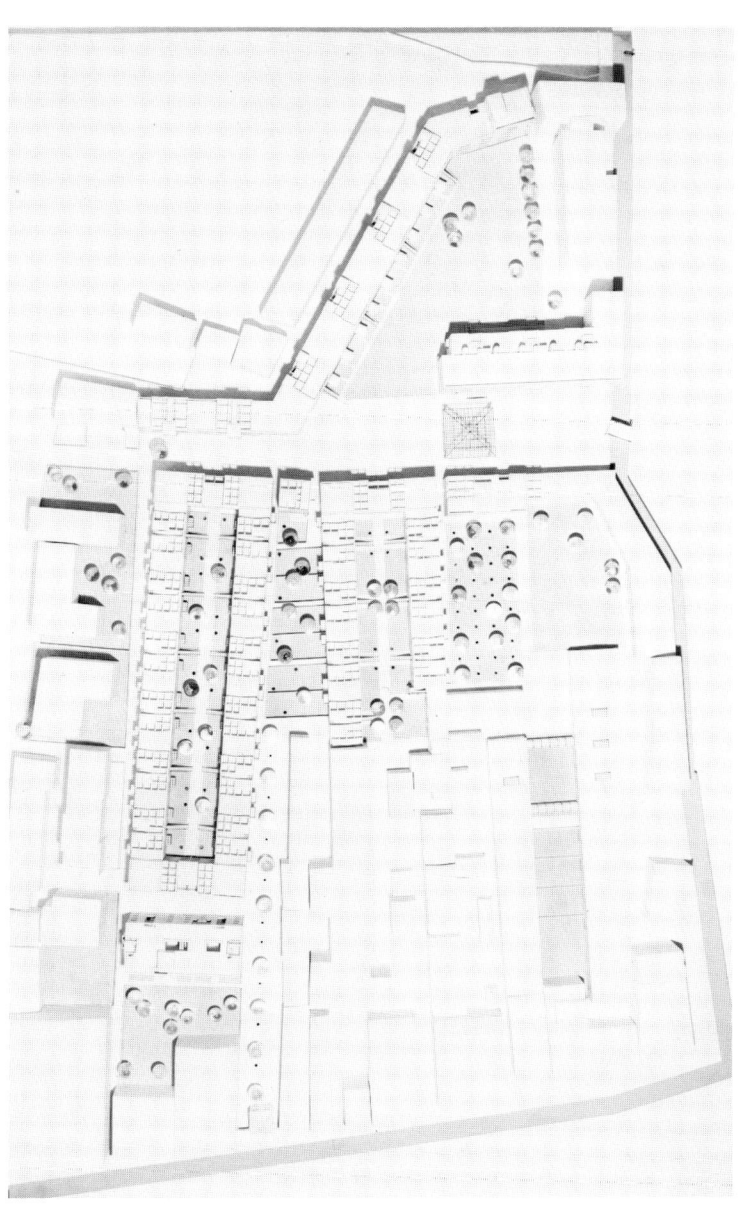
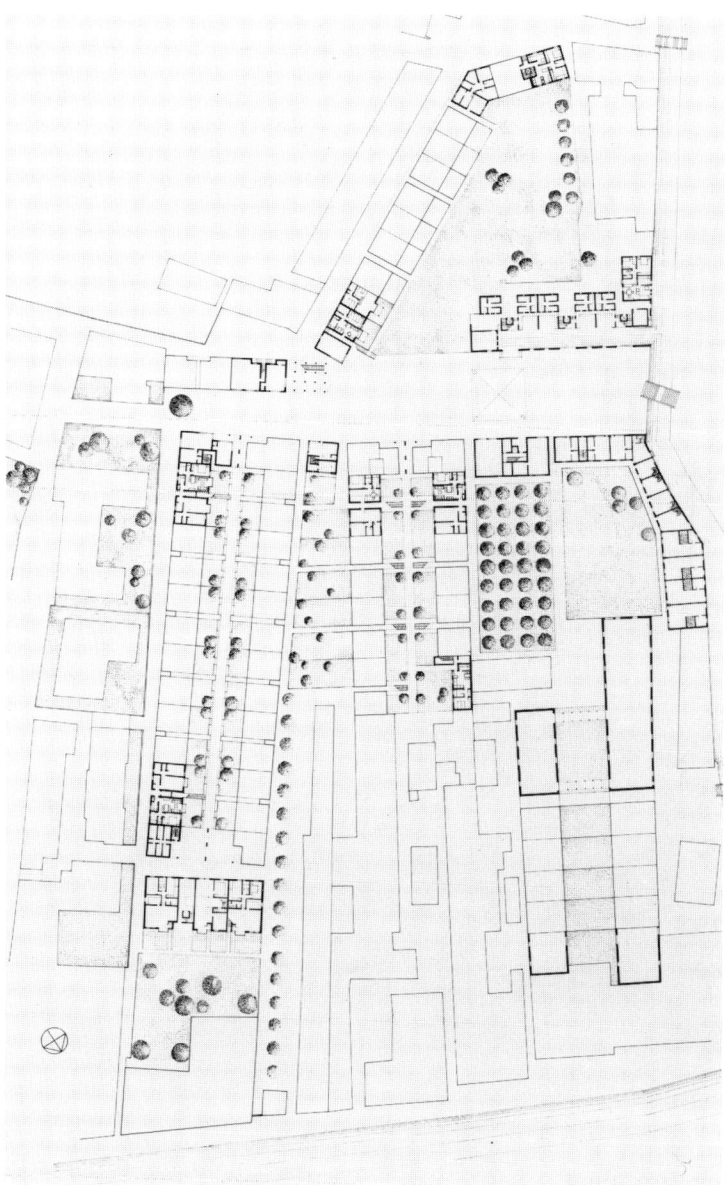

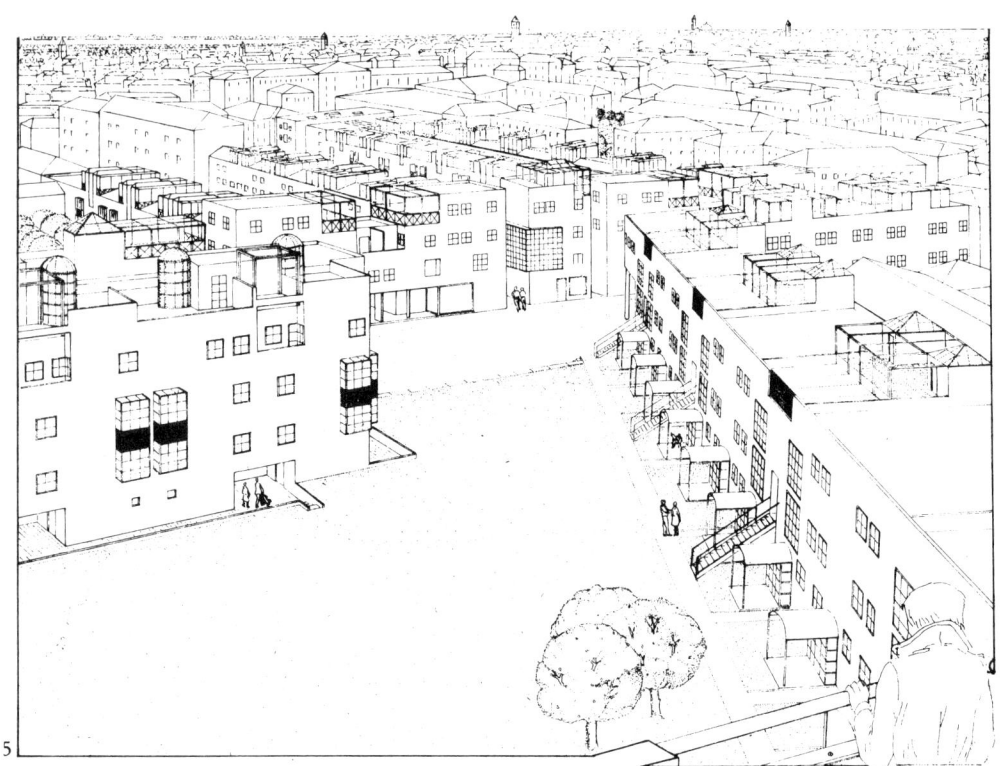

5. View from east towards the Campo Lungo.
6. Profile AA.
7. Interior of the boathouse beneath the orthogonal building on Rio della Crea.
8. View of the new Calle between the new project and the site of the Region.

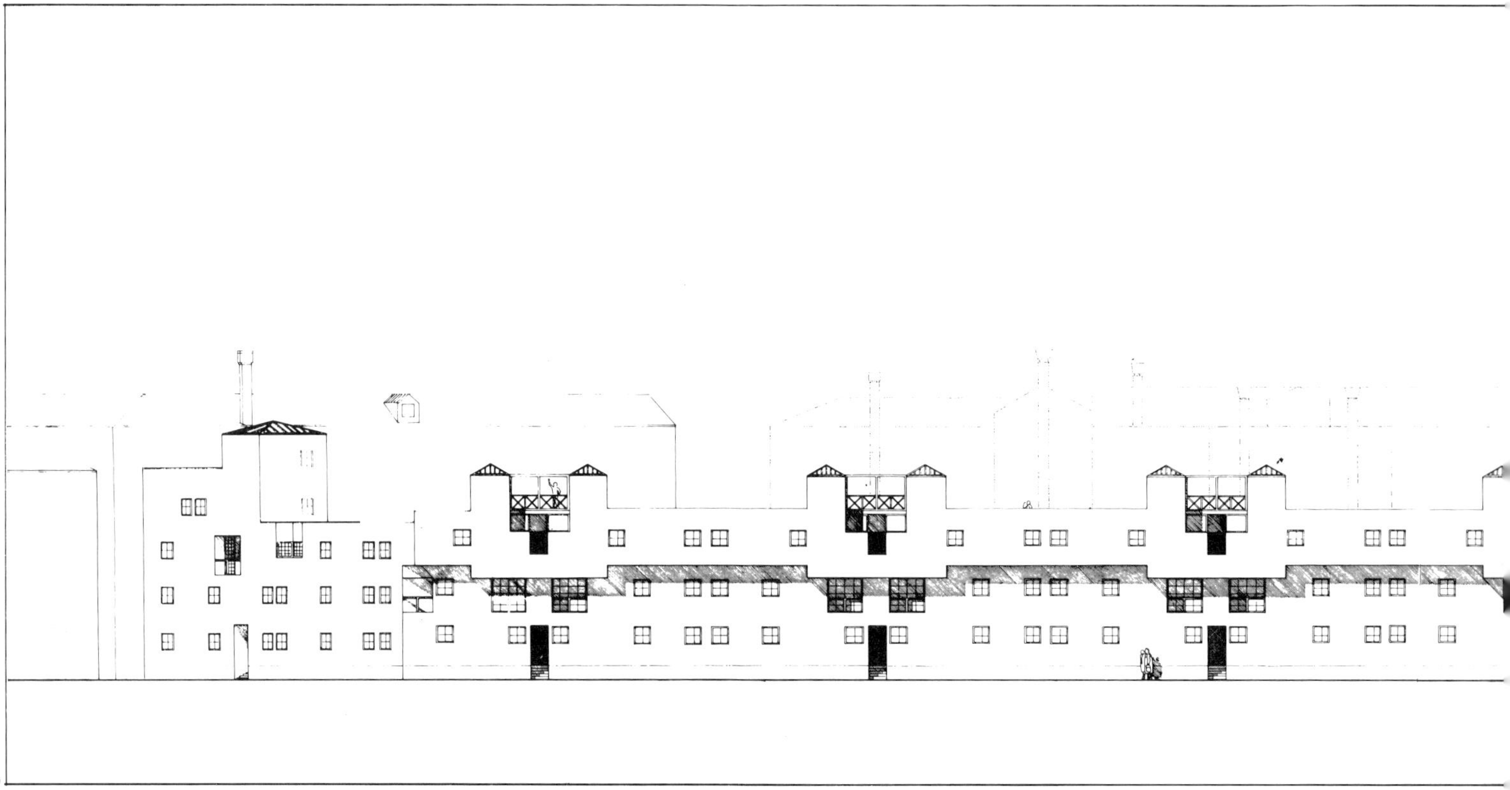

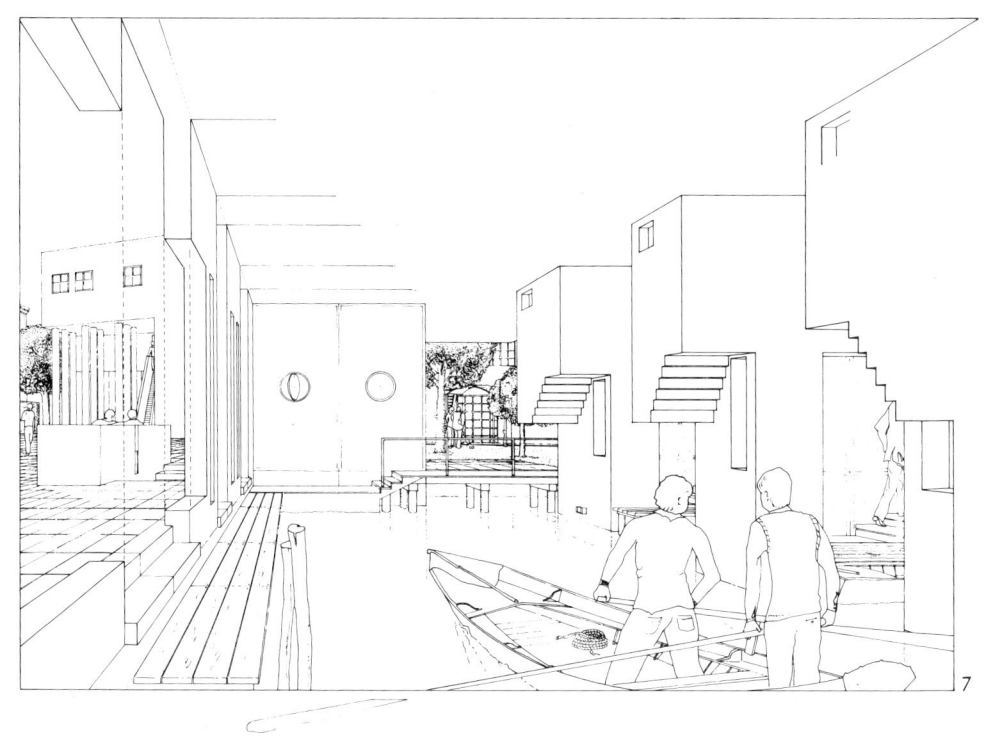
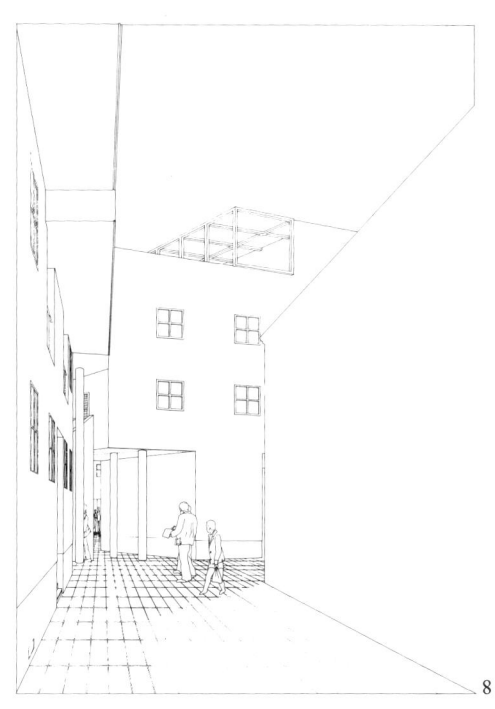

7

8

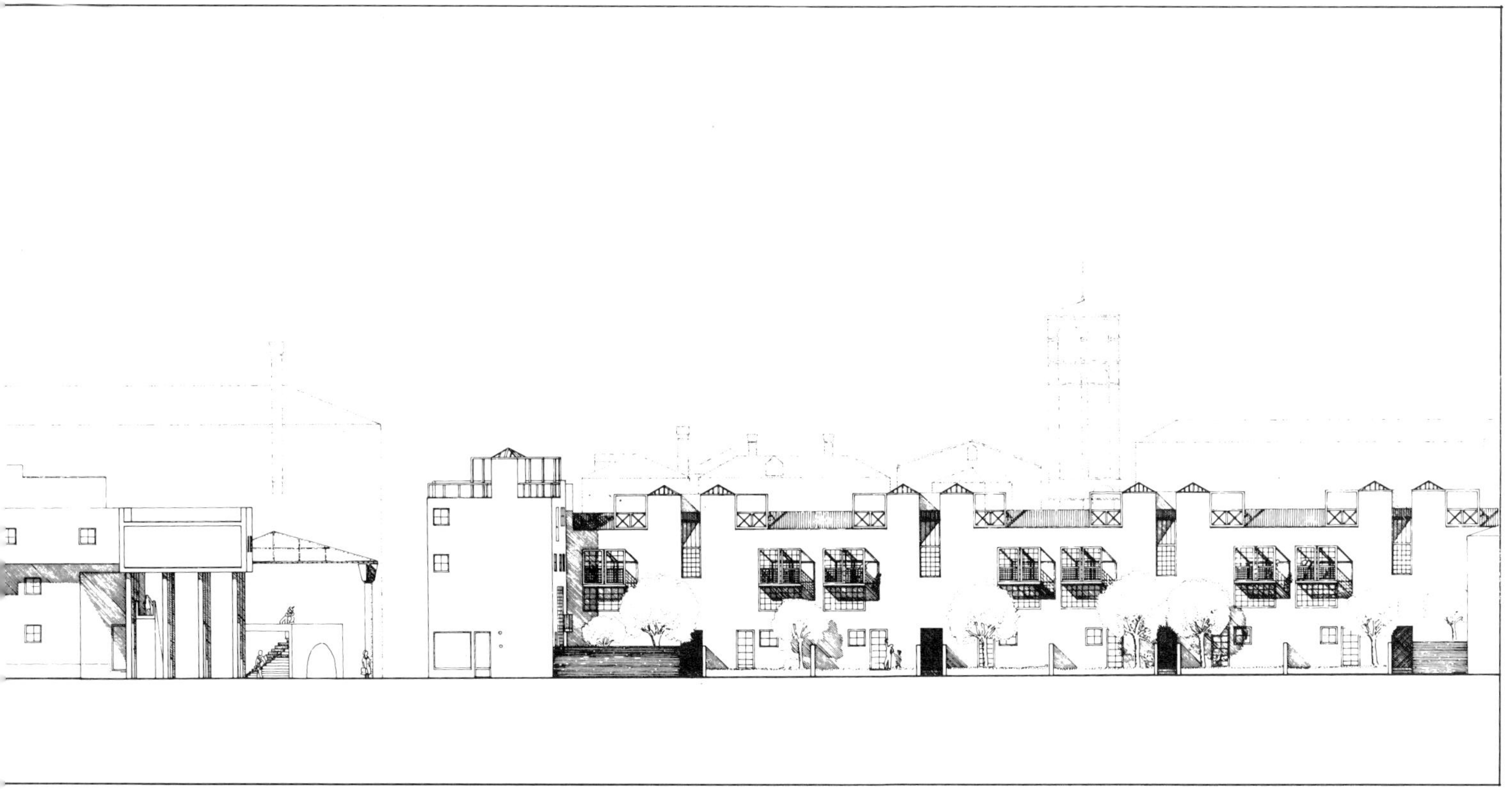

85

9. Profile BB. 10. Section CC.

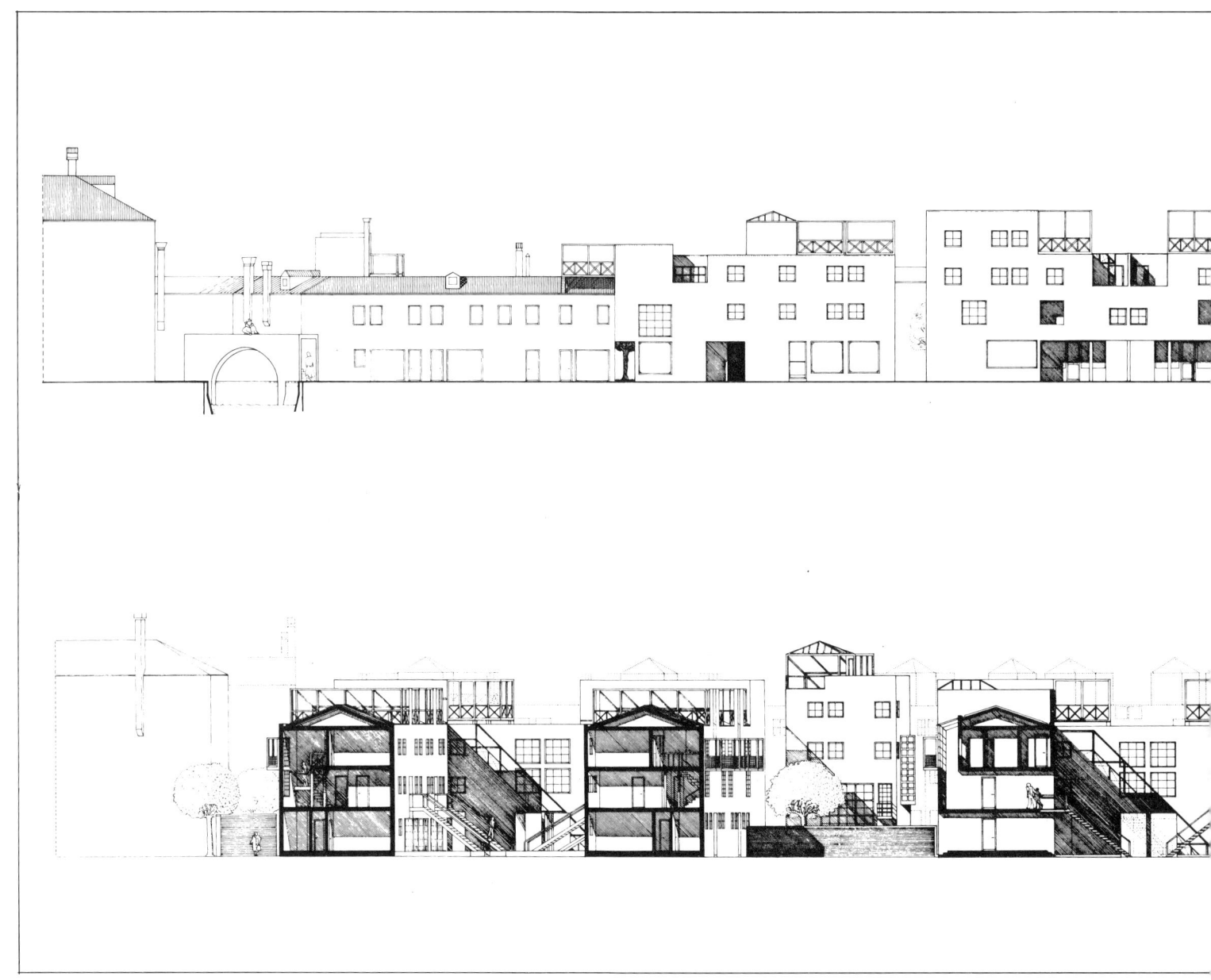

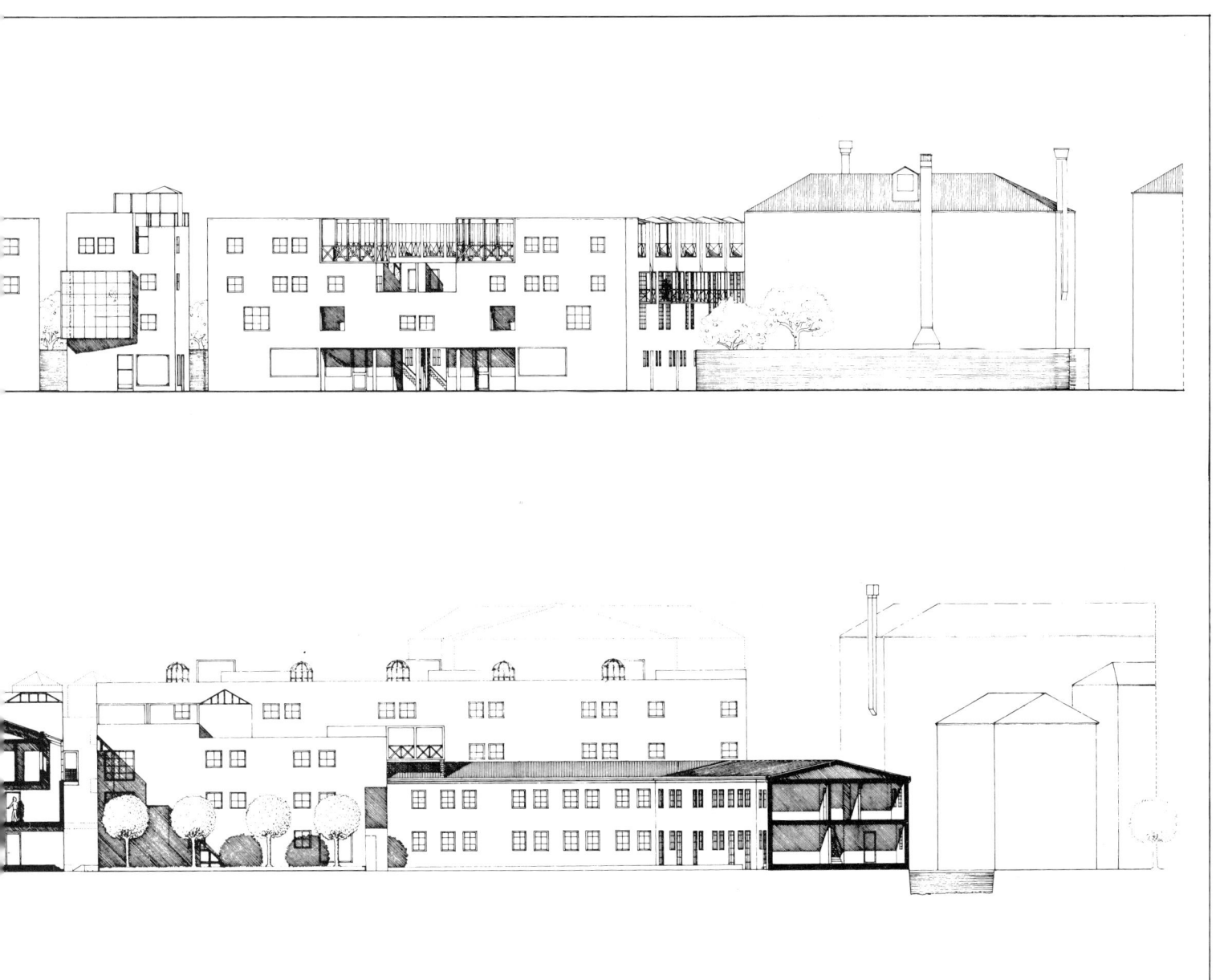

11. *Perspective view from south-east.*

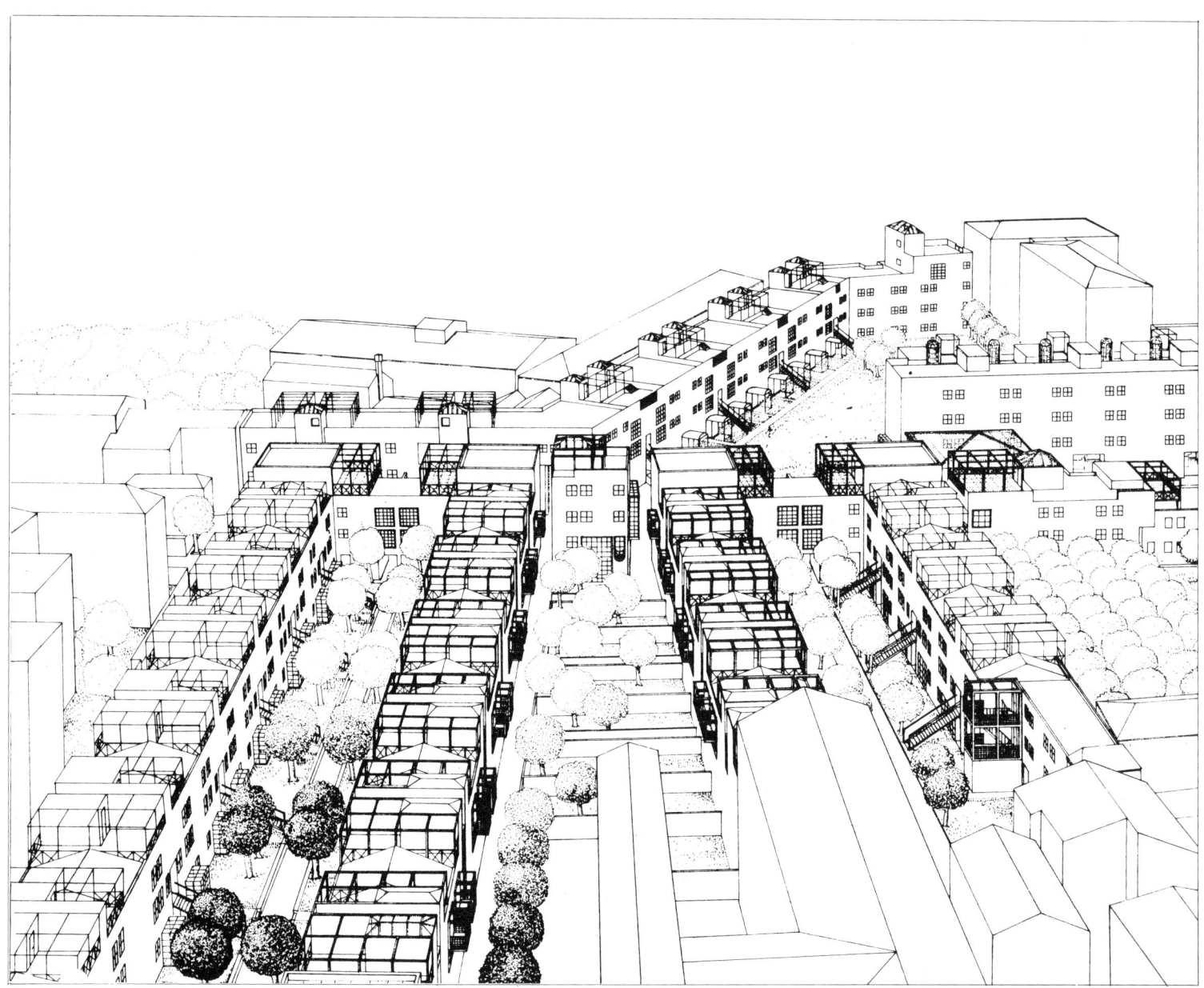

Residential building in Berlin

West Berlin is a city of fragments. It is itself a fragment of an ancient urban unity, of the ancient city of stone barracks. The impossibility of physically reconstructing that unity is offset within each of us by a process of interpretation and recollection. Berlin has become, in the European consciousness, one of the most literary of cities; it has focussed in itself the most radical sense of the laceration by the events of the last half-century of the unity of the urban structures of the ancient cities of Europe.

Our concern in the plan we present here has been to use the idea of urban unity to maintain an ambiguous relationship, in an unresolved tension, a divided memory. We have sought to put forward a reconsolidation of the concept of fragment on a new scale, to work above all on the relation between recomposed architectural wholes in order to create a sense of the reciprocal necessity of their parts, so as to overcome the widespread impression of being luxury suburbs emanated by the newer zones of reconstructed Berlin. Even the materials we have used (the klinker used as a facing material in two shades of colour ranging from yellowish-grey to brick-red, the greyish-blue metal structures) are a highly subjective reference to a fragment of the city's history.

The first operation was to consolidate the five "sticks", planned but not yet built, as urban elements. This consolidation is also the reversal of a principle of settlement, that of parallel and independent sticks, without any attempt to extend this principle to the entire system of the site. Regulation of this system has been achieved by seeking to introduce different levels of articulation into the system itself. The corner towers, the great portals, one for access and the other for passage through the square, the layering of continuous masonry elements and metal structures, all have the aim of establishing hierarchies in the language of the large block.

The second operation was the enhancement of the environmental qualities of the Landwehrkanal through the creation of a square, bounded by the facade enclosing the block of the five stick buildings and a building set at right angles to it, which presents itself as a bridgehead and recompositional element for the existing group of buildings. This square is characterized by the prominence given to the chimneystack of the Pumpwerk as a focal reference point and by a pond placed symmetrically in relation to the enlargement of the Landwehrkanal by the Von der Heydt villa: the pond will be raised and linked with the canal by a small waterfall circulating the water.

The third operation consisted in the location of the youth service structure in the eastern triangle. It consists of a large enclosure bounded by a double wall in the form of a transparent-vaulted portico, of which both the interior and exterior can be used. The open spaces are articulated into varying dimensions of use. As a whole, the outdoor area can be used as a large walled garden.

The fourth operation consisted of the attempted recomposition of the elements around the Pumpwerk. The southern entrance from Lützowstrasse is regulated by a low building unifying the various fragments and leading through a public entry in a glazed gallery into the inner tree-lined courtyard. The lower blocks could house a nursery school and kindergarten. The machine room for the Pumpwerk is completed towards the east by a glazed awning and conceived as a small museum. The entrance from number 10 Genthinerstrasse, where there is a particularly fine building, is emphasized by gardens running alongside the new Pumpwerk being built and leading into the inner tree-lined courtyard. The courtyard of the industrial blocks at 8/9 Genthinerstrasse is connected with the courtyard of the old pump house, eliminating some single-story buildings and completing the head of the ex-inspector's house.

An orthogonal building projecting from 42 Lützowstrasse bounds the area of the recomposition: it opens out with a broad aperture towards the new pump house and its dimensions and appearance link it with the industrial building on the inside of number 8 Genthinerstrasse.

Finally a link enclosing the site along the Schöneberger Ufer is envisaged, with the creation of a large green space inside.

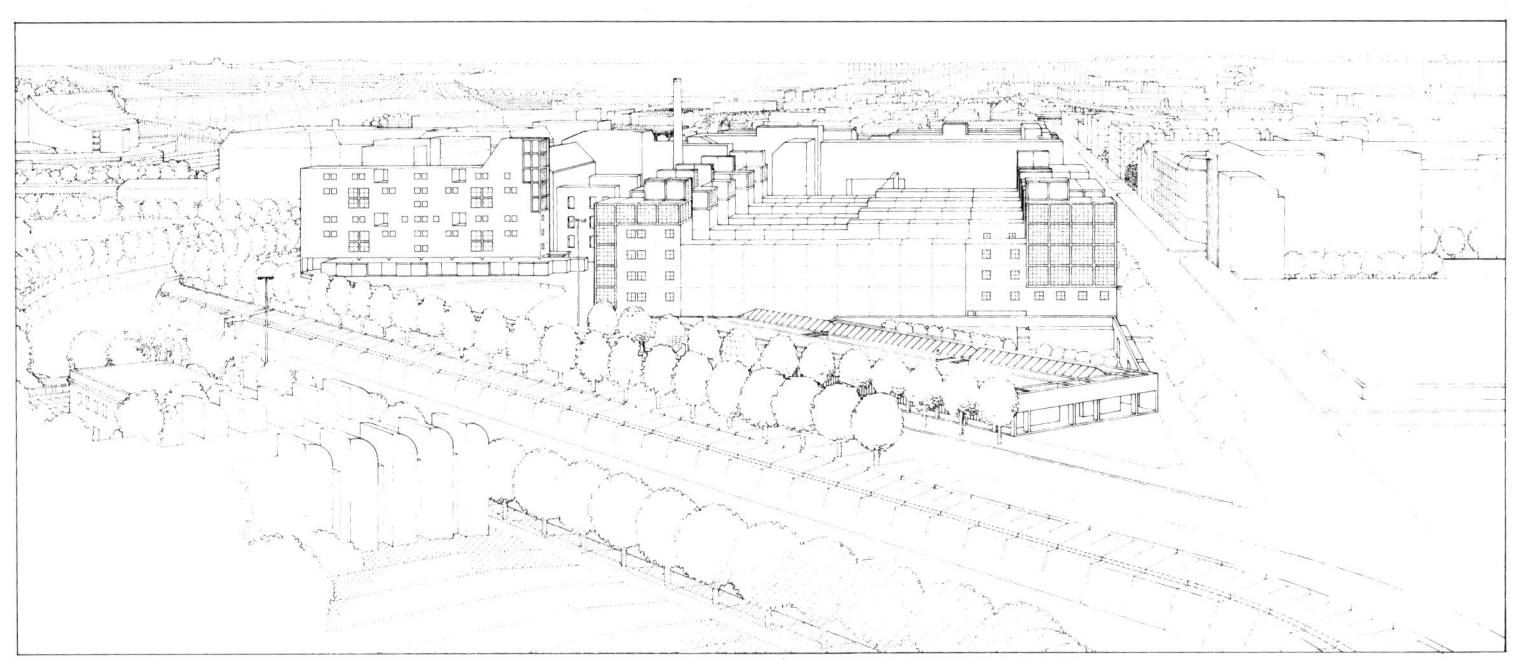

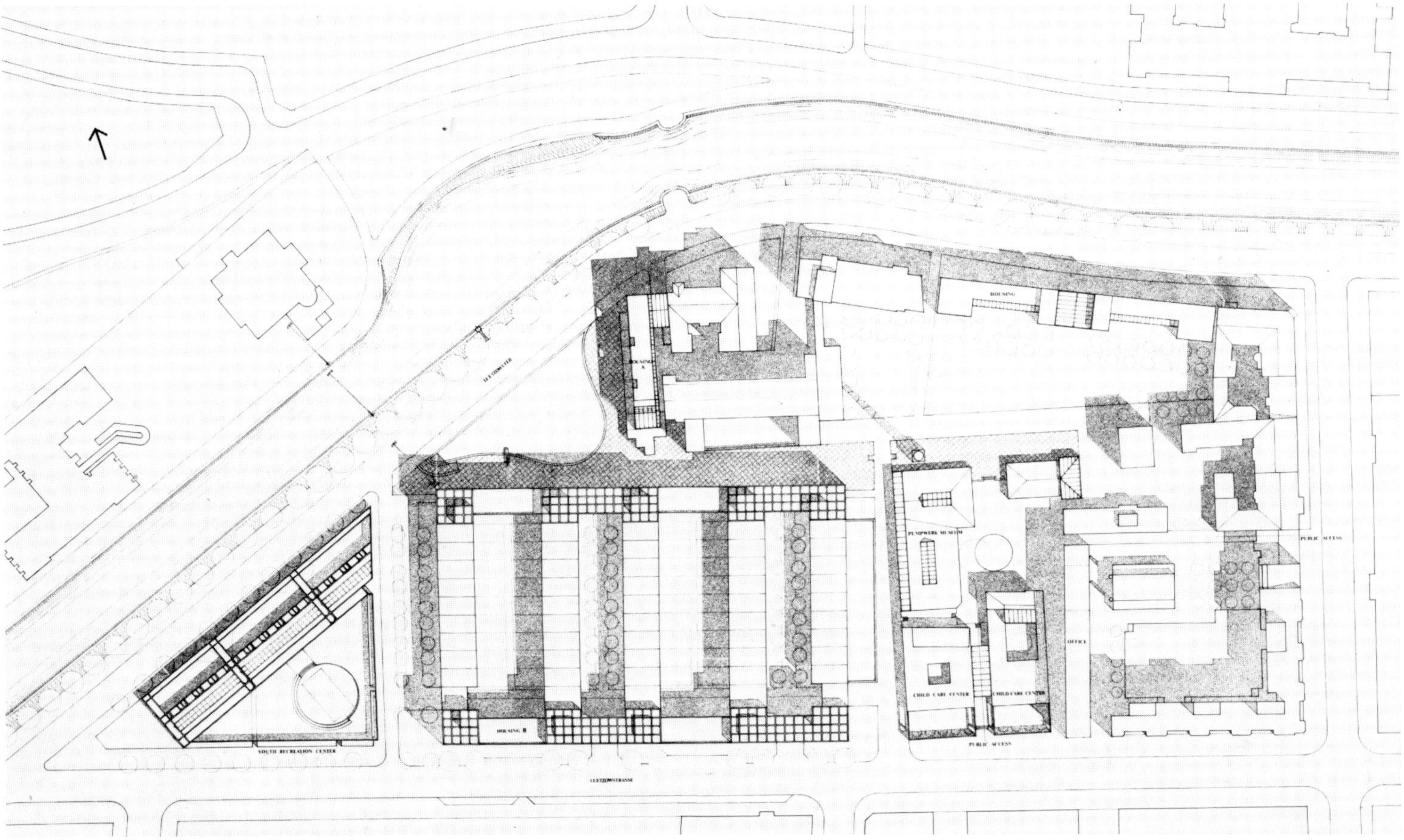
HOUSING
HOUSING A
PUMPWERK MUSEUM
PUBLIC ACCESS
OFFICE
CHILD CARE CENTER
CHILD CARE CENTER
PUBLIC ACCESS
HOUSING B
YOUTH RECREATION CENTER
LUETZOWSTRASSE

1. *Perspective general view.*
2. *General plan.*
3. *Elevation of Lützowstrasse.*
4. *Longitudinal section XX.*
5. *Cross section YY.*

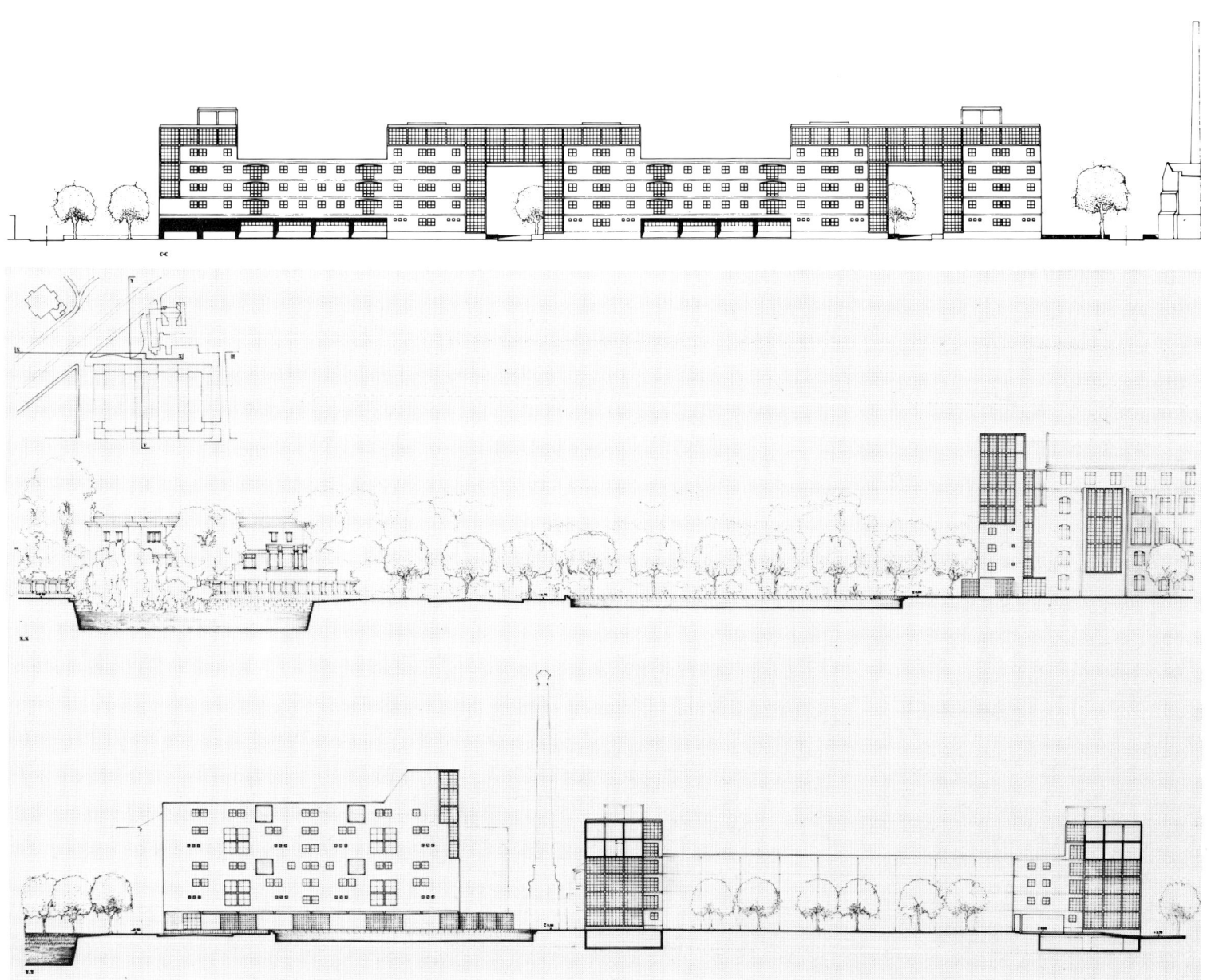

6. Axonometric of the corner of the Pumpwerk museum.

7. Axonometric of youth centre.

8. Perspective view from the Landwehrkanal towards the square.

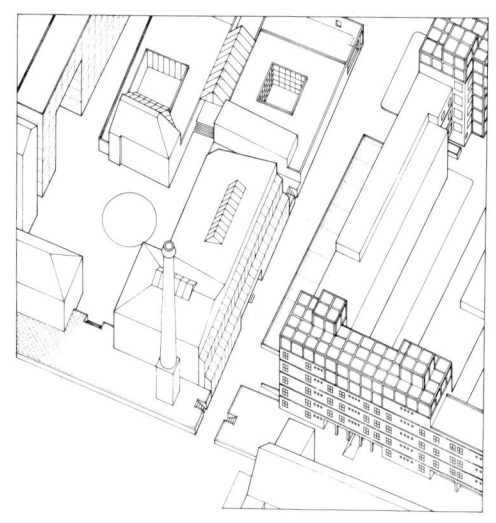
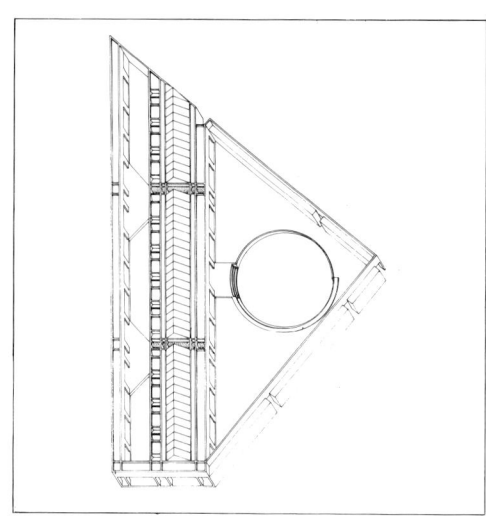

New centre
for G. G. Feltrinelli Foundation
in Milan

1. *View of present state.*

The aim of the Feltrinelli Foundation is to collect, catalogue and make available for public reference texts and documents related to the history of Marxism and of the workers' movement generally. The collection has brought together important public and private collections.

The Foundation supplements these activities by organizing study seminars, courses and other didactical activities. Its functions involve the general archives, the unified archives created from bequests, a reading room, catalogues, lecture rooms for courses of study, and offices and workrooms for the restoration work, bookbinding, microfilming etc. inherent in preserving documents, and finally a conference hall equipped with simultaneous translation booths for both internal and public use.

All these features combine to distinguish the Foundation as a focal point of the city's cultural life. The site designated for the Foundation's new centre is rich in historical and monumental elements. It is the clear space between S. Maria alla Porta, Via Gorani and Via Brisa, created by war-time destruction and by the lucky failure to implement previous plans for the area.

The Roman city emerges on this site in the form of ruins of the baths and fragments of masonry which were probably part of the imperial palace. The Gorani tower dates from the Middle Ages and is in a decrepit state: it is part of the system of look-out towers still visible in the ancient city centre (the towers of Ansperto, of Via Meravigli and of Via Mercanti, under the 18th century covering of the Palazzo dei Giureconsulti). The remains of the entrance to the courtyard of Palazzo Gorani belong to the 18th century: it is part of the sequence of closed courtyards once extending from S. Maria alla Porta to Via Brisa.

These "monuments" are the emblematic remains of the transformations that have affected this site, the physical witnesses of the site's layout in other clearly defined periods. The town plan envisages planning permission for building over 6,500 square metres, inclusive of flooring. The detailed plan we have proposed for the entire site will not only define the volumes of the Foundation but will also offer a design for the area in front of the Gorani tower as a public square, a final arrangement of the archaeological elements and completion of the screen formed by S. Maria alla Porta.

The plan envisages the construction of five tower-buildings in the central area of the square. They will have square bases with sides measuring 10.80 metres and a height of 19 metres: set around the Gorani tower, they will reinforce its significance in an interplay of relationships and cross-references. The bases of the towers delimit a square quadrangle, the focus of the layout of the entire complex. Looking onto it are the entrance to the reading room, the study rooms, the descent to the archaeological area, as well as the library tower, with its trapezoidal base which serves as a link with the archaeological area. The reading rooms and the meeting room constitute a constructed base, enclosed by the tower buildings and completing the screen of buildings which starts at Via Brisa and peters out a little before reaching Via Gorani.

Entry to the conference hall will be from S. Maria alla Porta, so as to facilitate organization of seminars or other functions open to the general public.

On the side towards Via Brisa, the paved square, excavations, archaeological remains and recreation spaces constitute exceptional elements in the context of the ancient centre of Milan, relating the project's functioning to a continuous dialogue between the city's present functional needs and the tissues, fragments and meanings of the historical city.

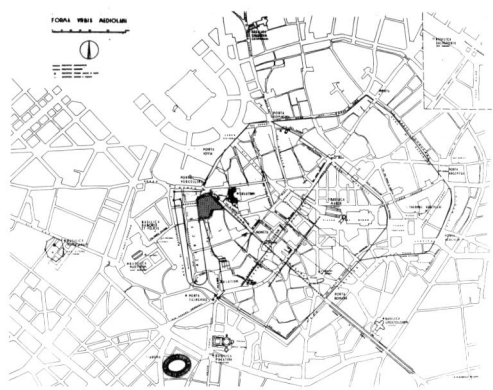

2. Location of the project site.

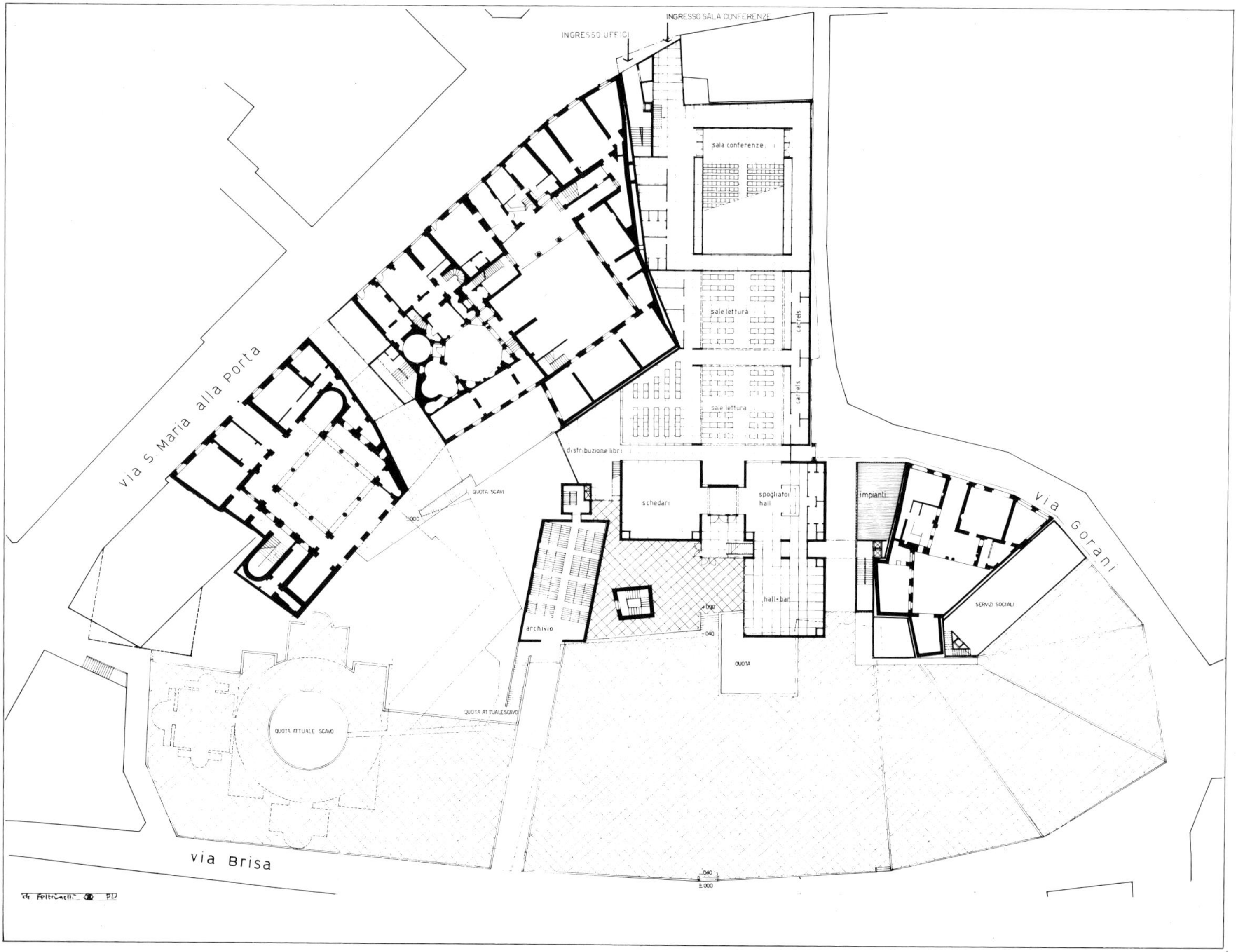

3. General plan: ground-floor plan.

4. Perspective general view from Via Brisa, first solution.

5. Photo of model of the first solution.

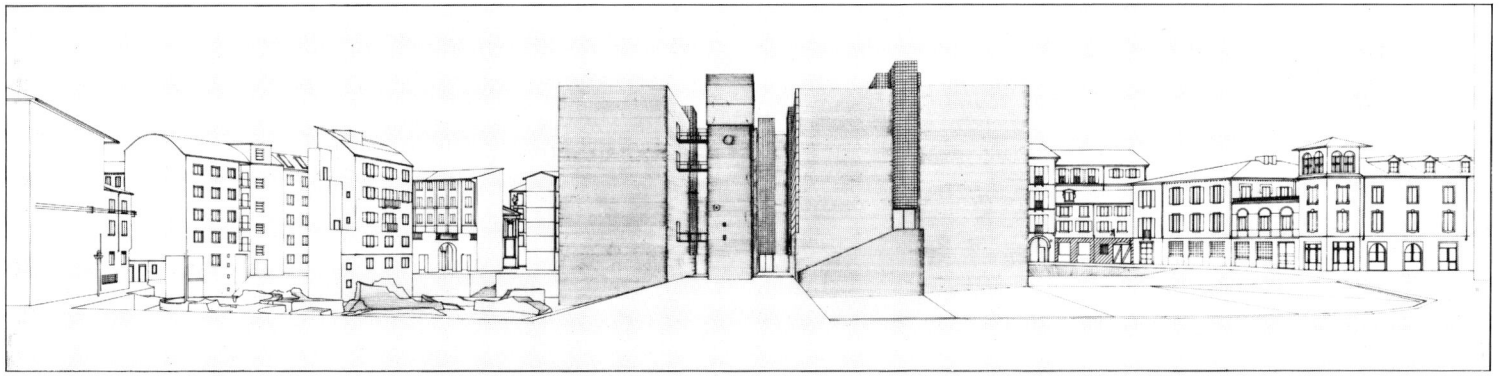

6. *Axonometric of the first solution.*

7. *View of corner of Via Gorani and Via Brisa.*

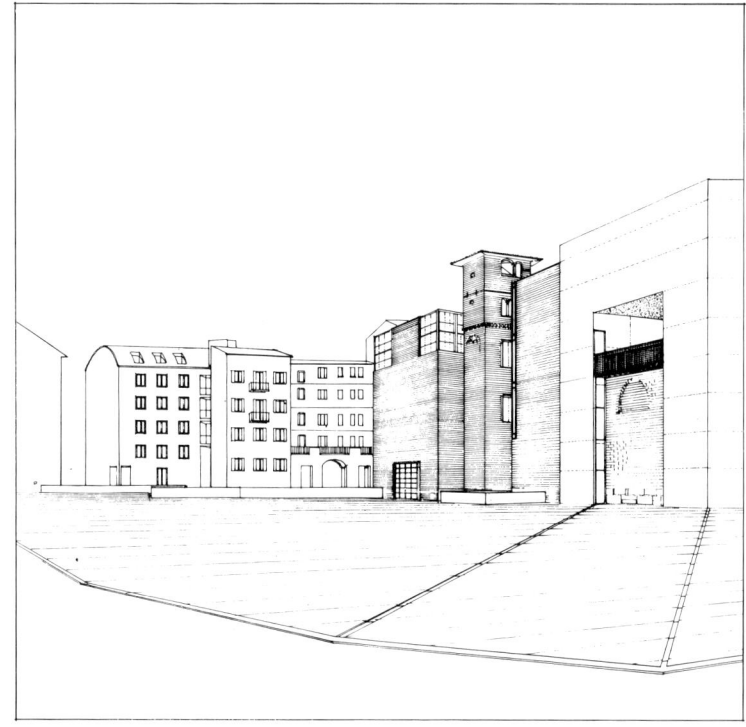

Business centre in Milan

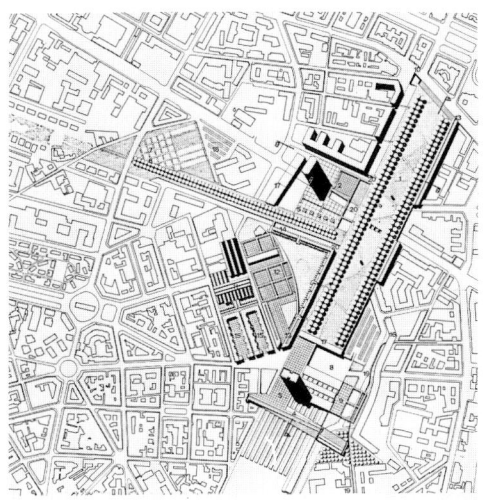

1. *General plan.*

The zone once intended as the business centre is one of the largest gashes in the city's built-up area. While the possibility of concentrating further offices in this zone has been diminishing with time, and the service thoroughfares meant to intersect in the heart of the business centre have failed to materialize, at the same time the use of the railways for a regional underground service has emerged and is now in process of execution. This plan involves construction of an underground railway-line crossing the city and connecting at six stations between la Bovisa and Porta Vittoria.

This regional underground line, known as "il passante" (the through-system), has two stations in this area. As one of the points of the new regional centre (and to avoid further congestion in the old city centre) the area of the ex-business centre has been organized as a large empty space around which the boundaries of the built-up area are redefined.

A large embankment gives a unified form to the space left empty. A rise 120 metres wide and about 700 metres long, with its top about 7-10 metres above the level of the existing roads, stands out as a "bastion" between the ancient city and the developing city. The upper space, a large elongated lawn bounded by two rows of trees, is bordered at one end by a building that closes off the square opposite Porta Garibaldi station and at the other by a covered gallery on Via Fabio Filzi, giving access to the stations of the MM3 underground line and the through system of Piazza della Repubblica. The area bounded by the large lawn is hence also the urban space between the two stations of the through system. To the north, on the same level as the embankment, an offshoot extends beyond Via Sassetti and slopes down to the gardens of Via Restelli. In its flyover section this offshoot creates a garden over services and amenities provided on the square below, and where it descends to the level of the city it skirts the area of the plant nurseries, which is envisaged as a permanent site for the circus and fairground installations, partly by making use of existing structures.

The square under this offshoot is located between the town hall and the embankment. It is crossed by Via Melchiorre Gioia and linked with the roof-level of the amenities. It comprises sports amenities, commercial structures and services (restaurants, canteens etc.) for people working in the area.

Another square is located beyond Porta Garibaldi station near the viaduct crossing the railway. The viaduct, partially roofed, is to be transformed into a covered market to serve the residential areas on either side of the railway.

The station of Porta Garibaldi remains accessible along its front on the present level. The space in front of it is bounded by a building for tertiary use, such as integrating the offices of the state railways or other functions.

Along the margin towards the old city centre, residences will adjoin the central space, as new buildings within blocks to be restructured. These buildings have two facades: the higher one towards the city and the lower one facing the central space.

Alongside the station of Porta Garibaldi, the screen of existing high-rise buildings is completed to create a link with the embankment where it extends beyond Corso Como, so that a portal to be built will give access to the station square.

Along its other side, the Island is completed with low-cost housing arranged along the edges of the embankment, connected with it by means of raised terraces. The clear space resulting on the inside is equipped with urban amenities.

The existing factory buildings of the Brown-Boveri company are crossed by a road axis. It is envisaged that part of this will be retained to form a covered square for commercial and artisan businesses.

The upper horizon of the embankment will not only constitute an unusual urban space in Milan, but also provide new ways of tackling problems of traffic and movement in the area.

2. *Overhead view of the model.* 3. *Longitudinal section.*

2

3

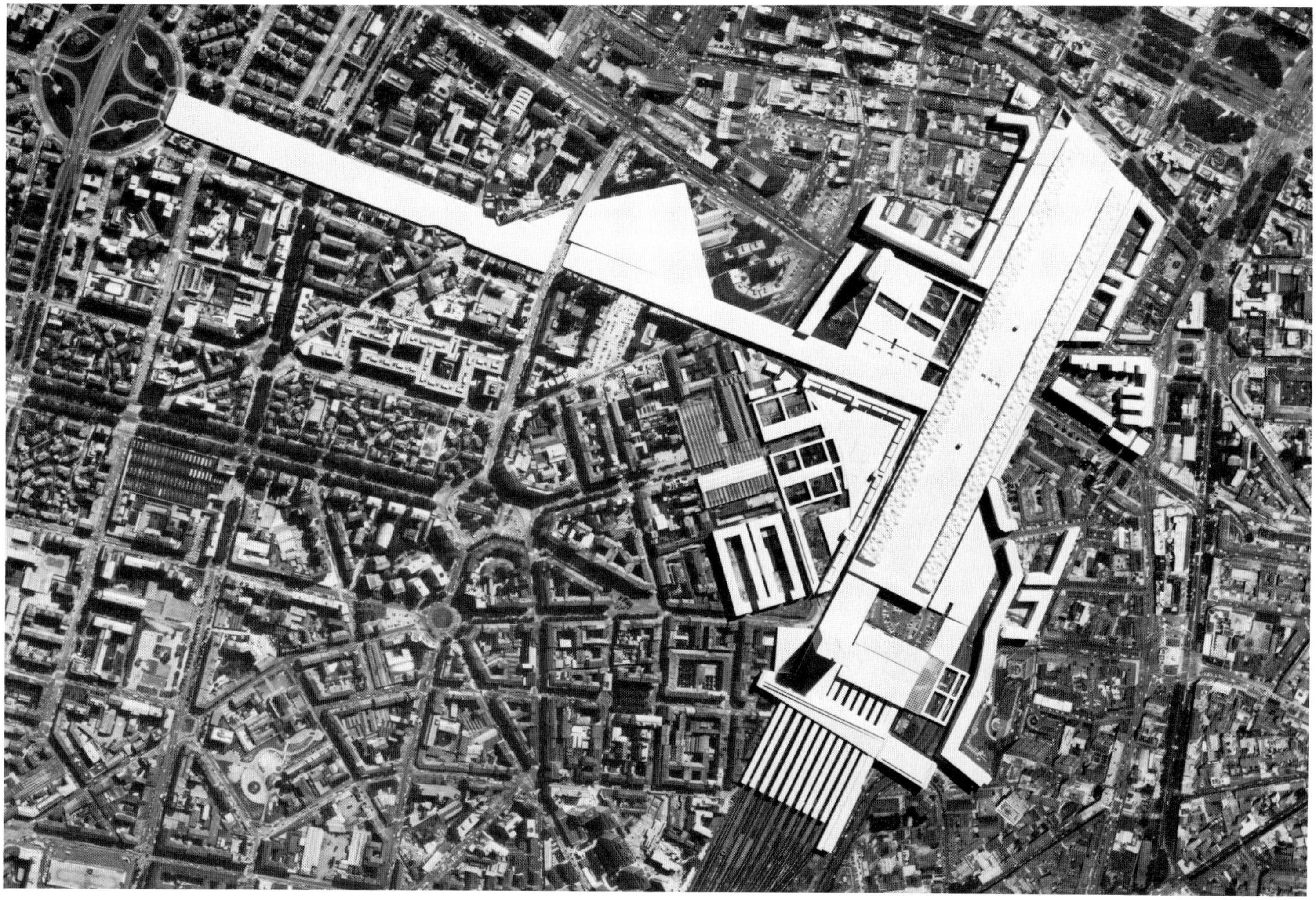

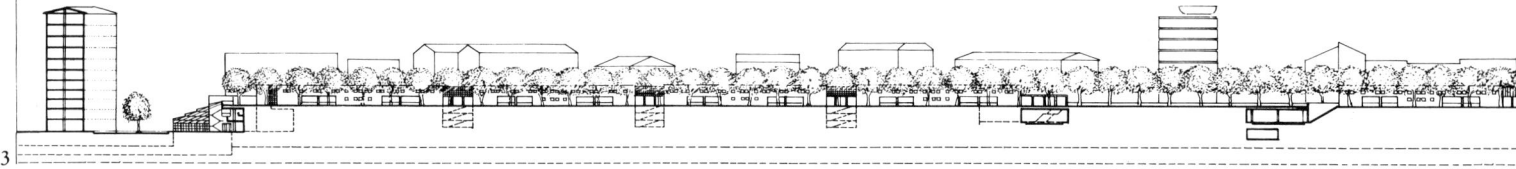

4. Model, view of Porta Garibaldi station.　　5. "Through" system.　　6. Connections.

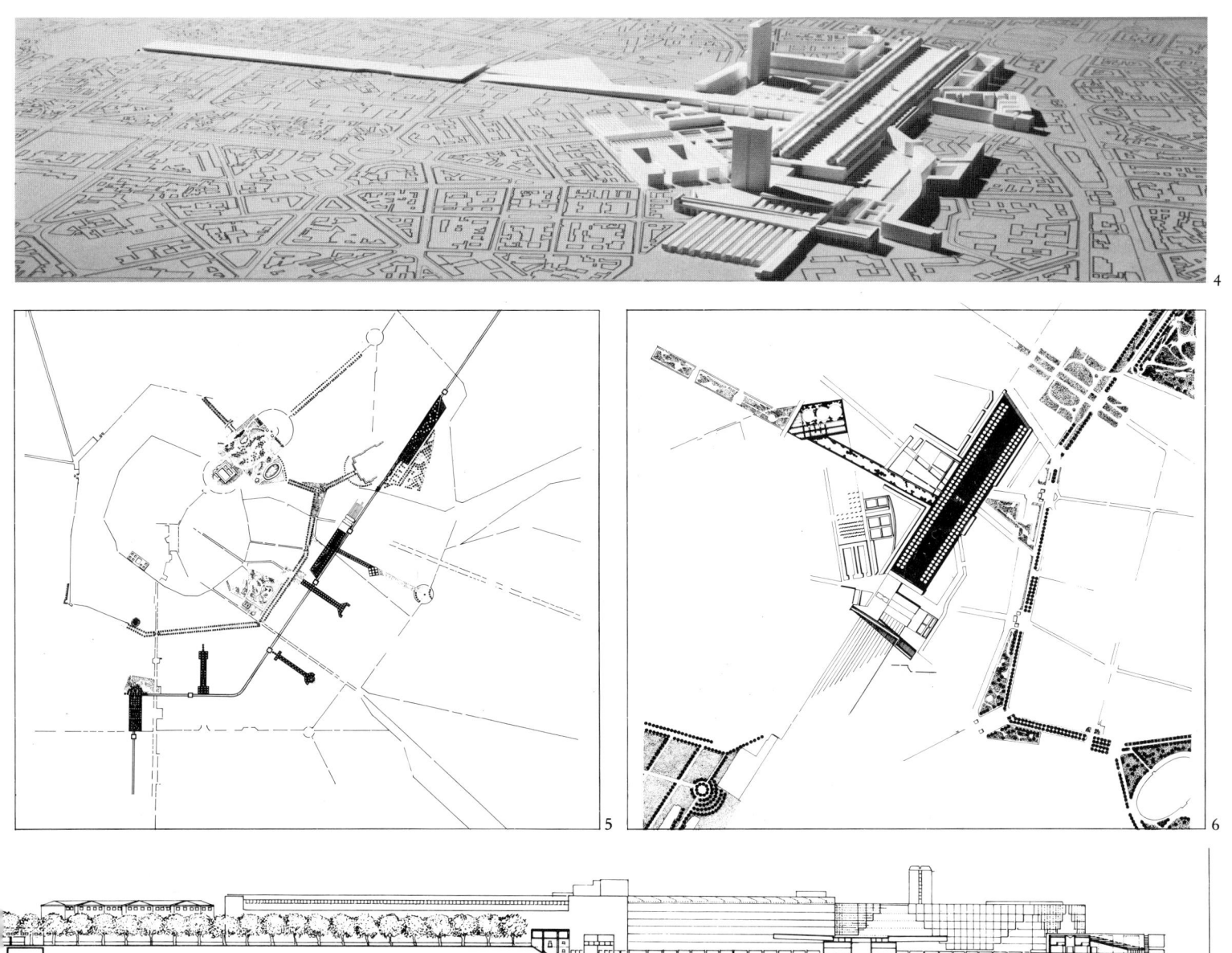

7. *Cross section.*
8. *Tree-lined embankment, bus stop, Alitalia air terminal.*
9. *Strada Garibaldi, Viale L. Sturzo, parking.*

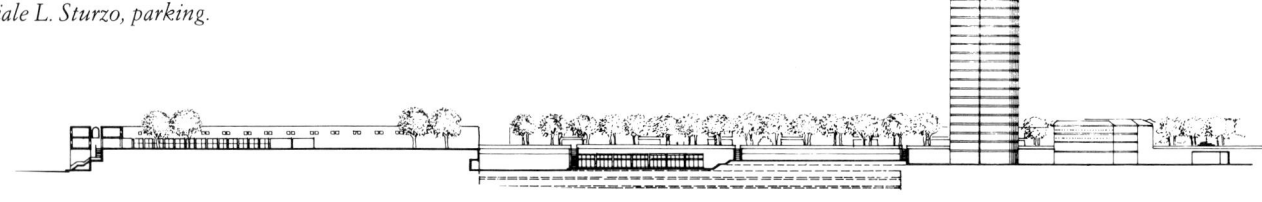

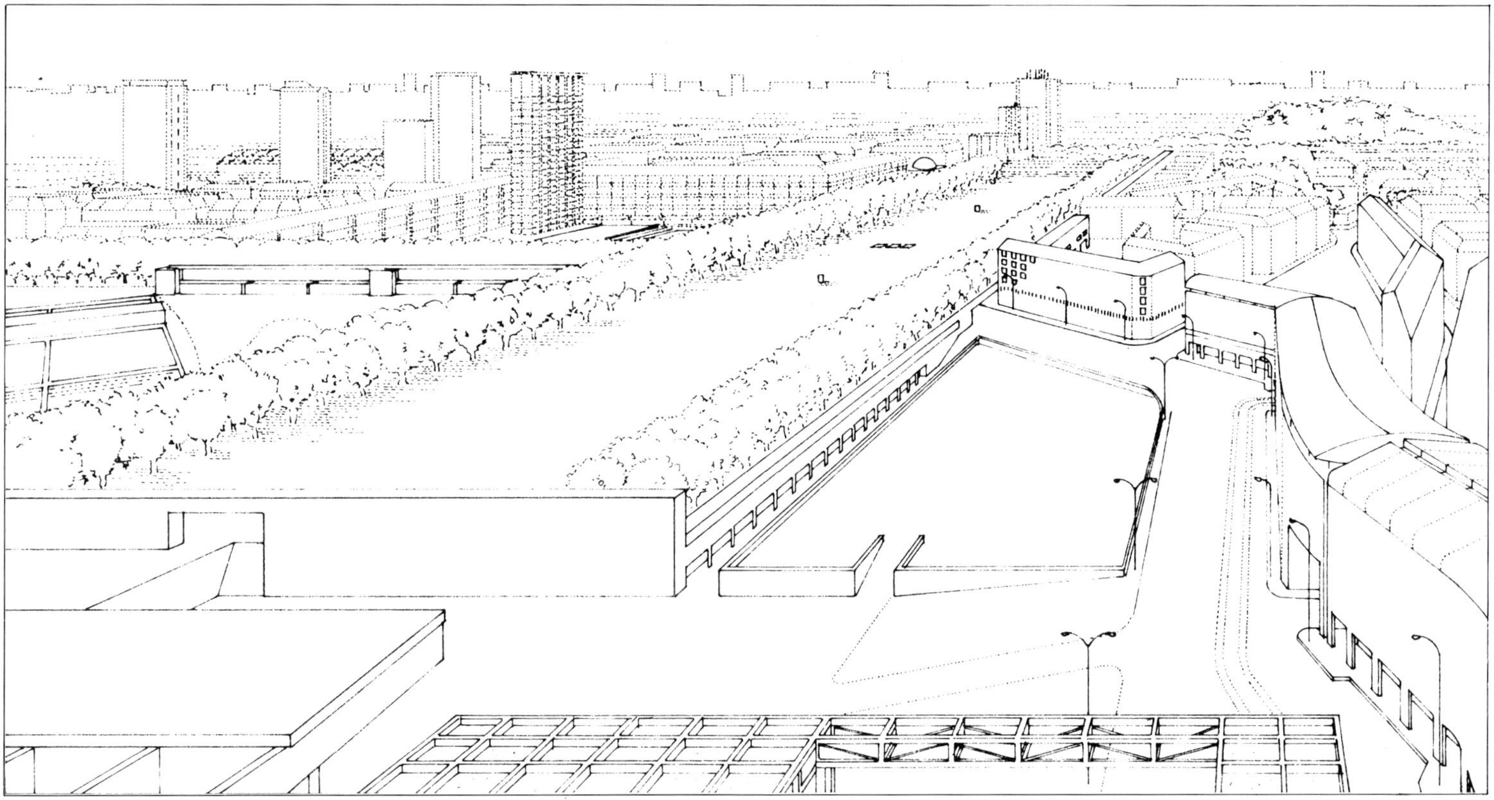

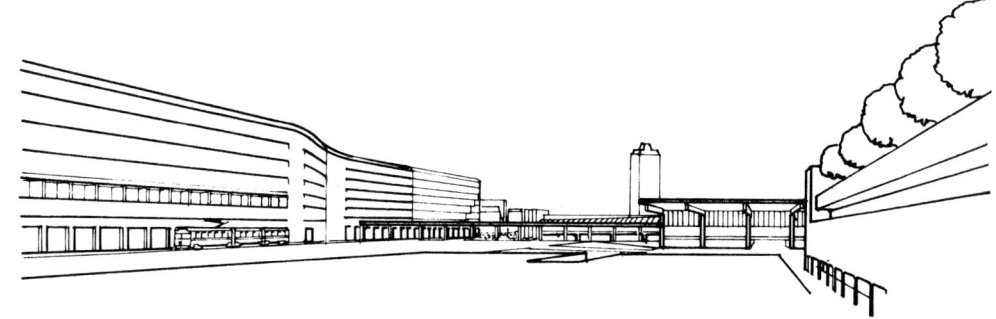

IVI Chemical Research Centre at Quattordio di Alessandria

The subject tackled was a research centre run by a big paint factory. The factory, located in a hilly zone of Piedmont (near Alessandria), is a large complex of buildings erected and modified continually over the last fifty years. The land available for the research centre lies behind it and outside the fence enclosing the factory complex; access is from a provincial road about 11 metres lower than the factory level.

The problem was therefore to link the new building with the existing ones by using and emphasizing the factory enclosure and the diagonal layout of the access road. It was decided to lay out the building on the diagonal of the corner of the factory fence, an orientation further emphasized by a large metal reservoir, and by developing the building on a single stepped level so as to create a continuous link between the levels of the road and the factory and affirm the volumetric presence of the new research building.

The typological plant is structured on three parallel strips. The two outer ones contain the series of laboratories with their relevant services and offices, while the central part contains general services. Two corridor-staircases connect the three blocks and determine the general layout. Below the corridor-staircases there are shafts for the service plants and a mechanical system for transporting heavy objects on the different levels. Above the corridors, there are volumes containing ventilation systems for expelling air from the laboratories. In the two ends of the threefold structure, the offices are located below while the central plant and a test-room for pilot experiments are above.

The vertical structures are in unfaced brickwork, with metal door and window fittings, while the roofing provides access for inspection of installations located on it and terminates in a Keller-type metal grid above the waterproofing of the roof.

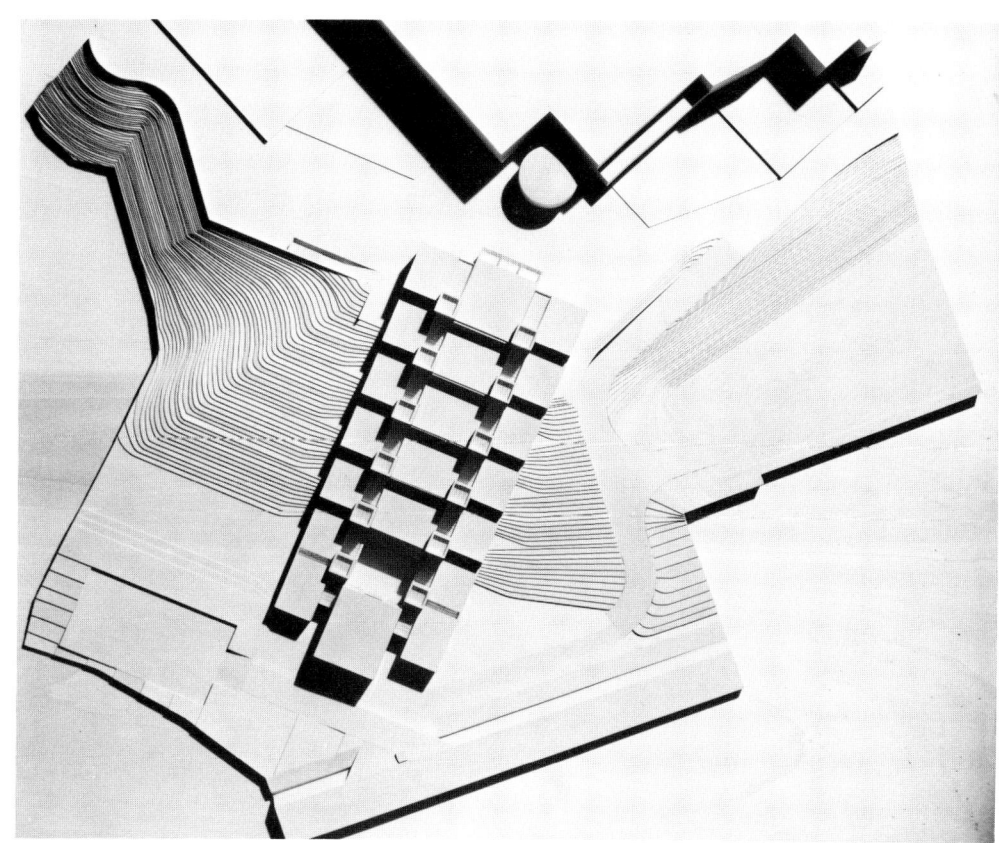

1. *Overhead view of model.*

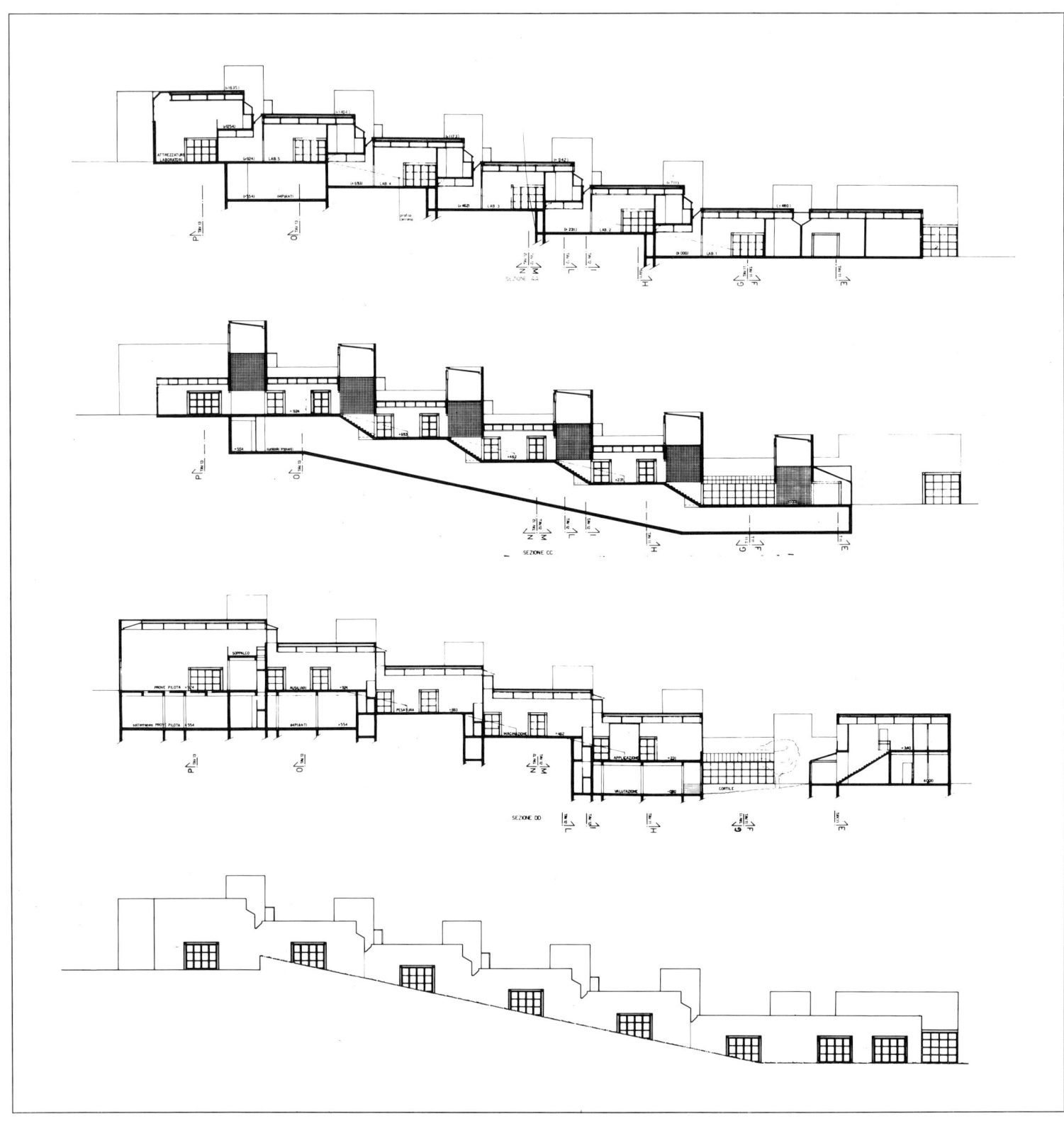

2. *Longitudinal section and elevation.* 3. *General plan and transverse sections.*

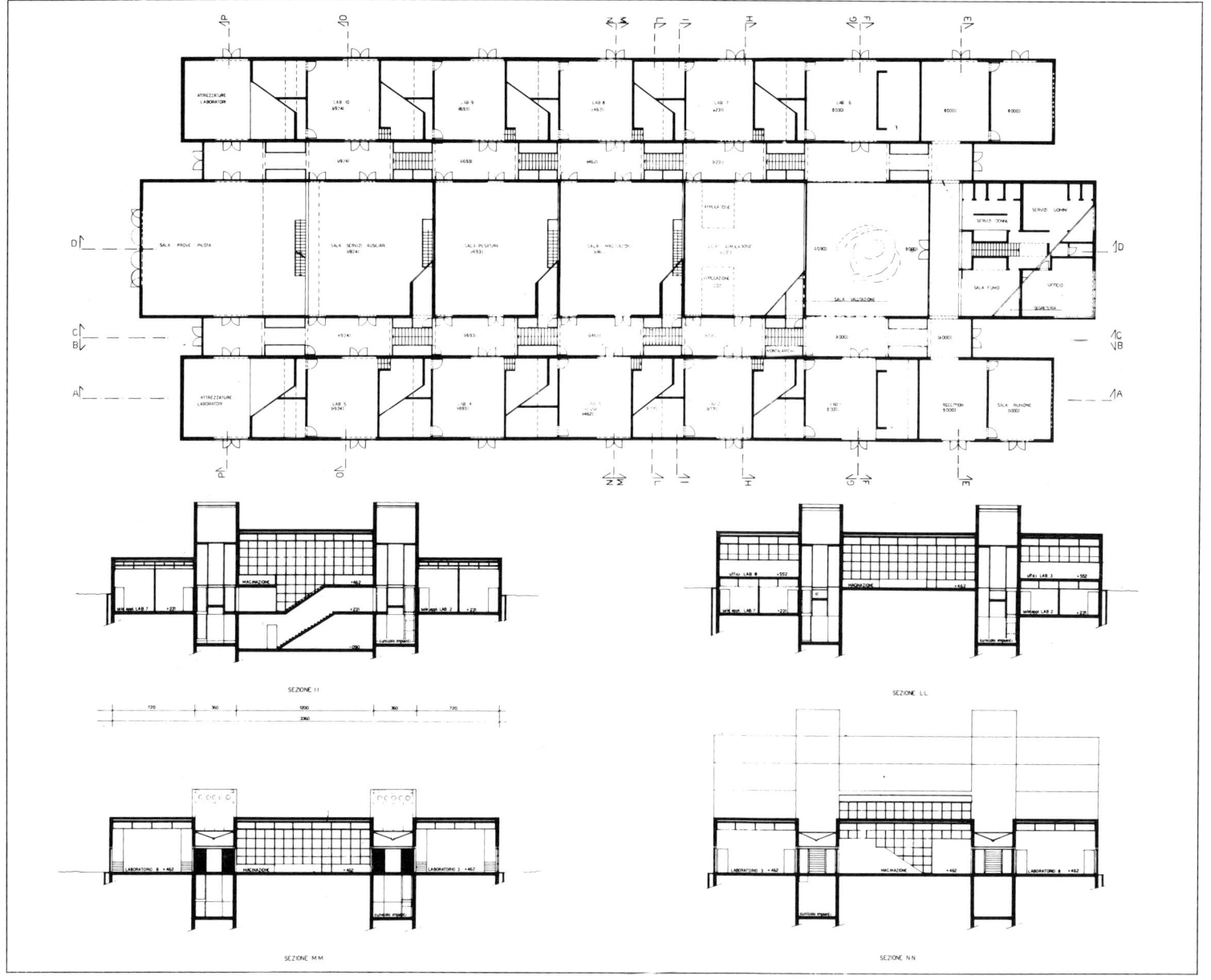

4. Perspective cross section through corridor.
5. Photo of front of model.

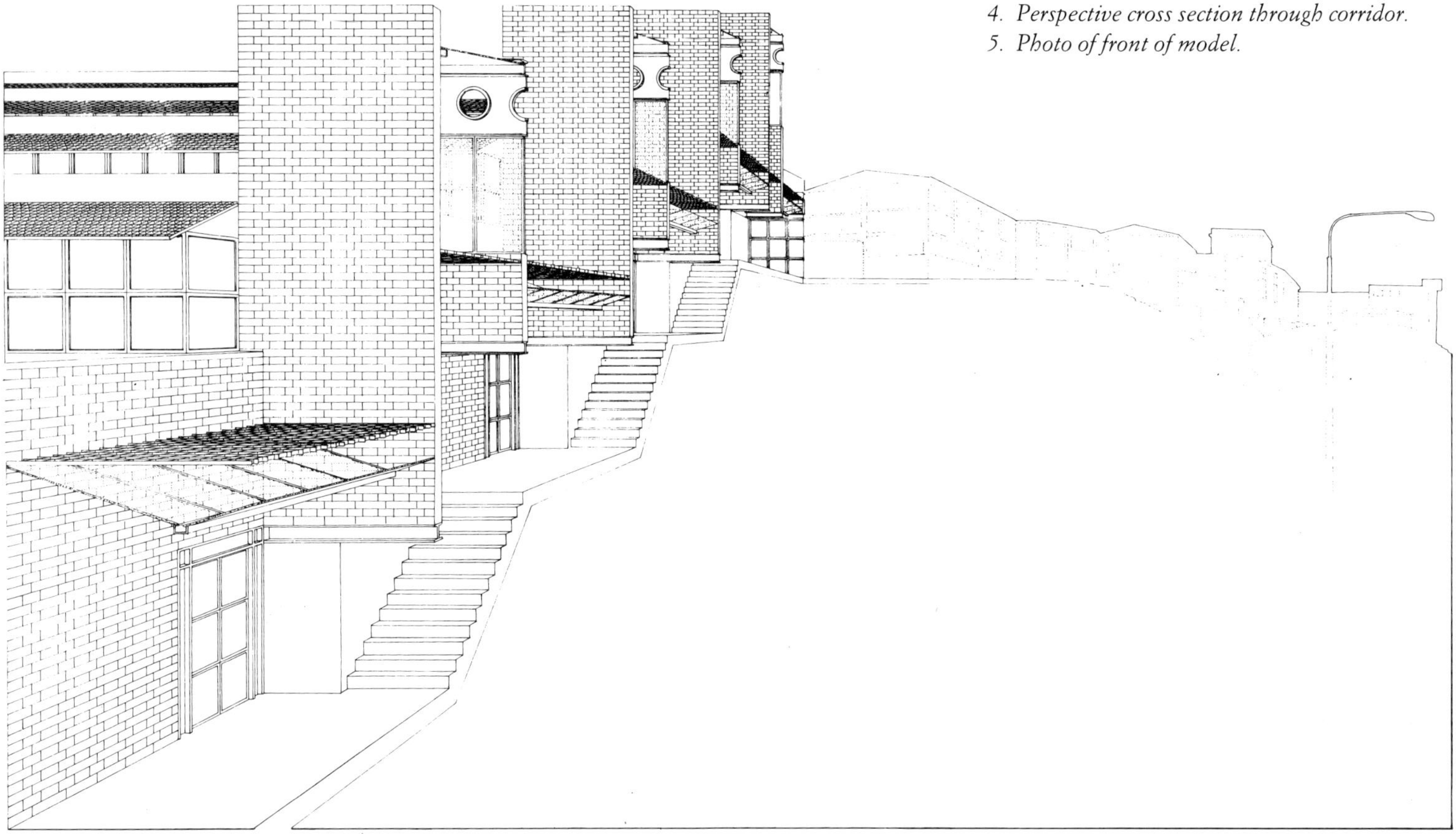

Collaborations

Design nos. 1-84 were executed by Vittorio Gregotti, Lodovico Meneghetti and Giotto Stoppino with the exception of the following:
1. with E.N. Rogers and G. Stoppino.
2. 3. 90. with G. Stoppino.
5. with F. Buzzi.
70. 71. 72 with L. Airaldi, M. Allione, F. Buzzi and S. Rizzi as external collaborator.
75. with P. Brivio, U. Eco and M. Vignelli. G. Stoppino and M. Vignelli.
85. with Ufficio Tecnico La Rinascente.
From nos. 86 – 100 collaborators were:
86. P. Brivio, H. Matsui and F. Purini.
87. H. Matsui and F. Purini.
88. V. Parmiani and B. Paulis.
89. F. Amoroso, S. Bisogni, H. Matsui and F. Purini.
91. G. Pollini with S. Azzola, H. Matsui and from 1979 with R. Brandolini and C. Fronzoni.
92. S. Bisogni, H. Matsui and P. Nicolin.
94. H. Matsui.
95. P. Cerri and P. Nicolin.
96. G. Samonà and G. Pirrone.
97. F. Barbagli, E. Battisti, P. Calza, G. Dallerba, E. Detti, G.F. Di Pietro, G. Fanelli, T. Gobbò, R. Innocenti, M. Mazza, H. Matsui, M. Mocchi, F. Neves, F. Purini, P. Sica, B. Viganò and M. Zoppi.
98. 99. B. Viganò.
100. The design for the Università della Calabria was the award-winner in a competition in 1974. The design team consisted of E. Battisti, V. Gregotti, H. Matsui, P. Nicolin, F. Purini, C. Rusconi Clerici and B. Viganò.
Collaborators on the executive plan:
S. Azzola, C. Castello, V. Casanova.
Structures: G. Ballio, A. Castiglioni, G. Colombo, G. Grandori.
Engineering: Tekne VRC.
Town planning: Laris spa.

From 1974 Vittorio Gregotti formed, with Pierluigi Cerri, Hiromichi Matsui, Pierluigi Nicolin and Bruno Viganò, a design office, Gregotti Associati. In 1976 Bruno Viganò left the partnership and in 1977 Pierluigi Nicolin followed suit, while in 1981 the architect Augusto Cagnardi joined it.
Collaborators on designs by Gregotti Associati are:
101. R. Cecchi.
102. R. Collovà, I. Rota, Cepro spa., Laris spa.
103. O. Bohigas, Martorell, Mackay.
104. R. Cecchi and I. Rota.
106. S. Azzola, G. Clerici, I. Rota.
107. S. Azzola, R. Cecchi, V. Casanova, C. Castello, I. Rota.
111. S. Azzola, R. Cecchi, V. Casanova, C. Castello, H. Matsui, I. Rota.
115. S. Azzola, R. Cecchi, G. Clerici, I. Rota.
116. S. Azzola, V. Casanova, G. Clerici, I. Rota.
121. S. Azzola, R. Cecchi, V. Casanova, C. Castello, G. Clerici, I. Rota.
122. D. Ferretti, F. Semi, N. Valle Bellavitis.
123. J. Matsui.
124. R. Cecchi, C. Fronzoni, A. Gobbi, I. Rota; garden consultant E. Casasco.
125. S. Azzola, R. Cecchi, A. Gobbi.
126. C. Castello.
127. C. Castello, T. Brenner.
128. S. Azzola, R. Cecchi, V. Casanova, R. Spagnolo.
129. S. Azzola, E. Casagrande, C. Magnani.
130. E. Casagrande, C. Magnani, F. Messina, G.F. Trabucco, P.A. Val, N. Ventura.
131. S. Azzola, R. Cecchi, Laris, A. Cagnardi, R. Cattaneo, M. Gasca Queirazza, A. Marcarini.
132. S. Azzola, R. Cecchi, R. Brandolini, T. Brenner, V. Casanova, C. Castello, C. Fronzoni, E. Puglielli.
133. E. Casagrande, C. Magnani, F. Messina, G.F. Trabucco.

134. F. Cervellini, S. Petruccioli, S. Azzola, R. Cecchi, R. Cattaneo.
139. S. Azzola, R. Cecchi, R. Brandolini.
141. E. Battisti, M. Dezzi Bardeschi, M. Mattei, R. Cattaneo, E. Puglielli, R. Spagnolo.
142. R. Cattaneo, E. Puglielli.

Work nos. 1 - 84 were designed by Vittorio Gregotti, Lodovico Meneghetti and Giotto Stoppino, associated architects from 1953 to 1968. From 1974 to 1976 Vittorio Gregotti was associated with Pierluigi Cerri, Hiromichi Matsui, Pierluigi Nicolin and Bruno Viganò; from 1977 to 1981 with Pierluigi Cerri and Hiromichi Matsui, and from 1981 with Pierluigi Cerri, Hiromichi Matsui and Augusto Cagnardi.

Works and projects

1. 1951
9th Triennale - Installation
and organization of the room
"Measure and greatness of man"
Milan

2. 1953
Room for a young person
Novara

3. 1953
Shop
Vigevano

4. 1953
One-family house
Lesa

5. 1953
Pavilions at the trade fair
Novara

6. 1953
Sforza house
Stradella

7. 1953
10th Triennale
Plywood furniture
Milan

8. 1953
Transformable cinema
Novara

1

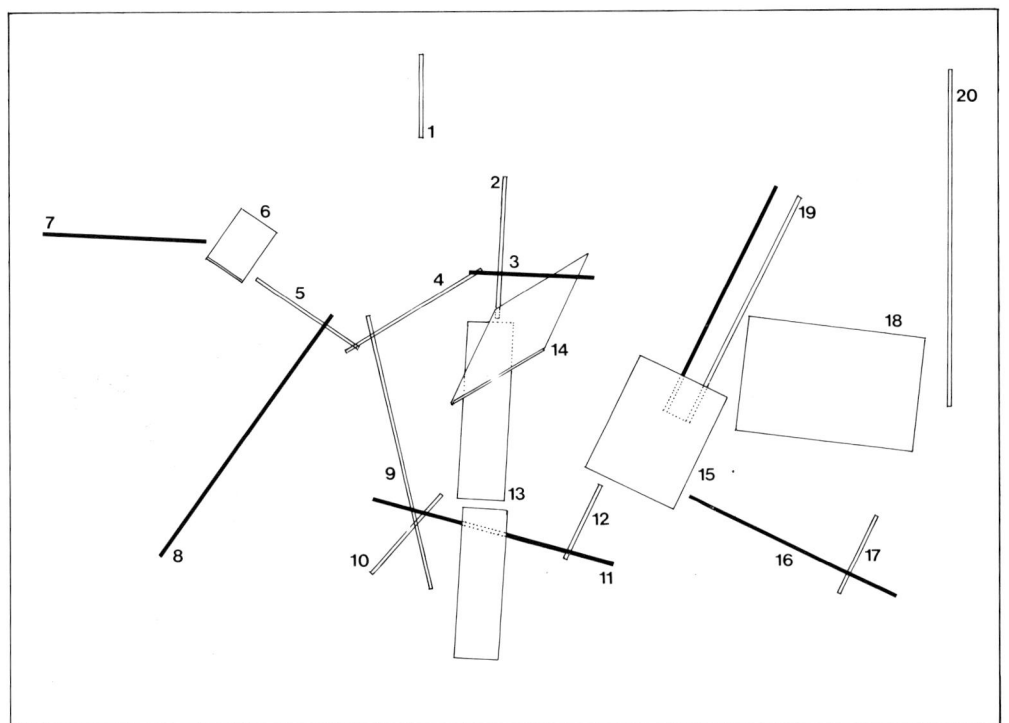

1

9. 1954
House at Borghetto
Novara

10. 1954
Rosetta house
Novara

11. 1954
Agricultural machinery shed
Gargagna

12. 1954
Office furnishings
Mortara

13. 1954
10th Triennale - Standard furnishings for INA-casa state housing
Milan

14. 1955
Interior
Novara

15. 1955
Entrance services for a textile factory
Novara

16. 1955
Games table in curved timber

7

16

17. 1955
Competition for formation of a list of INA-casa designers

18. 1955
Fontana house
Novara

19. 1955
Meeting-room for the town hall
Novara

20. 1955
Tower building for mixed use
Novara

21. 1955
Clothes shop
Novara

22. 1955
Clothes shop
Vigevano

23. 1956
Multi-story residential building in Via Sant'Adalgiso
Novara

24. 1956
Standard furnishings for clothes store, curved timber

21

25. 1956
Bronze handles for Vis
type doors

26. 1956
Residential nucleus for employees
of Bossi spa
Cameri

27. 1956
Interior
Novara

28. 1957
Group of four-story buildings
IACP state housing
Gardone

29. 1957
Ten-story buildings for IACP state housing on the "Feltre" estate
Milan

30. 1957
Holiday house
Solcio di Lesa

31. 1957
Rental homes V.F.G.
Novara

32. 1957
Furniture for International competition
Cantù

33. 1957
Low-cost housing (IACP - state housing), four stories
Cameri

34. 1958
Bookcase with fitted centrepiece in solid curved timber

35. 1958
Building with dwellings for a cooperative with twelve members
Novara

36. 1959
National furniture competition
Lissone

31

37. 1959
"Cavour" armchair in layers of
solid curved timbers

38. 1959
Textile store
Cameri

39. 1959
Interior for the "Don Lisander"
restaurant
Milan

40. 1959
Competition for the municipal
theatre
Alessandria

41. 1960
Offices of the Banca Popolare
di Novara
Brà

40

42. 1960
House for the Mira brothers
Romagnano Sesia

43. 1960
Moralis house
Arona

44. 1960
Competition for the new Palazzo
di Giustizia
Verbania

45. 1960
Table lamp

46. 1960
12th Triennale - Example of rural home
Milan

47. 1960
Office building in the ancient town centre
Novara

48. 1960
12th Triennale - Table lamp
Novara

49. 1960
Stores for sanitary ware
Novara

50. 1960
Four-story
IACP-state-housing
Borgomanero

51. 1961
Clothes shop
Casale

52. 1961
Magni house at La Sacca
(first edition)
Lago Maggiore

51

52

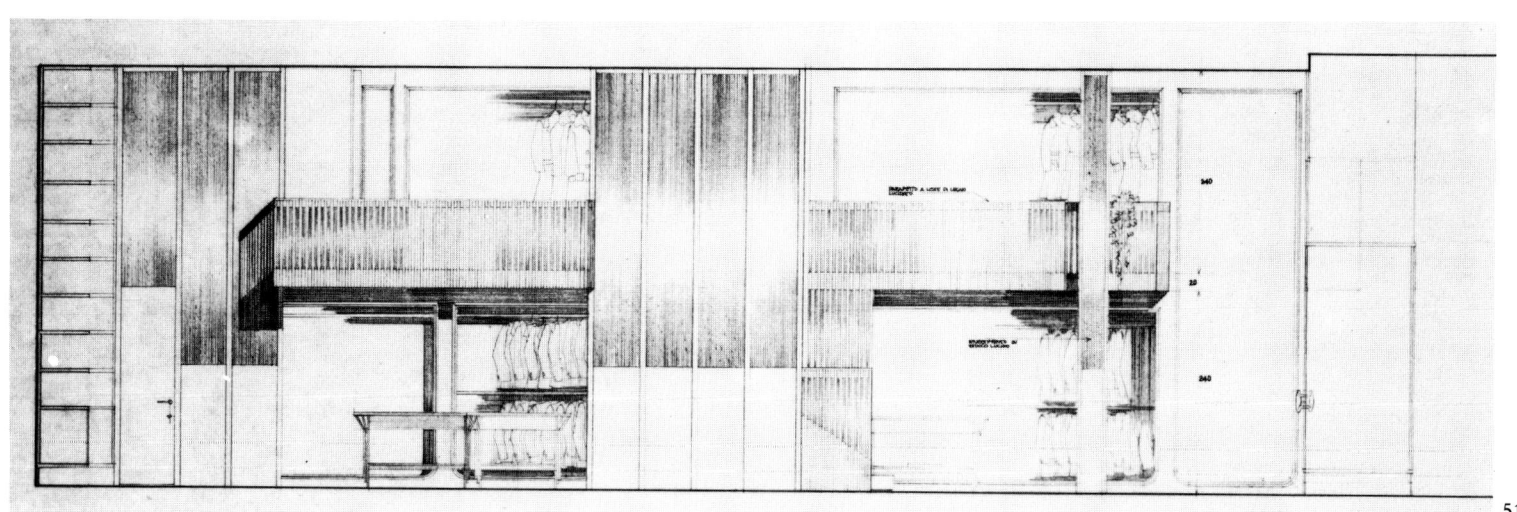

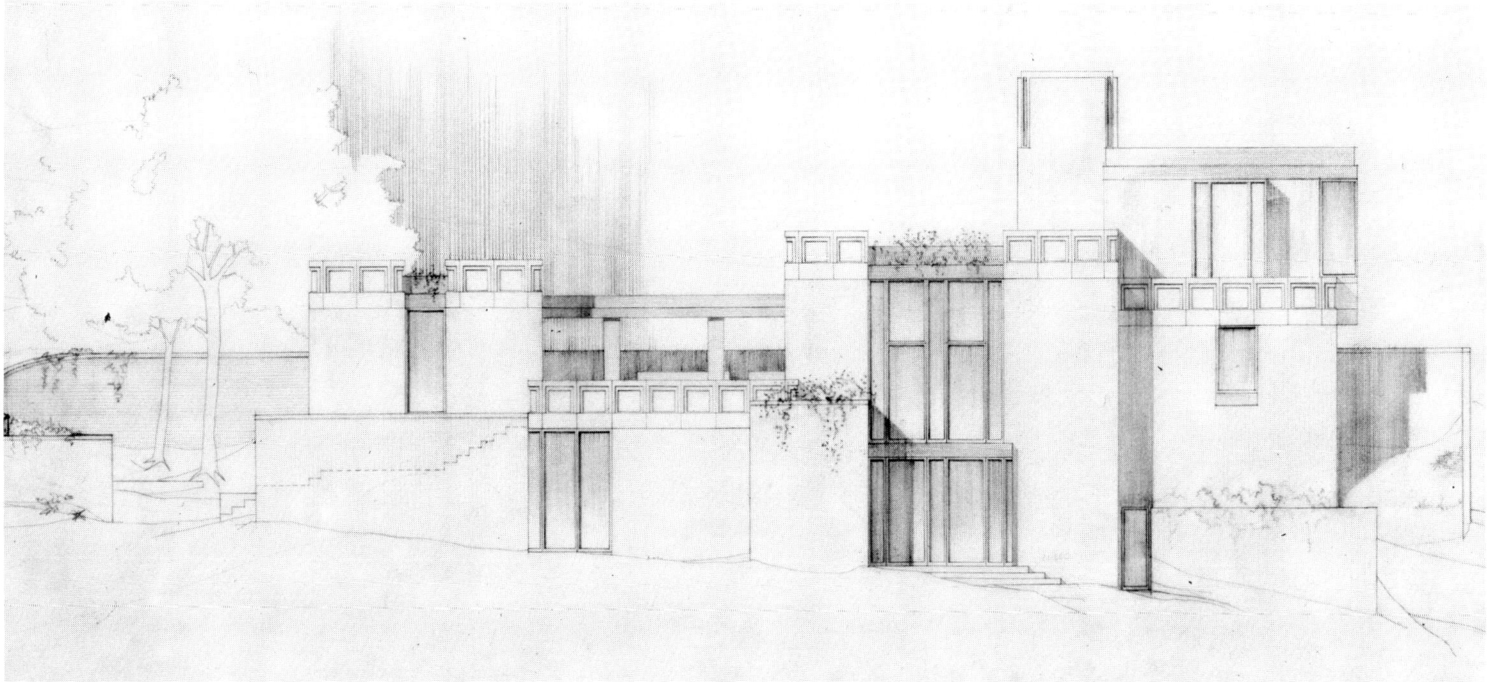

53. 1961
Magni house at La Sacca
(second edition)
Lago Maggiore

54. 1961
La Rinascente - Stool, chair and
armchair in cane
Milano

55. 1961
Furniture for International
competition
Cantù

54

56. 1961
Fregonara house at La Sacca
Lago Maggiore

57. 1961
House for two families
Portofino

58. 1961
Colombo interior
Novara

59. 1961
Four-story housing for employees
of Bossi spa
Cameri

60. 1961
Development of the town hall
Omegna

62. 1961
New centre for the Casa del Popolo
Trecate

64. 1961/62
Poretti house
Varese

66. 1962
E. G. interior
Novara

61. 1961
Extension of cemetery
Vespolate

63. 1961
Casa del Popolo, cinema, homes for cooperative
Romagnano Sesia

65. 1962
Duplex homes
Carimate

67. 1962
S. interior
Novara

64

68. 1962
Public transport station
Novara

69. 1962/63
Cooperative for council employees; dwellings in Via Palmanova
Milano

70. 1963
General town development plan
Novara

71. 1963
Plan for low-cost state housing
Novara

72. 1963
Detailed plan of the site of the ex-Perrone barracks
Novara

73. 1963
Detailed plan of surfaces and volumes
Oleggio

74. 1963/64
Cooperative for council employees; dwellings
in via D. da Settignano
Milan

75. 1964
13th Triennale - International introductory section
Milan

76. 1964
Detailed plan, old stadium site
Novara

77. 1964
Display of "Giovan Battista
Crespi, called Cerano" exhibition
Novara

78. 1964
Cooperative for council employees; dwellings in Via Montegani
Milan

79. 1964
Building cooperative "Marzia", apartments
Novara

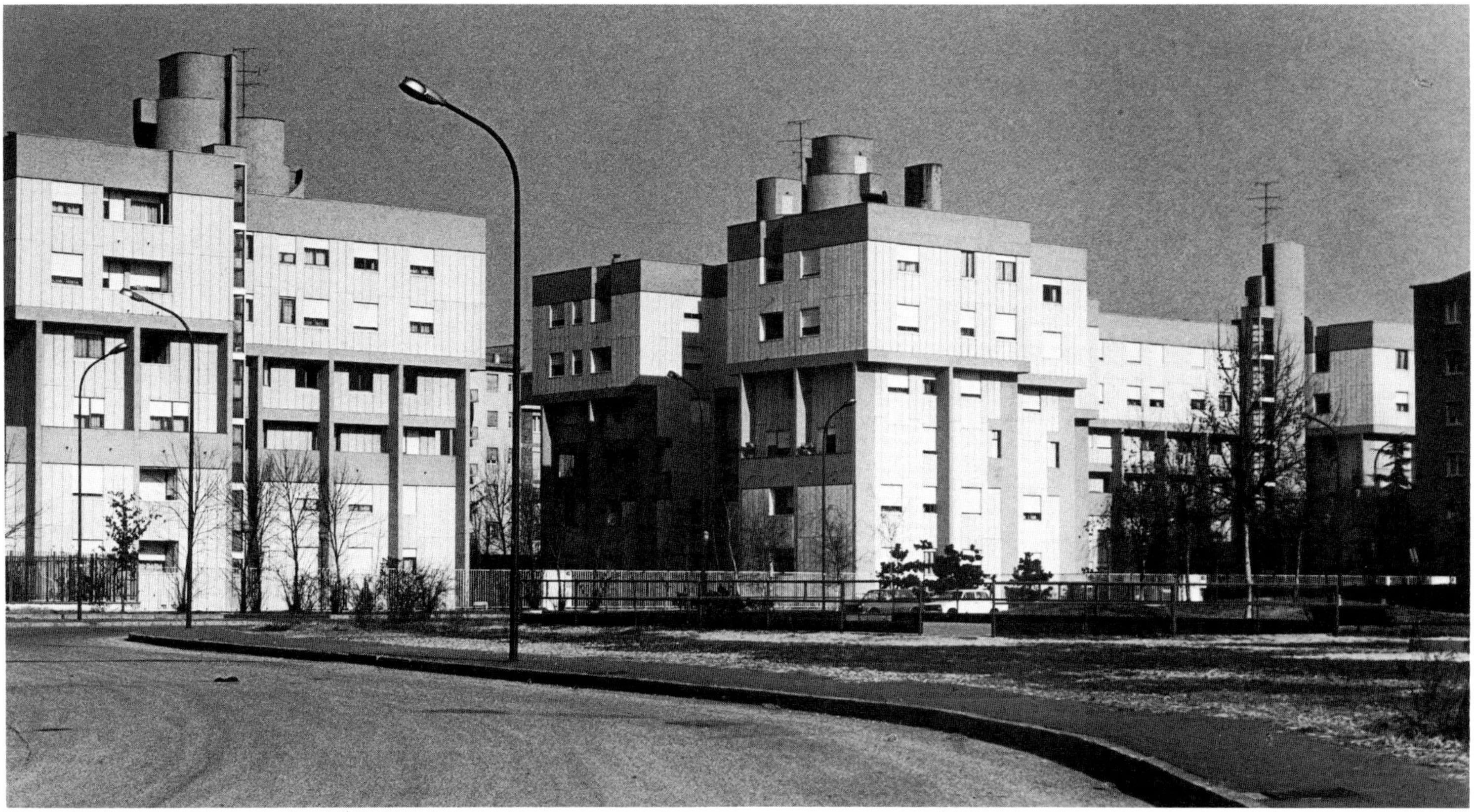

78

78

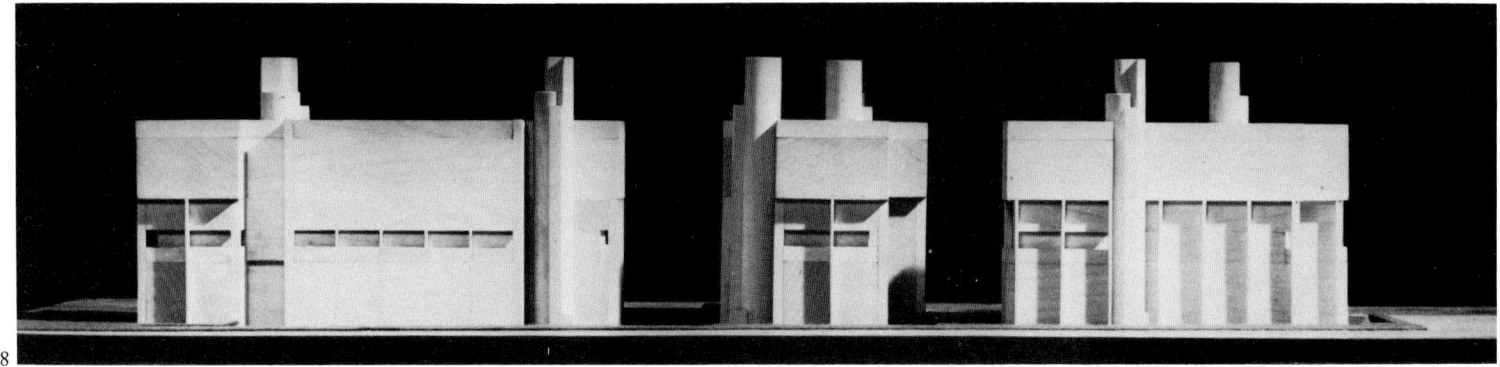

80. 1964
Standard lamp in series production by Arteluce
Florence

81. 1965
Display of "The home as dwelling" exhibition
Florence

82. 1965
Italsider pavilion at Milan trade fair
Milan

83. 1967
Tourist operators' company: church and square
Porto Rotondo

81

84. 1968
Bossi spa - Plan for a textile factory
Cameri

85. 1968
Architectural manual for UPIM department stores
Milan

86. 1969
La Rinascente group - Plan for the
new department stores
Turin

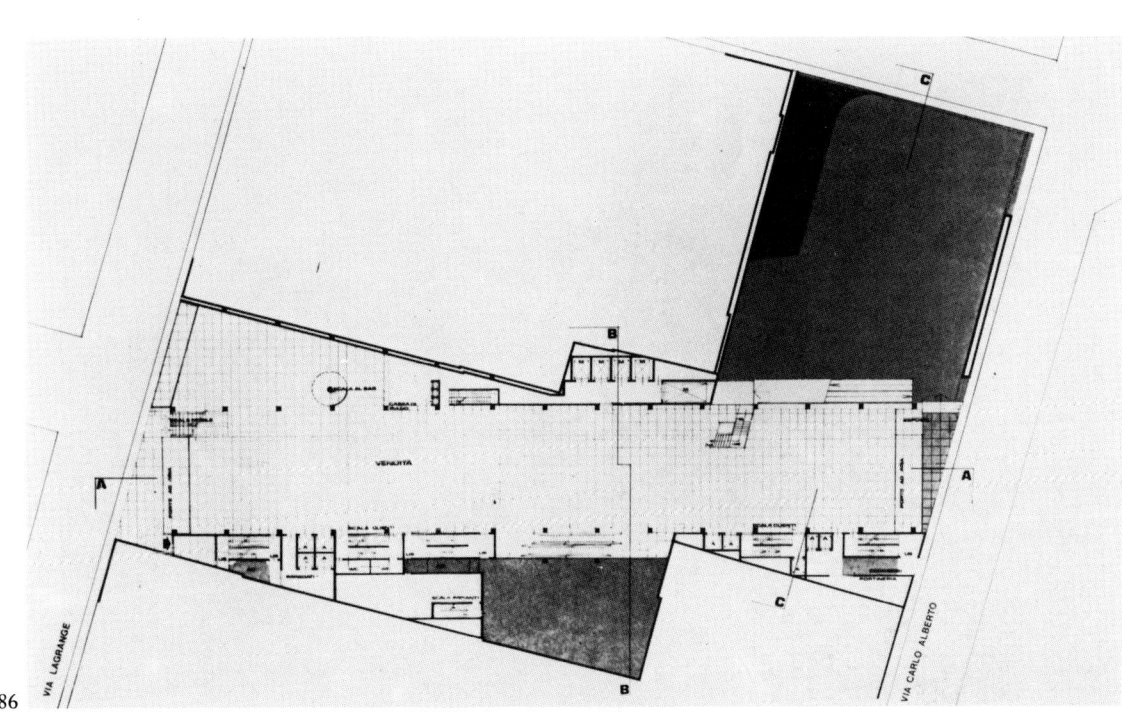

86

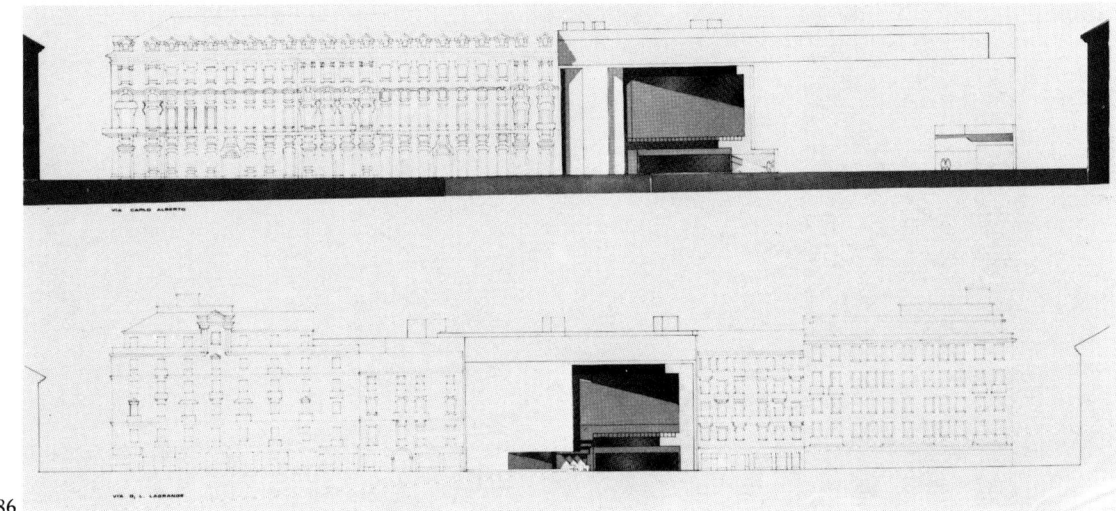

86

87. 1969
La Rinascente group - Plan for the
new department stores
Palermo

88. 1969
La Rinascente group -
Two food markets
Milan

89. 1969
IACP state housing -
Residential estate for 20,000
inhabitants
Palermo

90. 1969
Collective dwelling
Lucca

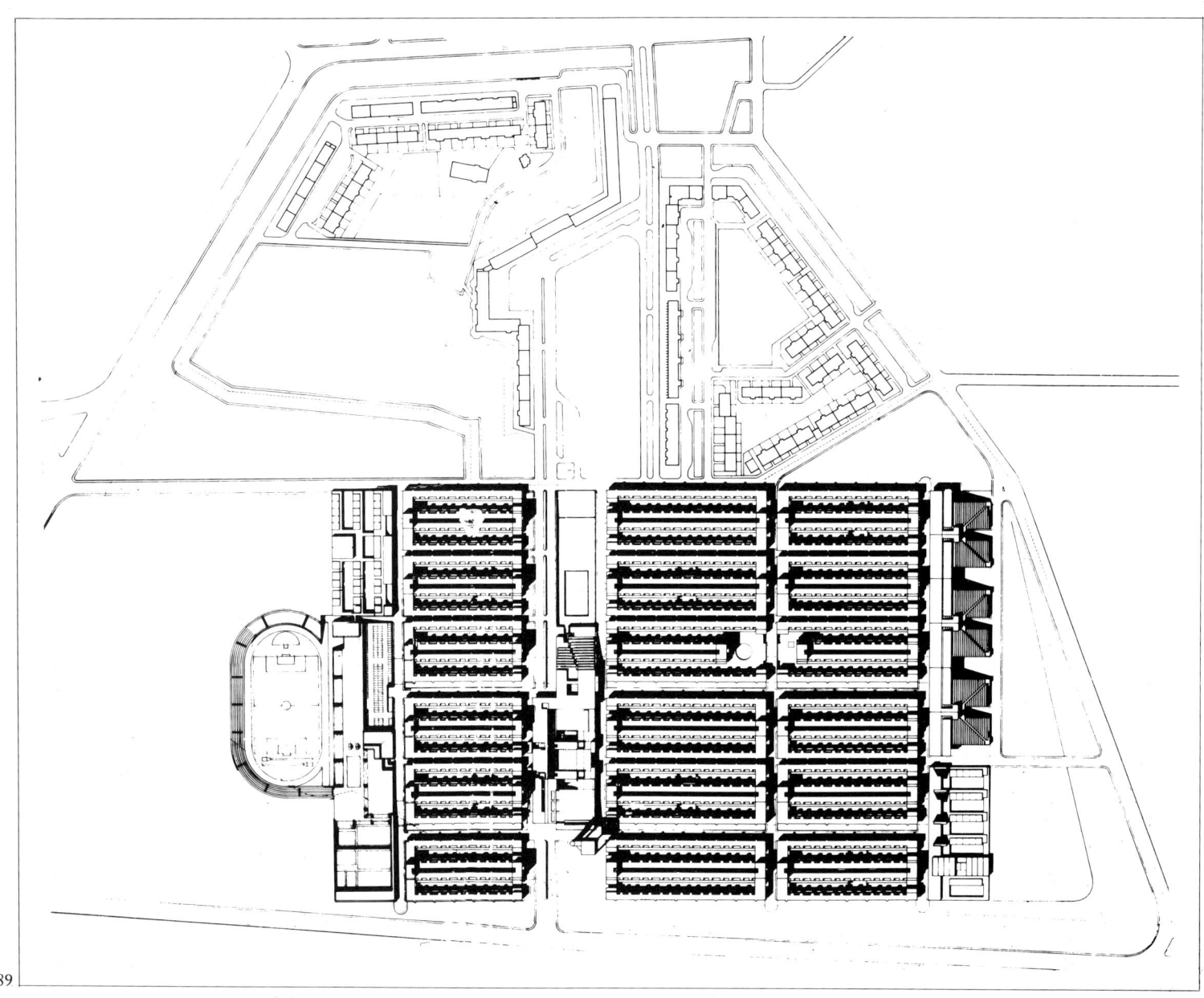

91. 1969
Palermo University - New Science
Departments at Parco d'Orleans
Palermo

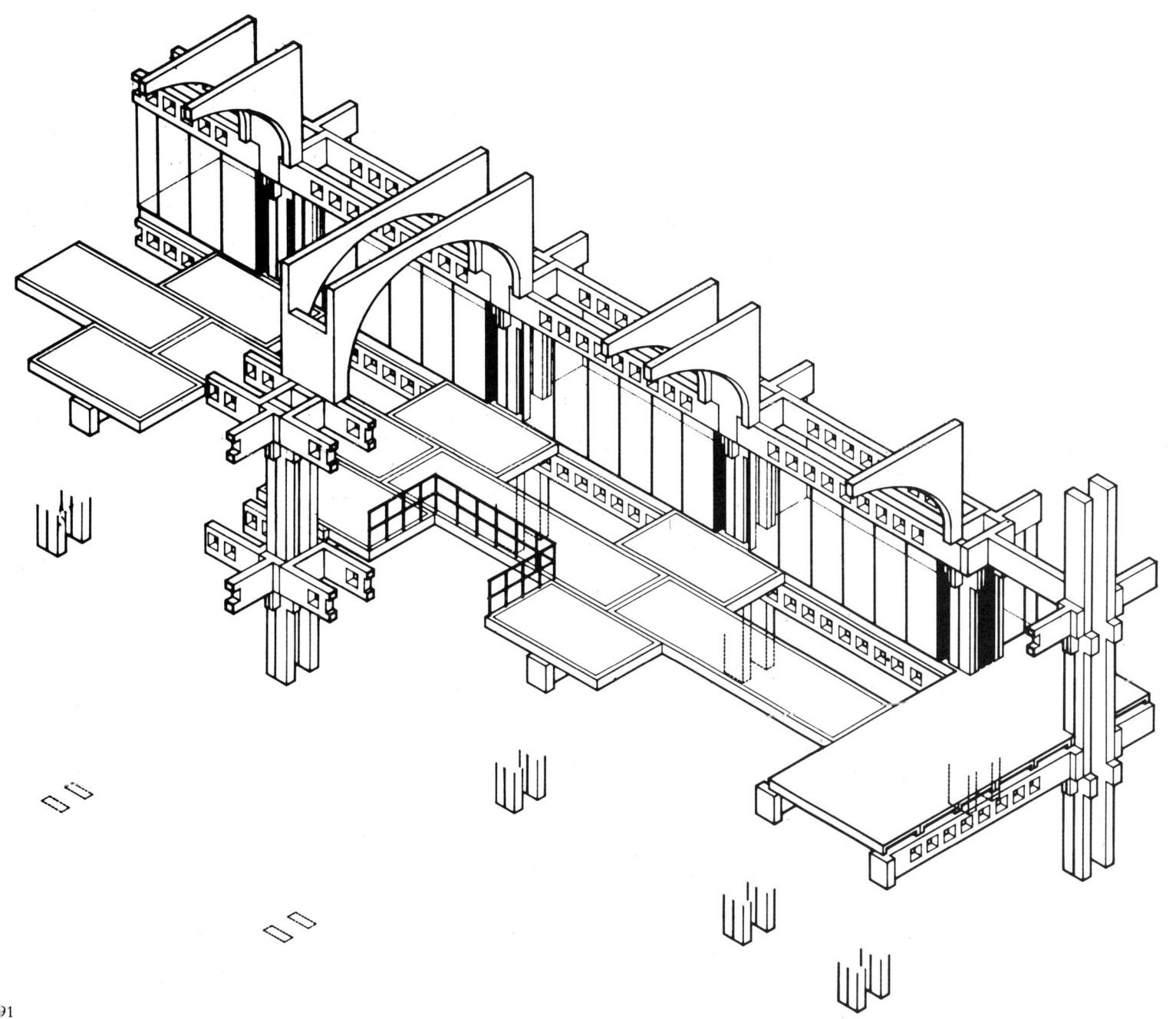

92. 1970
Competition for expansion of Vienna

93. 1970
Cartiere di Verona - Plan for a commercial and administrative centre
Milan

94. 1970
Bossi spa - Plan for a commercial and administrative centre
Mortara

95. 1971
Marco - Coordinated image for information supermarket
Milan

96. 1971
ISES Plan for public offices of new centre
Gibellina

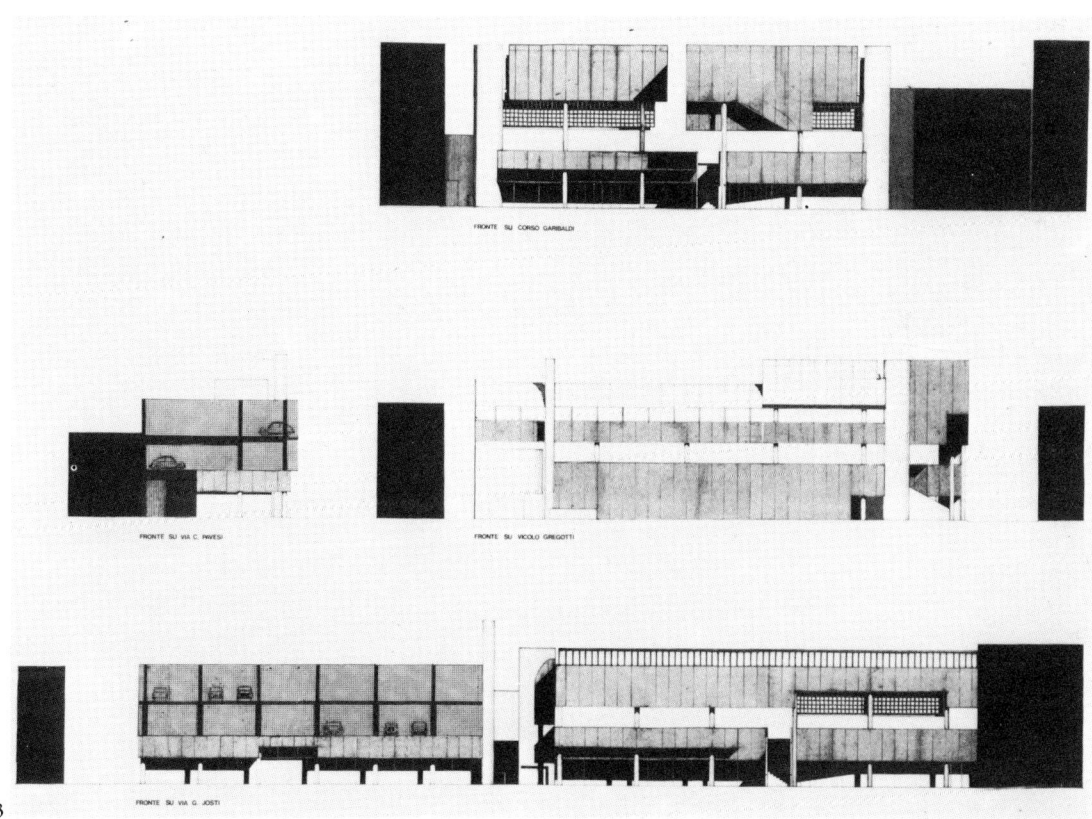
93

95

97. 1971
Florence University
Competition for new site
Florence

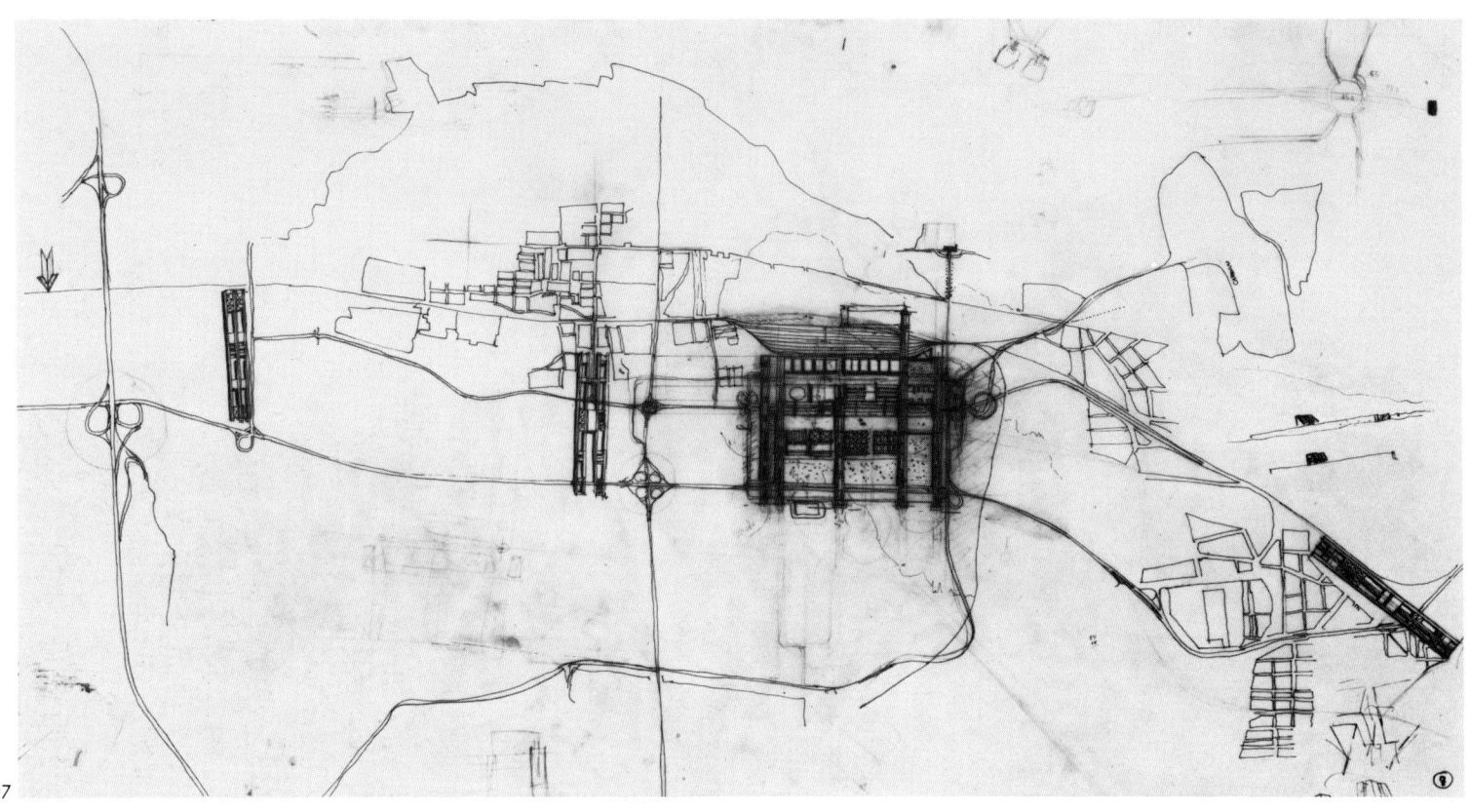

98. 1972
Gabel - Texile factory and offices
Rovellasca

99. 1972
Private home
Cantù

100. 1973
University of Calabria
Competition for the new site
Cosenza

101. 1974
Ricordi - Plan for a new sales oulet
Milan

102. 1974
Adda spa - Plan for integrated development of the Adda

103. 1974
Manilva sa - Tourist centre for 14,000 people
Malaga

104. 1974
Gian Giacomo Feltrinelli Foundation - Plan for the new centre
Milan

105. 1974
Portuguese Ministry of public works - Plan for a residential estate for 12,000 inhabitants
Setubal

106. 1976
Cefalù town hall - Detailed plan 167
Cefalù

107. 1976
Algerian Ministry of public works - Plan for the new regional public administration centre
Laghouat

108. 1976
Gabel - Plan for the new laundry and printworks
Como

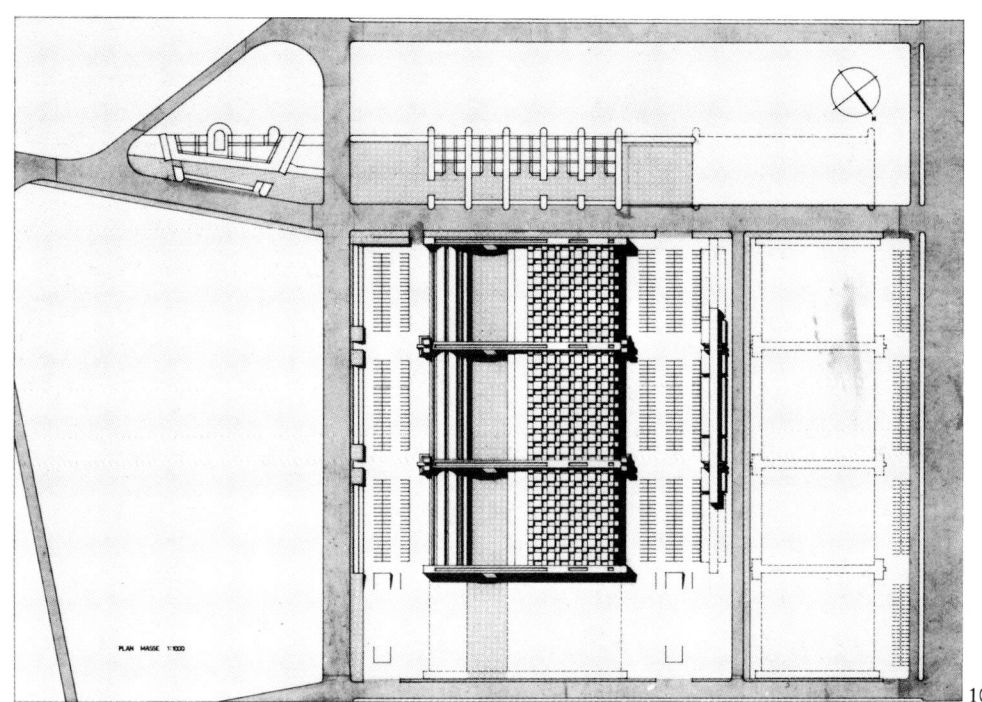

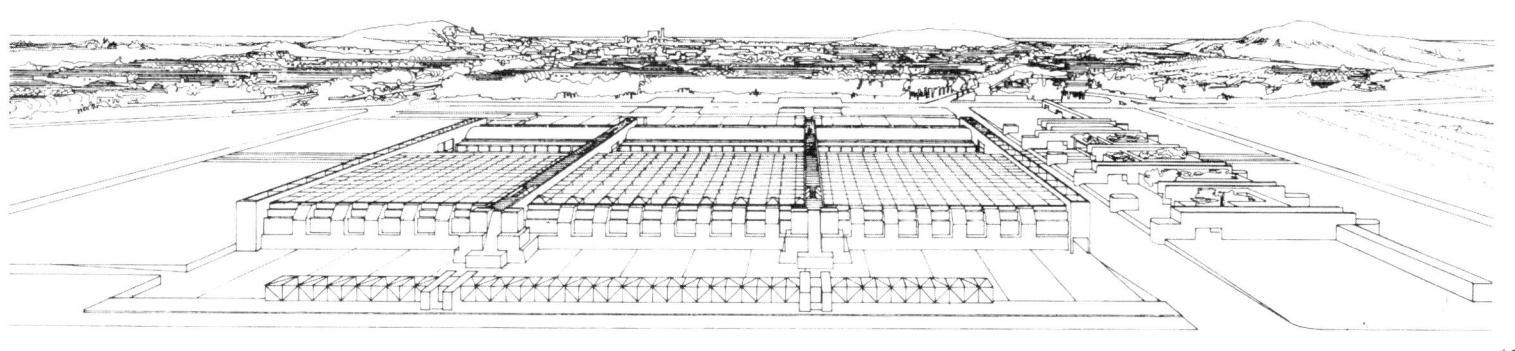

109. 1976
Restructuring of
G. A. apartment
Milan

110. 1976
Missoni - Sales outlet
in Via Montenapoleone
Milan

111. 1977
Gruppo Montedison - Plan for a
research centre
Naples

112. 1977
Exhibition for the sculptor
Arnaldo Pomodoro at the
Modern Art Museum
Paris

109

110

113. 1977
Fiat ANFIA - Exhibition of Italian automobile coachwork
Turin

114. 1977
University of Calabria - Detailed plan
Cosenza

115. 1977
Detached house
Oleggio

116. 1977
Design for a detached house
Novara

117. 1977
Cedit - Designs for ceramics
Milan

118. 1978
Marisa shop in Via Sant'Andrea
Milan

119. 1978
Fiat ANFIA - Exhibition of Italian automobile coachwork
Rome

120. 1978
Industrial Design Zentrum - Display of Peter Behrens exhibition
Berlin

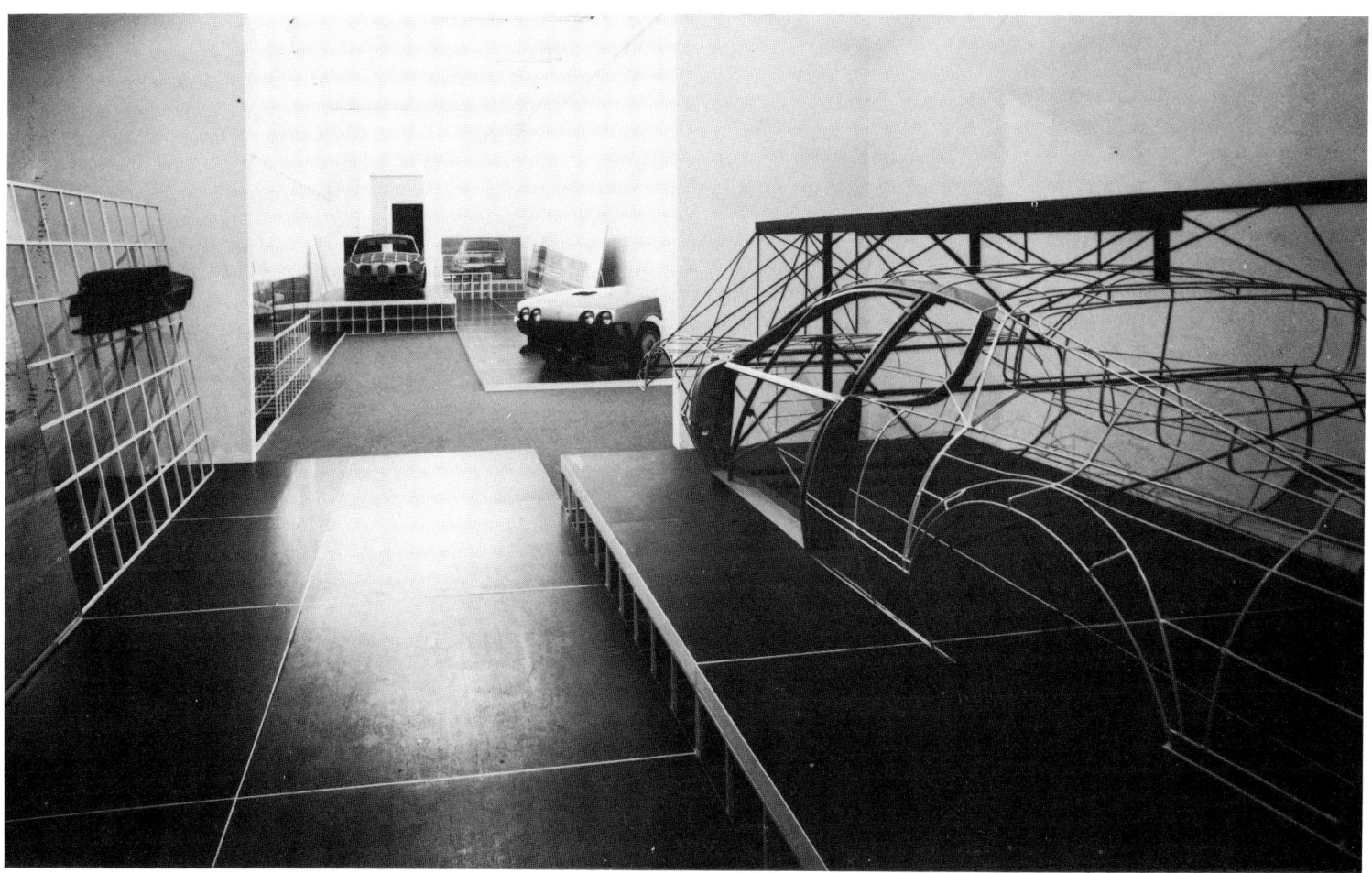

121. 1978
Dar al Hanan Institution, Saudi
Arabia-Design for a school for
2,000 girls
Jeddah

122. 1979
Mounting of the Venice
"'79 exhibition - Photography"
Venice

123. 1979
Italian Foreign Ministry - Design for the new Italian cultural institute
Tokyo

124. 1979
Comune of Abbiategrasso - Plan for rearrangement of Fossa Viscontea park
Abbiategrasso

125. 1979
Librex shop - Restructuring and interiors
Milan

123

126. 1980
Missoni - Design for new sales outlet
Paris

127. 1980
Zegna - Design for new sales outlet
Paris

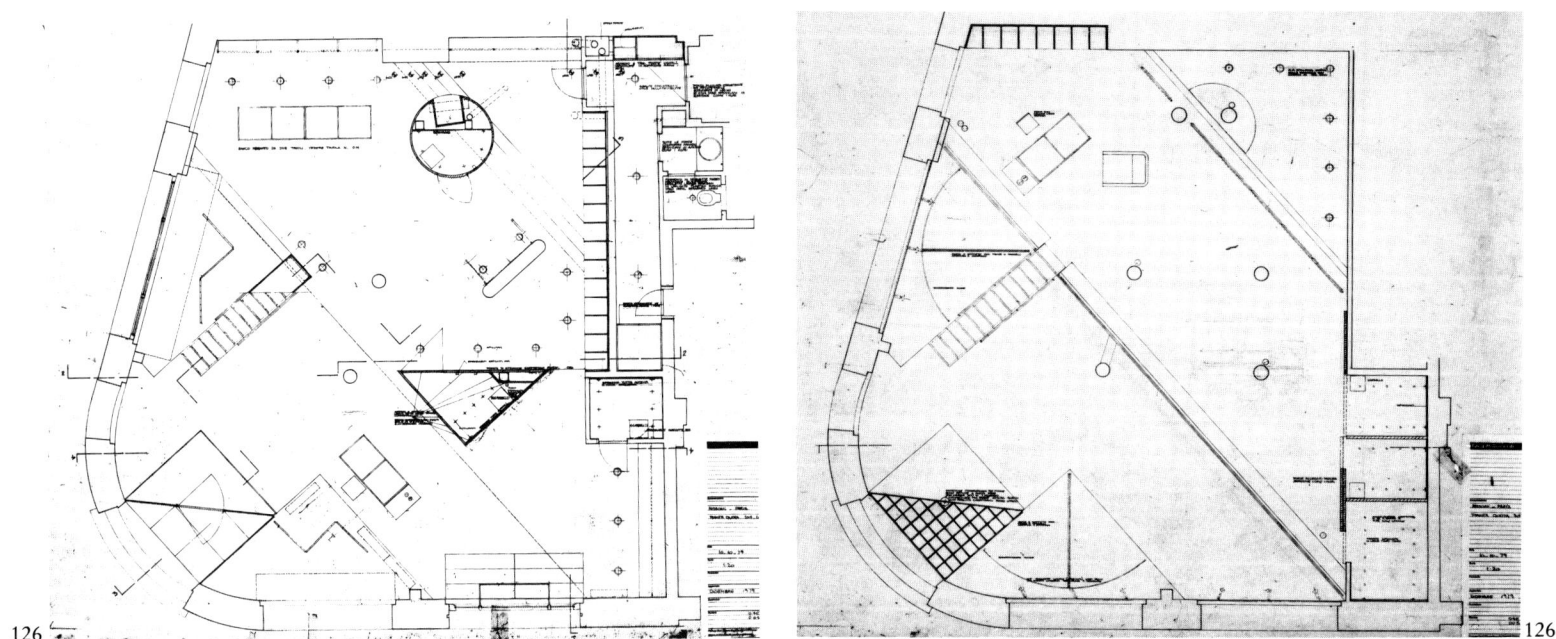

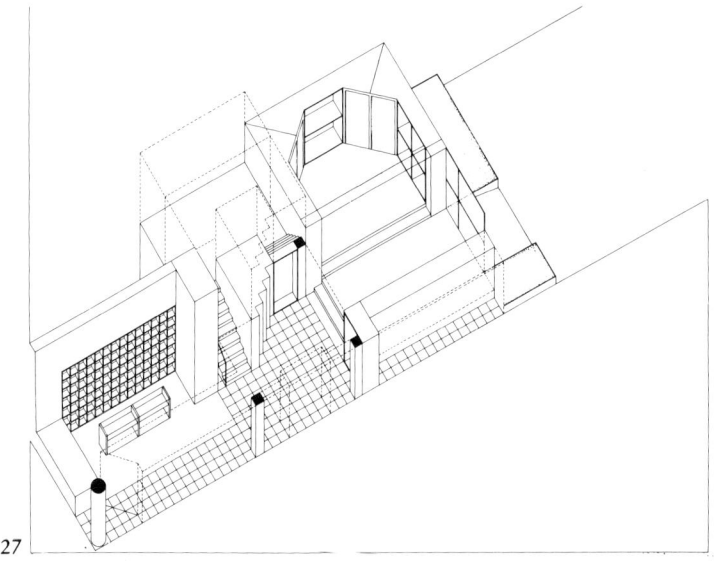

128. 1980
Bossi - Extension of offices
for textile factory
Novara

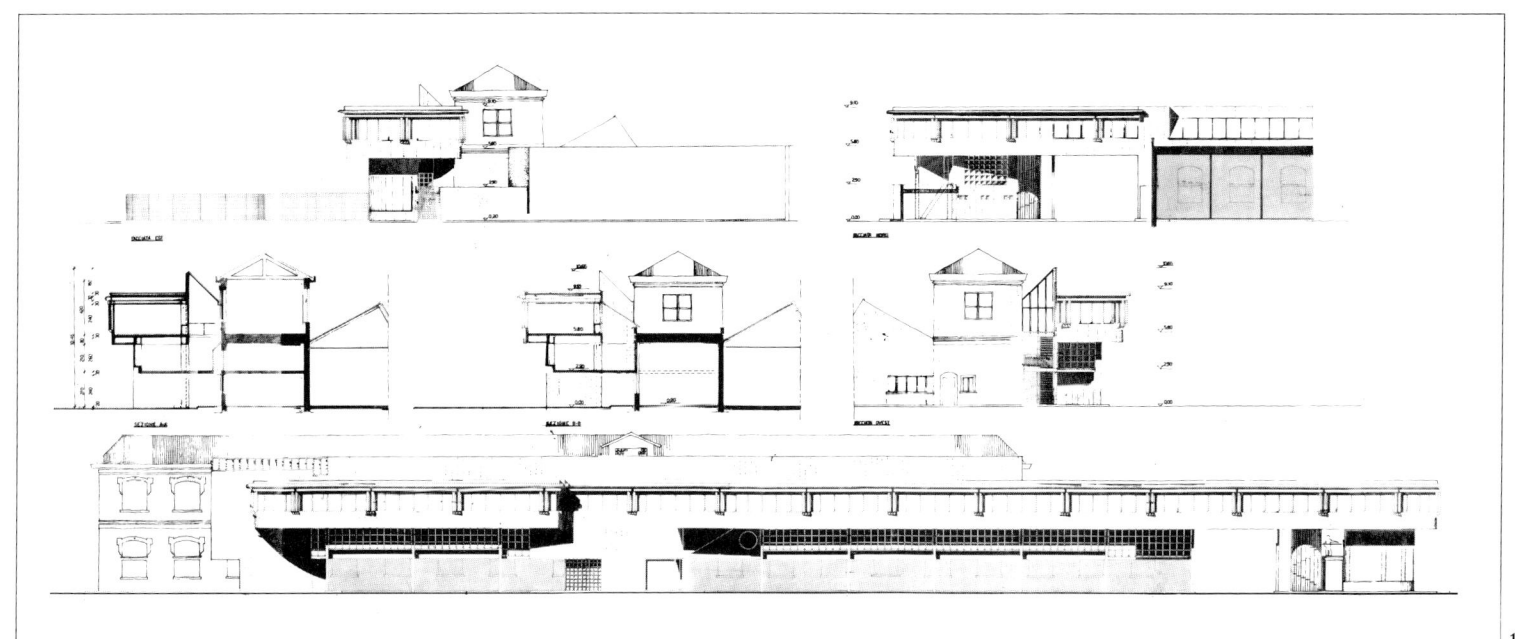

129. 1980
A.C.T.V. - Design for new boat yards on the Giudecca
Venice

130. 1980
Comprehensive project for access studies and detailed plan of Isola del Tronchetto
Venice

131. 1980
Restricted competition for new layout of the ex-Varesine site and Isola district
Milan

132. 1980
Internationale Bauausstellung Berlin 1984 - Restricted competition for Lützowstrasse
Berlin

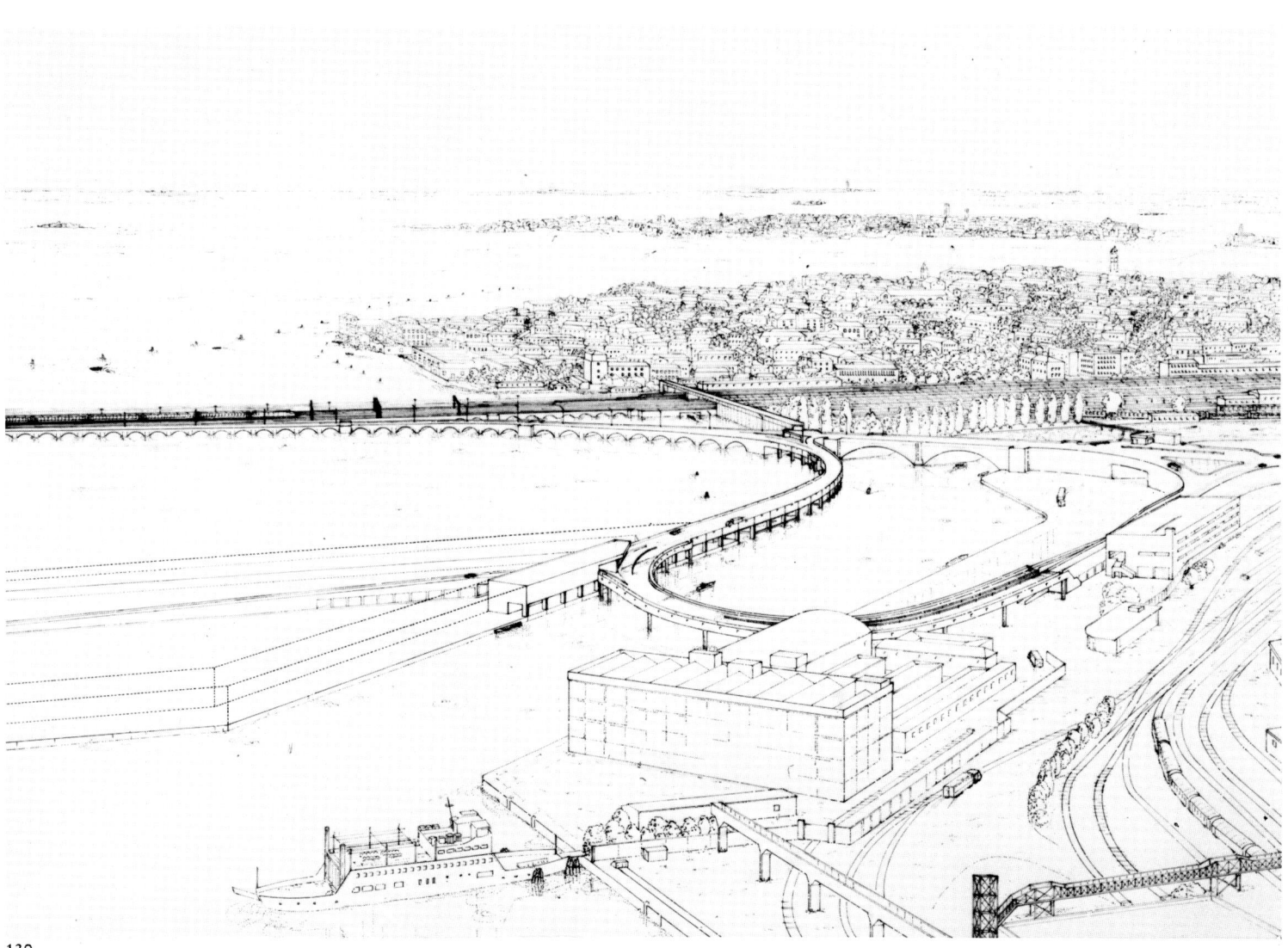

130

133. 1981
Beni Immobili Italia - Design for new residential block at Cannaregio
Venice

134. 1981
Republic of San Marino - Plan for new layout of arrival centre and restructuring of transit system
San Marino

135. 1981
Zucchi - Display for exhibitions
Frankfurt

136. 1981
Aurora - Display for exhibitions
Milan

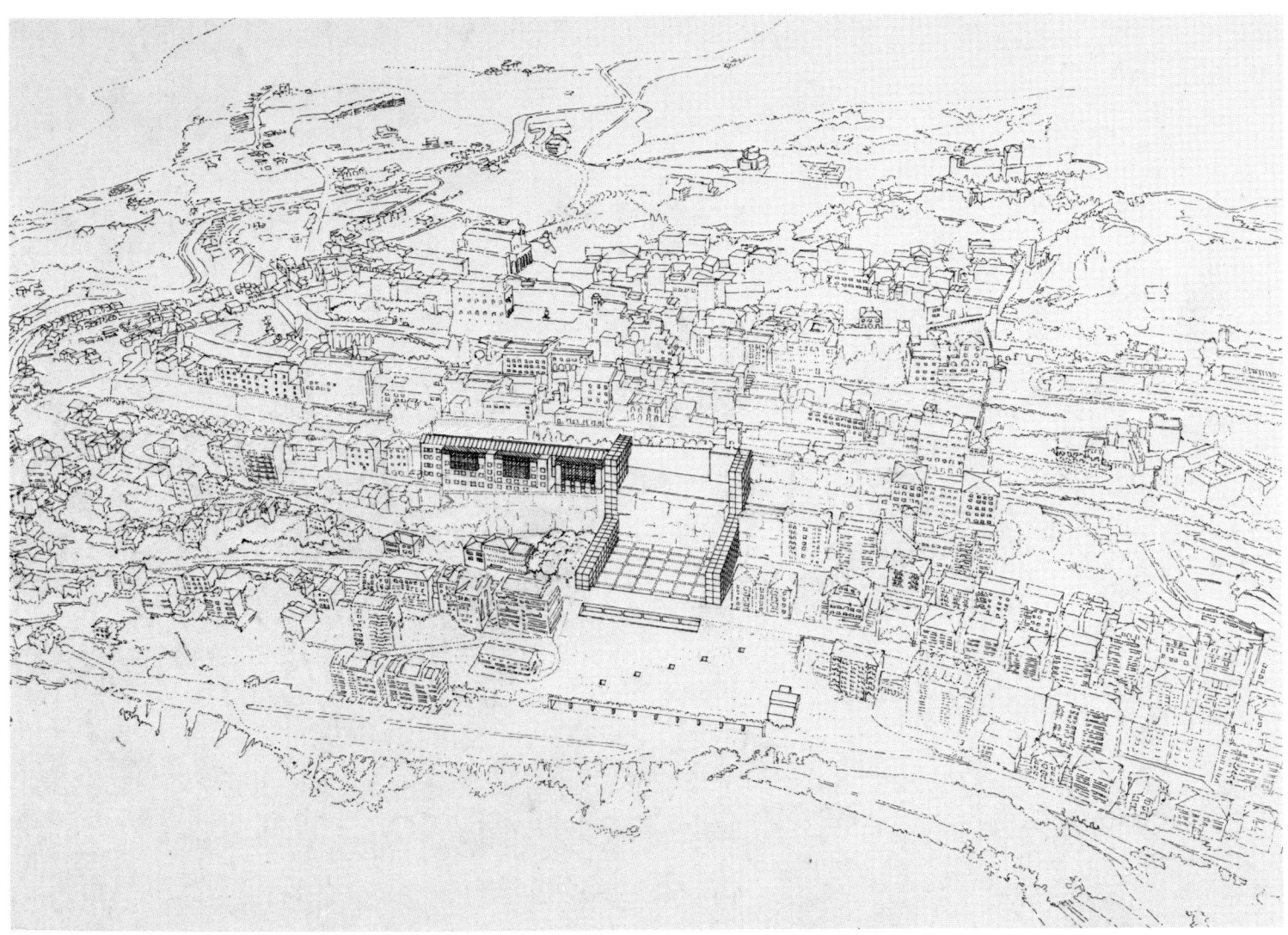

134

137. 1981
Mounting of display for the restoration of the Brera altarpiece by Piero della Francesca
Milan

138. 1981
"Identité Italienne - Italian art since 1959" - Display and graphics at the Centre Pompidou
Paris

139. 1981
IVI Chemical research centre
Quattordio

140. 1981
Display for manufacturers of office furniture at the 21st furniture trade fair
Milan

138

140

141. 1981
Layout of the site of the Nuovo
Museo d'Arte Contemporanea
Florence

142. 1981
Plan for a school centre for senior
high school
Sassuolo

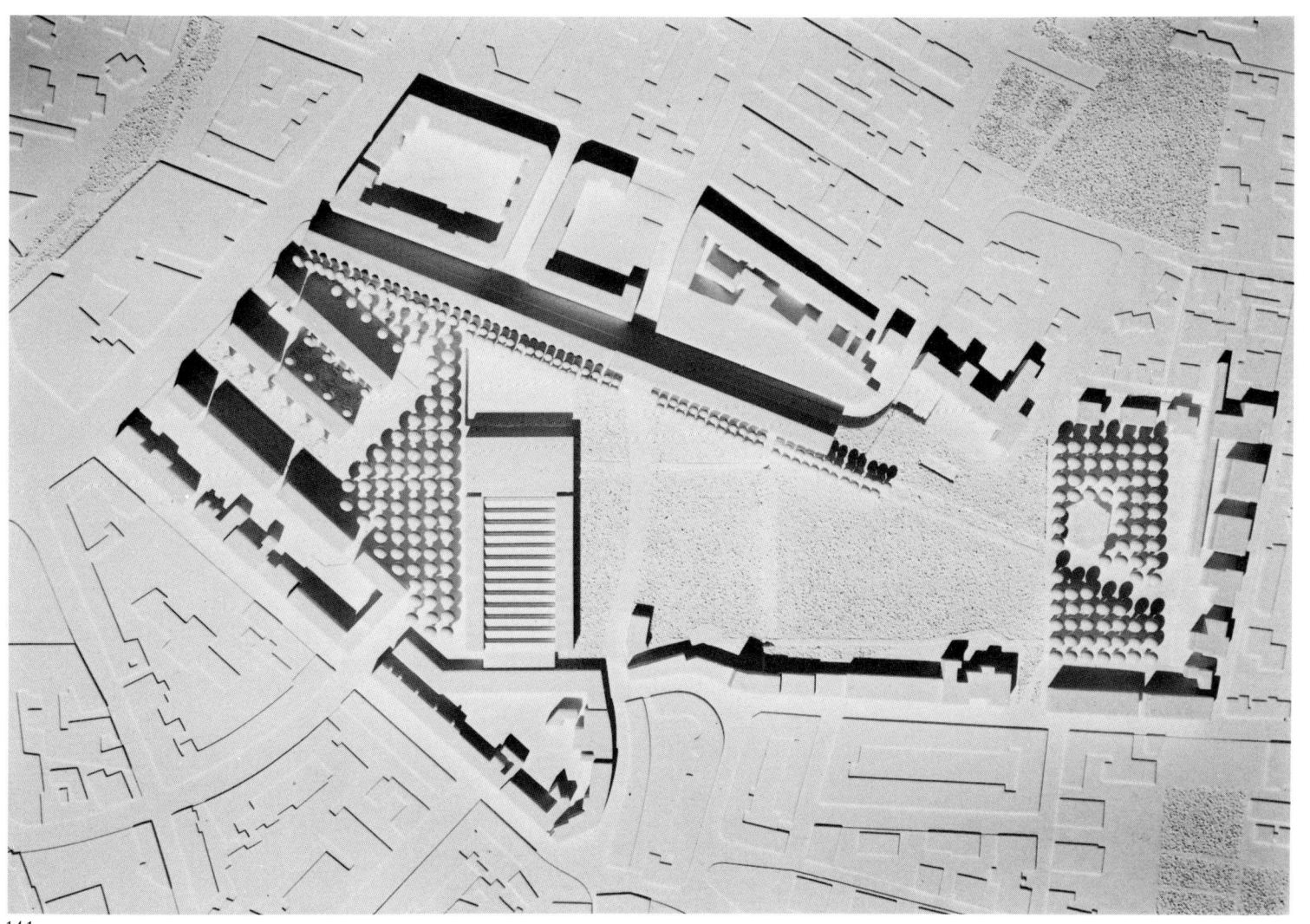

141

Photographic credits

Aldo Ballo, Milan: pp. 95, 98, 101, 104, 113, 143, 149.
Ballo & Ballo, Milan: pp. 44/45.
Gabriele Basilico, Milan: pp. 124, 138 (n. 110).
Casali, Milan: pp. 126, 129.
Roberto Collovà, Palermo: p. 49.
Giorgio Colombo, Milan: p. 148 (n. 138).
Carla De Bernardi, Milan: pp. 93, 139.
Antonia Mulas, Milan: pp. 35, 36, 39, 40.
Sala Dino, Milan: p. 112.

Printed on behalf of Gruppo Editoriale Electa
by Fantonigrafica, Venice